The Confiscation of
American Prosperity

The Confiscation of American Prosperity

From Right-Wing Extremism and Economic Ideology to the Next Great Depression

Michael Perelman

HC
106.83
.P47
2007

First published in 2007 by
PALGRAVE MACMILLAN™
175 Fifth Avenue, New York, N. Y. 10010 and
Houndmills, Basingstoke, Hampshire, England RG21 6XS.
Companies and representatives throughout the world.

PALGRAVE MACMILLAN is the global academic imprint of the Palgrave Macmillan
division of St. Martin's Press, LLC and of Palgrave Macmillan Ltd. Macmillan® is a
registered trademark in the United States, United Kingdom and other countries.
Palgrave is a registered trademark in the European Union and other countries.

ISBN-13: 978-0-230-60046-1
ISBN-10: 0-230-60046-8

Library of Congress Cataloging-in-Publication Data is available from the Library
of Congress.

A catalogue record of the book is available from the British Library.

Design by Scribe, Inc.

First edition: October 2007

10 9 8 7 6 5 4 3 2 1

Contents

Acknowledgments

A number of people have helped me with this book. I want to thank some of the most important, including Michael Pollack, Richard Ponarul, Nomi Prins, Robert Cottrell, Fred Lee, Wendy Diamond, Harry Trebbing, Salim Rashid, J. Andrew McKee, David K. Levine, Michele Rubin, Rich Wagner, and Edward Roualdes. Most of all, I am grateful to Blanche Perelman, who has tolerated a great deal to make this book possible.

The best lack all convictions, while the worst
Are full of passionate intensity.
—W. B. Yeats, The Second Coming

Though those different plans were, perhaps, first introduced by the private interests
and prejudices of particular orders of men, without any regard to, or foresight of,
their consequences upon the general welfare of the society; yet they have given
occasion to very different theories of political economy.
—Adam Smith

Prologue

For the last three and a half decades, a tiny minority of people has captured the lion's share of the fruits of economic growth in the United States. At the same time, the middle class is disappearing and much of the rest of society is rapidly falling behind, producing a level of inequality that has not been seen since the eve of the Great Depression. Business leaders, along with most politicians and economists, celebrate this new state of affairs and pretend the benefits are certain to trickle down soon to the rest of society.

This book does not belabor the obvious injustices of inequality; instead, it describes the extent of this confiscation of wealth, how the perpetrators managed to pull it off, and, finally, how this confiscation is setting the stage for a catastrophic depression. Leaders in the world of business and government, as well as professional economists, seem oblivious to the dangers ahead. The extreme inequities in society breed a hubris that prevents them from even considering the possibility that they are contributing to a catastrophe. All the while, the economics profession seems unable to comprehend the depth of the problem.

Unless strong actions are taken, the calamity that currently afflicts the poor is certain to trickle up, engulfing even the very rich. I do not mean that the very rich will become destitute; only that the losses they will eventually experience will far outweigh the vast amount of extra wealth and income they now claim for themselves.

Despite the dangers ahead, the United States still possesses the most powerful economy the world has ever known. The unique conditions that once made the U.S. economy so effective are already beginning to unravel. People in power commonly realize that the U.S. economy has fallen considerably short of its promise. In terms of traditional measures, such as Gross Domestic Product, the economy has modestly progressed, but the rate of growth is disappointing at best, especially considering the proliferation of new technologies. The quality of life for the majority of society has deteriorated.

In many respects, the gross inequities of U.S. society are coming to resemble some of the more impoverished countries in the world. Amidst splendid opulence, we find declining industries, unemployment, and even squalor. With so much potential, providing a decent standard of living for everybody should be a simple matter.

Despite these unpleasant symptoms, the deeper problems are not yet obvious. The dangers that I will explore do not appear in the media—not even in the business press.

In his justly famous farewell address, President Eisenhower called the main problem identified in this book as the "disastrous rise of misplaced power." At the time, he was referring to the military-industrial complex. Today the pathology has advanced much further. The complex now includes a vast network of corporate power, political parties, well-financed think tanks, and religious movements. This network has also enjoyed the support of much of the media and even a good part of academia. These parties did not have identical goals in mind, but they all shared a distaste for the sociopolitical climate of the late 1960s. The result was a conservative revolution.

The United States had already been on a steady path to the right. Indeed, since the election of Franklin Roosevelt in 1932, every Democratic administration with the exception of Lyndon Johnson's has been more conservative—often far more conservative—than the previous Democratic administration. Similarly, every elected Republican administration, with the single exception of George Herbert Walker Bush's, has been more conservative than the previous Republican administration. Although the national election in 2006 appears to be a repudiation of the right-wing agenda, the most important factors in the election were the disastrous war in Iraq and a multitude of scandals that damaged the Republicans.

Given this relentless drift to the right, the policies of Richard Nixon now appear to the left of those of Bill Clinton. Yet by the time Nixon took office, business was distraught. Many business leaders at the time were under the impression that socialism would soon triumph in the United States. The first part of the book will explain this paradox.

In the early 1970s, business successfully launched an aggressive campaign to take a firmer hold on the levers of power. Instead of the gradual drift toward more conservative economic policies, revolutionary changes became the order of the day. Within a couple of decades, a right-wing revolution had swept aside much of the New Deal.

These right-wing revolutionaries professed conservative ideals, including a more modest role for the state. In practice, their willingness to use state power was hardly modest, except insofar as the state might otherwise inconvenience the interests of the corporations and the super-rich. Backed up by the strict dogma of economic theory, conservatives categorically promised markets would cure all social ills. Markets, however, pay attention only to commercial activities, ignoring considerations such as quality of life or environmental degradation. Markets also disempower people from making political choices.

Rules and regulations provide a counterweight to market forces, creating a means to keep the harmful effects of markets in check. By this standard, the United States certainly has the most market-friendly economy in the world.

Regulations can protect people's health and safety and limit fraud; however, rules and regulations are not necessarily positive. They can also be used to shore up the corporate power to the detriment of society. The right-wing revolution has gone a long way toward dismantling the protective regulatory layers, while hardening the pro-corporate parts. This book emphasizes the importance of regulations as a check on some of the destructive speculative forces that can unleash depressions.

This reformulation of the ground rules of the system has given birth to a grotesque form of crony capitalism, which has been metastasizing for many decades. Under this crony capitalism, markets lack the capacity to discipline the most powerful players, which is supposedly one of the greatest benefits of capitalism. A wave of corporate manipulation and government favoritism will eventually wreak havoc on the economy.

This book explains the evolution of this system, while analyzing the deeper but often less obvious consequences of this deformed economy. It also shows the inevitability of a disaster so extreme that it will devastate even the most affluent who are benefiting the most from the current economy. The last part of the book explains why economists are unable to come to grips with this dangerous slide into disaster.

The trajectory of *The Confiscation of American Prosperity* resembles a crime story. The first part, "The Plunder," describes the caper. The second part, "The Plot," shows how brilliantly it was organized. The third part, "Retribution," explains how it is going to blow up in the faces of the perpetrators, and finally the book turns to the presumptive cops on the beat, the economists, who should have known to have spoken up.

But this is not really a crime story. Although a few of the major players may have violated the law, most of what happened was perfectly legal. People combined raw power with dazzling tactics to engineer a right-wing takeover. While they mastered the short-term tactics necessary to achieve their objectives, their ambition and greed blinded them to the long-run consequences of their actions.

Overview

The first part of this book describes how the conservative revolution permitted a small number of people to plunder the lion's share of three decades of economic growth—perhaps the greatest confiscation of wealth and income in the history of the world.

The second part begins with the economic crisis in the late 1960s that pushed business to go on the offensive. Economists refer to the period following World War II as the "Golden Age" because conditions at the time were so exceptional. During that period, both business and the majority of the economics profession had been under the impression that with proper management, including government intervention in the economy, the good times could last forever.

Unfortunately, this faith was groundless. Business, political, and economic leaders were caught unaware of the inevitable unraveling of the Golden Age. No market economy, even with the most intelligent management, has ever achieved the kind of stability people came to expect during the Golden Age. Instability, even if punctuated by periods of calm, is a natural part of capitalism.

As the Golden Age ended, profits shrunk. At first business became despondent, then launched a furious campaign to reshape the social and economic structure of the United States in an effort to restore corporate power to its pre-Depression level. The victory from this campaign was even more impressive because the right wing managed to induce many people to support an agenda that was sure to undermine their own economic welfare. The right succeeded in this effort in large part because the deteriorating economic conditions left many working-class people confused and angry. Taking advantage of this mood, the right-wing electoral machine caused many people to lose sight of their own economic interests by effectively railing about the contentious social conditions of the 1960s.

By the time Richard Nixon came to office in 1968, everything seemed aligned to allow conservatives to take political power. The Democrats had discredited themselves with an unpopular war and had done little to address the real needs of their political base. Building upon the grassroots movement begun in the wake of Barry Goldwater's defeat in 1964, the Nixon administration launched a frontal attack on the New Deal coalition by appealing to the culture war of the day. Now the rich and powerful appeared poised to win support for their agenda.

These divisive machinations seemed to have cleared the way for an economic revolution, except a problem remained. Although part of the working class was antagonized by the upheavals of the 1960s, a growing antiwar movement and an energized civil rights movement presented serious challenges. The emergence of the environmental movement with the broad sympathy of much of the middle class complicated matters even more. Nixon moved to placate the environmental movement to appear to be more inclusive. Within this contentious political climate, he did not dare to carry out a broad offensive against labor.

Suddenly, the conflict took a decisive turn. A small group of business interests carefully engineered a conservative takeover of the main organs of power in the United States beginning in the 1970s. Using a combination of well-financed think tanks, racist demagoguery, and sophisticated political maneuvering, business countered the modest progressive successes of the 1960s. These institutions worked to change the political climate of the country by influencing the media. Even more importantly, business used its newfound powers to counter a falling rate of profit by turning back many of the reforms dating back to the New Deal.

The third part concentrates on how the right-wing revolution set in motion the destructive forces that are responsible for many of the difficulties that the U.S. economy already faces and on why the future damage will be far more extreme. I will also explain why not just ordinary working-class people will suffer from its harmful consequences, but even the intended beneficiaries of the right-wing revolution—business and the very wealthy—will pay a price.

In some cases, the costs of the right-wing revolution are already relatively obvious. For example, the obscene military budget crowds out important social and economic programs while military adventurism promises to make even greater demands on the economy in the future. In other cases, such as the undermining of the educational system, the effect is less immediate but just as devastating.

The right-wing revolutionaries express vehement hostility toward the government. Indeed, the ability of the government to regulate some of the worst business abuses is now practically nonexistent. Today, public agencies are less capable of protecting the environment, providing education, and promoting science and technology—all of which are essential ingredients of a vibrant economy. All the while, business shamelessly wallows in generous government subsidies and other forms of favoritism.

In the fourth and final part, I discuss the impotence of the economics profession. This part recounts the evolution of the economics profession in the United States, including the long-standing suppression of critical voices. Despite intense and even acrimonious debate about minor issues, economics evolved into a narrow orthodoxy. I also discuss how the largely ideological nature of modern economics has more or less led the discipline into a dead end, leaving it incapable of dealing with the emerging economic catastrophe.

Part I

The Plunder:
The Extent of the Confiscation

Chapter 1

The Great Capitalist Restoration

The New Inequality

Right-wing extremism represents a serious threat to economic prosperity, so much so that even the intended beneficiaries of this movement will eventually pay dearly. So far, the major economic impact of the right-wing revolution has magnificently rewarded those who sit at the pinnacle of the economic pyramid, while the rest of society has not fared very well. This chapter discusses the extent of inequality before exploring the dangers that lie ahead.

Despite a historically slow rate of growth, between 1970 and 2003 the Gross Domestic Product adjusted for inflation almost tripled, from $3.7 trillion to $11.7 trillion (President of the United States 2006, Table B-12, p. 296). Because the population also increased by about 35 percent during that same period, per capita income grew more slowly than the Gross Domestic Product. On average, per capita income still has more than doubled—but not for everybody.

Hourly wage earners certainly did not benefit from the economic growth. According to government statistics, hourly wages corrected for inflation peaked in 1972 at $8.99 measured in 1982 dollars. By 2005, hourly wages had fallen to $8.17, although they rose modestly during that period using a different measure of inflation (President of the United States 2006, Table B-47, p. 338).

In a pathbreaking series of studies, economists Thomas Piketty from the French research institute, CEPREMAP, and Emmanuel Saez of the University of California at Berkeley produced a veritable treasure trove of data for researchers interested in the distribution of income. Using data from the Internal Revenue Service, Piketty and Saez reported gross pretax income for taxpaying units measured in 2000 dollars. This income excludes all government transfers to taxpayers—such as, Social Security, unemployment benefits, welfare payments, and so on—as well as employees' payroll taxes, and capital gains. Their data are especially valuable because, unlike most data sets, these provide information about the highest incomes.

These data show that for the bottom 99 percent of taxpaying units, the average income stood at $36,008 in 1970, then peaked in 1973—at the same time as hourly wages—at $38,206. This figure bottomed out in 1993 at $33,087. By 2004, average income for the bottom 99 percent recovered somewhat to $37,295 but was still below where it had been three decades earlier (Piketty and Saez 2006; see also Johnston 2003, 38–39; Krugman 2002).

Of course, not everybody in the bottom 99 percent fell behind, but the losses among the vast majority were sufficient to counterbalance the gains of the most fortunate members of this group. Also, as Piketty and Saez warn, the data require some refinement. Part of the shrinkage in the income per capita for the bottom 99 percent of the population results from a decline in the number of people within the average taxpaying unit. Also, the exclusion of capital gains creates a further understatement of income, especially among the most affluent of the bottom 99 percent.

As a result, taking individuals instead of tax returns as the unit of measurement, the average income of the bottom 99 percent has not decreased; but probably 90 percent of the population were worse off in 2004 than in 1970. During the same period, the top 10 percent increased its share of total income from about 31.51 percent in 1970 to 42.91 percent in 2004—that is, an increase of 11.40 percentage points.

Even among the richest 10 percent of the population, the unseemly distribution of income is increasingly skewing toward the richest of the rich. During the same 1970–2004 period, the share of the top 1 percent rose from 7.80 percent of total income in 1970 to 16.21 percent in 2004, an increase of 8.41 percentage points, meaning that this group enjoyed almost three-quarters of the entire 11.40 percentage point increase of the top 10 percent.

Even higher on the economic pyramid, this skewed pattern of income reproduces itself. The share of the top 0.1 percent increased from 1.94 percent of total income to 6.95 percent. This increase of 5.01 percentage points means that the top 0.1 percent of households captured almost 44 percent of the total increase of the share of income of the top 10 percent (Piketty and Saez 2006, Figure 3).

Moving up even further, the top 0.01—a mere 13,100 tax-paying households—increased its income share from 0.53 percent in 1970 to 2.87 percent in 2004, not much below where it stood on the eve of the Great Depression. This increase of 2.34 percentage points represented almost 21 percent of the total gains of the entire top 10 percent. Looked at from another perspective, between 1972 and 2001, this group saw its wages and salaries increase fifteen-fold (Dew-Becker and Gordon 2005, 104).

Keep in mind that in their article, Piketty and Saez did not include capital gains but they do in their supplemental data on the Web. There, they show that including capital gains boosts the income share of the top 1 percent in 2003 from 16.2 percent to 19.5 percent (Piketty and Saez 2006). As Jonathan Swift wrote back in 1733: "Big fleas have little fleas upon their backs to bite them, and little fleas have lesser fleas, and so ad infinitum." Alas, today, the big fleas are on the backs of their smaller brethren.

Other studies confirm the findings of Piketty and Saez. For example, in 1970 the top 10 corporate CEOs earned about 49 times as much as the average wage earner—again, only counting direct pay. By 2000, the ratio had reached the astronomical level of 2173:1. The rate of growth of executive pay has far outstripped the rate of growth of profits. For example, between the periods 1993–95 and 2001–03, compensation for the top five executives of public companies' relative to those companies' total earnings more than doubled from 4.8 percent to 10.3 percent (Bebchuk and Grinstein 2005).

Despite the decline in their average well-being, the bottom 90 percent probably still received about 30 percent of the increase in the Gross Domestic Product because of population growth. Even so, the Piketty and Saez data suggest that the wealthiest stratum of the nation was able to devour the majority of the $7 trillion growth in the economy between 1970 and 2002. In addition, the Gross National Product (GNP) does not exactly equal the income figures of the Internal Revenue Service, but the numbers are close enough to conclude that the top 10 percent of the population received the lion's share of all economic growth between 1970 and 2000.

These 13,100 richest families in America had about the same income as the poorest 25 percent of the households in the country (Piketty and Saez 2006; Krugman 2002). Of course, membership in this elite group was not unchanging, but it was probably relatively stable. Certainly, few of these fortunate people ever fell into the bottom 25 percent.

Such extreme inequality conjures up images of a world of old inherited wealth in which people passively live off relatively stable investments. That picture would be misleading. What seems to be driving this new inequality is a dramatic increase in labor income. I do not mean that those who live off of their investments have disappeared. These coupon clippers are still with us, but they are now joined by people who enjoy stratospheric salaries (see Piketty and Saez 2006).

For example, in 2006 the five leading Wall Street firms—Bear Stearns, Goldman Sachs, Lehman Brothers, Merrill Lynch, and Morgan Stanley—awarded an estimated $36 billion to $44 billion worth of bonuses to their 173,000 employees. The bulk will go to the top 1,000 people. Two executives alone account for almost $100 million (Herbert 2007). Worldwide, an estimated 3 billion people live on $2 per day. This $36 billion would be enough to allow about 1.4 million people to more than double their annual income.

One study examined the average pay for the top five executives in 1,500 firms included in major stock indexes. The average pay for these 7,500 people in 2001 was $6.4 million, numbering more than half of the 13,100 taxpayers in the top 0.01 percent, who, coincidentally, made an average of $6.4 million each in 2001 (Bebchuk and Grinstein 2005; Dew-Becker and Gordon 2005).

Of course, $6.4 million is not all that much money in the new world of inequality where big fish expect to earn more than other big fish. The payroll for major league baseball, football, and basketball players averages $2.48 million per player (Dew-Becker and Gordon 2005). The elite players earn many times this average. Similarly, movie stars can earn tens of millions of dollars for performing in a single film. These celebrity salaries capture popular attention, but they are still relatively modest compared to the really big fish.

The world of finance offers the most stratospheric incomes. For example, James Simons of Renaissance Technologies made $1.5 billion in 2005. Twenty-five other hedge-fund managers made at least $130 million that year (Anderson

2006). To add insult to injury, ordinary taxpayers have to subsidize these out-landish salaries because corporations can deduct their costs on their tax returns.

Ownership of wealth is even more concentrated than income. With the burst-ing of the dot-com bubble in 2000, as would be expected, wealth inequality has temporarily fallen a bit. Even so, by 2001, the top 1 percent of households owned 40 percent of the financial wealth in the United States (Wolff 2004). Had the cal-culation of the wealth holdings of the richest 1 percent been made while the stock market was still expanding, the number would have been even more extreme than the reported 40 percent.

Next, I will show that the extent of inequality is even more extreme. I have no doubt that inequality will continue its upward climb in the absence of a serious recession or a rapid change in the political climate.

Even More Inequality

Some economists quibble with the way Piketty and Saez estimate income. By including transfers, such as Social Security and by using a different estimate of inflation, the incomes of the bottom 90 percent of the population can appear to have grown by about 20 percent between 1970 and 2002—or about a mere six tenths of 1 percent per year.

Such adjustments are relatively minor. In fact, I would argue that the unad-justed income data that Piketty and Saez use are actually excessively conservative in measuring how far the poor have fallen behind. Ordinary people must increasingly work longer hours to get the income they earn. For example, between 1970 and 2002, annual hours worked per capita rose 20 percent in the United States, while falling in most other advanced economies (Organisation for Economic Co-operation and Development 2004c, 6).

In addition, the reported income of the poorer segments of society does not account for the many extra expenses poor people pay. For example, the data ignores the late fees that banks and other corporations charge. In 2004, banks, thrifts, and credit unions collected a record $37.8 billion in service charges on accounts, more than double what they received in 1994, according to the Federal Deposit Insurance Corporation and the National Credit Union Administration. Banks continue to raise fees for late payments, low balances, and over-the-limit charges to as much as $39 per violation. Some banks even charge for speaking with a service representative. Naturally, these fees predominately fall on the poor (Chu 2005; Foust 2005).

Insurance companies charge more for people in poor neighborhoods. The poor also find themselves at the mercy of predatory lenders. To make matters even worse, their food costs more because they lack convenient access to grocery stores. Even though the government disregards these factors in assembling its statistics about wealth and income, they can be significant (Brookings Institu-tion 2006).

At the same time, middle-class people are already rapidly losing their pen-sions and medical benefits, while government programs upon which they depend, such as Medicare and Medicaid, are becoming less generous.

The Piketty and Saez data also seriously underestimate the welfare of the rich. For example, their income measure precludes capital gains, which represent a major share of the income going to the very rich. In addition, because measures of inequality depend on government data, efforts by the rich to avoid taxes make the distribution of income appear far more equal than it actually is (Titmuss 1962, 22). The Internal Revenue Service estimated that 16 percent of the legal tax obligation goes unpaid. We can rest assured that the vast majority of this short-fall comes from the wealthiest members of society.

Corporate executives have another reason to hide their income. Shareholders as well as the public at large do not look kindly when executives take advantage of their position. As a result, corporations go to great lengths to camouflage parts of executive income. For example, corporations often shower high-rank-ing officers with loans, which they later forgive (Bebchuk and Fried 2004, 116–17). The full extent to which camouflaging income makes inequality meas-urements seem less extreme will probably never be known.

Economists understand that what economist Max Sawicky calls do-it-your-self tax cuts are not particularly difficult to pull off (Sawicky 2006). For the most part, academic economics has done little to investigate either the extent or the effect of the multitude of tax-avoidance strategies.

The few academic studies that do exist offer shocking glimpses into this underworld of financial manipulation. For example, in a globalized economy, hiding money offshore is not particularly difficult. One recent study estimated that the world's richest individuals have placed about $11.5 trillion worth of assets in offshore tax havens. This amount is roughly equal to the annual Gross Domestic Product of the United States. Of course, citizens of the United States are not responsible for the entire $11.5 trillion, but then the report does not account for the assets that corporations stash in tax havens (Mathiason 2005).

Another scheme to avoid taxes is to underestimate tax liabilities by reporting inflated purchase prices on assets. This practice reduces reported profits when the assets are sold, lowering taxes on capital gains. One study estimated that this deception reduced capital gains by about $250 billion (Dodge and Soled 2005). This form of tax avoidance obviously serves to benefit the richest taxpayers, although it does not affect the Saez and Piketty results, which exclude capital gains.

Although the IRS occasionally convicts an unsophisticated offender, cheating on taxes is relatively safe for the rich and famous. The IRS also makes inequality worse by devoting a disproportionate share of its investigative energies to scruti-nizing those without substantial resources, especially poor people who declare an Earned Income Tax Credit (Johnston 2003, chap. 9). As hotel magnate Leona Helmsley arrogantly said, "Only the little people pay taxes."

Helmsley, I might add, served eighteen months in jail for her financial trans-gressions but not because of any diligence on the part of the government. Her tax fraud only came to light because of information uncovered in a civil suit filed by contractors she had refused to pay.

We should not be surprised that people resort to illegitimate means to avoid paying taxes. What is absolutely shocking is the extent to which Congress, often covertly, crafts special interest loopholes to allow the rich and powerful to avoid paying taxes. David Cay Johnston's outstanding book, *Perfectly Legal*, describes how thoroughly government has rigged the tax system to favor the rich (Johnston 2003). The government facilitates shenanigans, such as Helmseley's, by steadily increasing the complexity of the tax code by allowing skilled tax lawyers to devise even more loopholes.

In summary, the clever tactics of tax avoidance, which prevent the Internal Revenue Service data from capturing a good deal of the wealth and income of the top 10 percent of the population, also mask the extent of inequality in the United States. At the other end of the spectrum, measures of inequality also ignore the excessive costs borne by the poor.

Flying High in the Corporate Sky

Over and above tax-related distortions in the distribution of income, the wealthy have access to resources that do not even count as income. Because corporations must disclose some information, the rest of the world can enjoy a glimpse into their world of spectacular privilege. Consider executives' personal use of corporate jets:

> When William Agee was running the engineering firm Morrison-Knudsen into bankruptcy, he replaced its one corporate jet, already paid off, with two new ones and boasted about how the way he financed them polished up the company's financial reports. His wife, Mary Cunnigham Agee, used the extra jet as her personal air taxi to hop around the United States and Europe. When Ross Johnson ran the cigarette-and-food company RJR Nabisco, which had a fleet of at least a dozen corporate jets, he once had his dog flown home, listed on the manifest as "G. Shepherd." And Kenneth Lay let his daughter take one of Enron's jets to fly across the Atlantic with her bed, which was too large to go as baggage on a commercial flight. (Johnston 2003, 62)

This description seriously understates the extent of this abuse. Consider this fuller account of the RJR Nabisco case:

> After the arrival of two new Gulfstreams, Johnson ordered a pair of top-of-the-line G4s, at a cool $21 million apiece. For the hangar, Johnson gave aviation head Linda Galvin an unlimited budget and implicit instructions to exceed it. When it was finished, RJR Nabisco had the Taj Mahal of corporate hangars, dwarfing that of Coca-Cola's next door. The cost hadn't gone into the hangar itself, but into an adjacent three-story building of tinted glass, surrounded by $250,000 in landscaping, complete with a Japanese garden. Inside a visitor walked into a stunning three-story atrium. The floors were Italian marble, the walls and floors lined in inlaid mahogany. More than $600,000 in new furniture was spread throughout, topped off by $100,000 in objets d'art, including an antique Chinese ceremonial robe spread in a glass case and a magnificent Chinese platter and urn. In one corner of the ornate bathroom stood a stuffed chair, as if one might grow fatigued walking from one end to the other. Among the building's other features: a walk-in wine cooler; a "visiting pilots' room," with television and stereo; and a "flight-planning room," packed with state-of-the-art computers to track executives' whereabouts

and their future transportation wishes. All this was necessary to keep track of RJR's thirty-six corporate pilots and ten planes, widely known as the RJR Air Force. (Burrough and Helyar 1990, 94; see also Strauss 2003; Minow 2001)

David Yermack of New York University's Stern School of Business produced a paper with the delightful title "Flights of Fancy: Corporate Jets, CEO Perquisites, and Inferior Shareholder Returns" in which he investigated the relationship between this particular luxury and corporate efficiency. He found that the cost of corporate jets for CEOs who belong to golf clubs far from their company's headquarters is two-thirds higher, on average, than for CEOs who have disclosed air travel but are not long-distance golf club members (Yermack 2004).

Yermack's paper reported that "more than 30 percent of Fortune 500 CEOs in 2002 were permitted to use company planes for personal travel, up from a frequency below 10 percent a decade earlier." Since Yermack's study the problem has continued to escalate. Between 2004 and 2005, the reported value of personal use of corporate aircraft increased 45 percent, according to government filings of the 100 largest public companies (Fabrikant 2006).

Not surprisingly, Raghuram Rajan, the chief economist of the International Monetary Fund, gallantly came to the defense of the corporations. He suggested, without the slightest hint of humor, that these expenditures may have actually been justified because they encouraged executives to be more efficient (Rajan and Wulf 2004). This justification does not seem particularly credible since Rajan's study did not bother to distinguish between planes used for business or personal purposes, including use by retired executives.

In fact, the personal use of corporate jets does not seem to be correlated with profitability at all. Of course, some of the firms that supply their executives with corporate jets for personal use are successful, despite such wasteful excesses, but the use of corporate jets is correlated with poor performance. According to Yermack: "Firms that permit personal aircraft use by the CEO under-perform market benchmarks by about 4 percent or 400 basis points per year, after controlling for a standard range of risk, size and other factors" (Yermack 2004).

A *Wall Street Journal* article entitled "JetGreen" followed up Yermack's report. It described corporate jets "as airborne limousines to fly CEOs and other executives to golf dates or to vacation homes where they have golf-club memberships" (Maremont 2005). Although executives must report such personal use of corporate jets as income, they rarely disclose anything near the full cost. Besides, hiding golfing expeditions as business activity is not particularly difficult.

Golf Digest provided further evidence of the negative consequences of corporate jets. Every two years this publication informs the golfing public about who are the best golfers among executive leaders. A *USA Today* reporter investigated whether their companies performed as well in the business world as their leaders did on the golf links. The results were not surprising: of the companies run by the top twelve golfers, two-thirds fared worse than the Standard & Poor's 500 index in 2006 (Jones 2006).

Of course, high-level corporate executives enjoy many other perks besides free travel, including the provision of luxury boxes at sports stadia, chefs, yard work, and a multitude of other benefits that ordinary people would have to pay for on their own, if only they could afford them. *New York Times* business columnist Gretchen Morgenson described the excesses of Donald J. Tyson, former chairman of Tyson Foods, which ranged from the personal use of corporate jets to housekeeping and lawn care. Echoing Leona Helmsley, she appropriately titled her article "Only the Little People Pay for Lawn Care" (Morgenson 2005).

While those who want to minimize inequality point to paltry government programs that aid the poor, they never mention the hidden wealth of the wealthy. Sociologist Robert K. Merton, father of a Nobel Prize-winning economist, introduced the concept of the Matthew Effect. Writing in the context of the accumulation of scientific prestige by elite scientists, Merton called attention to a biblical passage from the book of Matthew: "For to everyone who has will more be given, and he will have abundance but from him who has not even what he has will be taken away" (Merton 1968, 58, citing Matthew 25:29). Today we are witnessing an economic Matthew Effect well beyond what anybody could have imagined only a few decades ago.

The Right-Wing Victory Paid Off—For Now

Nobody could deny that the business offensive has certainly paid off handsomely—at least for its intended beneficiaries. This alarming transfer of wealth and income has accelerated since the election of George W. Bush in 2000, although the rich suffered a slight, temporary setback with the collapse of the dot-com bubble early in his administration.

The increase of inefficiency has become so extreme that even the arch freemarketeer, Alan Greenspan, then Federal Reserve Chairman, was moved to express concern, telling a Senate hearing, "I think that the effective increase in the concentration of incomes here, which is implicit in this, is not desirable in a democratic society" (Greenspan 2004). Admittedly, one might question the Chairman's sincerity, especially considering his preferred remedies for inequality. For example, in response to a question about Social Security from Senator Schumer at a hearing before the same Senate committee a few months later, Greenspan responded, "I've been concerned about the concentration of income and wealth in this nation . . . and [the privatization of Social Security], in my judgment, is one way in which you can address this particular question" (Greenspan 2005).

Warren Buffett, perennially the second richest person in the world, offered more genuine expression of concern regarding the excessive tax cuts that have mostly benefited the rich. After surveying his clerk and secretaries, he found that he paid a far lower share of his income in taxes even though he did not attempt to minimize his obligations through tax planning (B. Stein 2006). Buffett offered some national statistics to shore up his analysis: "Corporate income taxes in fiscal 2003 accounted for 7.4 percent of all federal tax receipts, down from a postwar peak of 32 percent in 1952. With one exception (1983), last year's percentage is the lowest recorded since data was first published in 1934. . . . Tax breaks for corporations (and their investors, particularly large ones) were a major part of the Administration's 2002 and 2003 initiatives. If class warfare is being waged in America, my class is clearly winning" (Buffett 2004).

Many of the largest corporations pay no taxes whatsoever. One study of 275 profitable Fortune 500 corporations with total U.S. profits of $1.1 trillion over the 3-year period, 2001–03, found that 82 of these corporations

> paid zero or less in federal income taxes in at least one year from 2001 to 2003. Many of them enjoyed multiple no-tax years. In the years they paid no income tax, these companies reported $102 billion in pretax U.S. profits. But instead of paying $35.6 billion in income taxes as the statutory 35 percent corporate tax rate seems to require, these companies generated so many excess tax breaks that they received outright tax rebate checks from the U.S. Treasury, totaling $12.6 billion. These companies' "negative tax rates" meant that they made more after taxes than before taxes in those no-tax years. (McIntyre and Coo Nguyen 2004)

Twenty-eight of these companies managed to get a negative tax rate over the entire three-year period—meaning that the government actually gave them money. To make matters worse, the inequities are getting more extreme year by year: "In 2003 alone, 46 companies paid zero or less in federal income taxes. These 46 companies, almost one out of six of the companies in the study, reported U.S. pretax profits in 2003 of $42.6 billion, yet received tax rebates totaling $5.4 billion. In 2002, almost as many companies, 42, paid no tax, report-ing $43.5 billion in pretax profits, but $4.9 billion in tax rebates. From 2001 to 2003, the number of no-tax companies jumped from 33 to 46, an increase of 40 percent" (McIntyre and Coo Nguyen 2004).

Putting this erosion of corporate taxes into perspective, the authors of the report conclude: "Corporate taxes paid for more than a quarter of federal outlays in the 1950s and a fifth in the 1960s. They began to decline during the Nixon administration, yet even by the second half of the 1990s, corporate taxes still covered 11 percent of the cost of federal programs. But in fiscal 2002 and 2003, corporate taxes paid for a mere 6 percent of our government's expenses" (McIn-tyre and Coo Nguyen 2004). A follow-up study showed even worse erosion of taxes at the state level (McIntyre and Coo Nguyen 2005).

Gaining a perspective on the extent of the effect of cuts in personal income taxes may be easier. In 2005, President Bush campaigned to make his tax cuts permanent. If he succeeds, the benefits for just the top 1 percent of the popula-tion over the following 75 years will amount to an estimated $2.9 trillion (Kogan and Greenstein 2005). In other words, the tax cuts for this small segment of the population over this period would equal about one-quarter of the current annual GNP of the United States.

The lethal combination of tax cuts for the rich alongside growing burdens on the poor threaten to annihilate what is left of social mobility. In the words of Thomas Piketty who was mentioned earlier for his startling work on income inequality, "These new high-income tax cuts, together with all the previous tax cuts (including the repeal of the estate tax), will eventually contribute to rebuild a class of rentiers in the U.S., whereby a small group of wealthy but untalented children controls vast segments of the U.S. economy and penniless, talented children simply can't compete. . . . If such a tax policy is maintained, there is a decent probability that the U.S. will look like Old Europe prior to 1914 in a couple of generations" (Altman 2003).

I do not mean to imply that the right wing is totally indifferent about the unfairness of the present system of taxes. Without betraying a trace of irony, a famous *Wall Street Journal* editorial wailed about "the non-taxpaying class," complaining about the "lucky duckies" who avoided their tax obligation (Anon 2002).

The lucky duckies in question were people who were too poor to earn enough to pay taxes, not the affluent beneficiaries of the right-wing revolution. And what a revolution it was! Even if we correct for population growth and transfer payments while ignoring all the reasons why the gains of the wealthy may be an understatement, we can still safely say that the right-wing revolution represents the largest transfer of wealth and income in the history of the world—far larger than what occurred during either the Russian or Chinese revolutions. After all, neither China nor Russia had an economy that came anywhere near $7 trillion, which is the amount by which the annual Gross Domestic Product in the U.S. economy grew between 1970 and 2002.

In terms of wealth, the differences are far more severe because creating an annual income flow requires a much greater level of wealth comparable to the difference between the annual rent of a house and its purchase price. Yet government policies continue to promote an even more extreme redistribution of wealth and income to the rich.

The words of John Taylor, a conservative American politician and political commentator two centuries earlier, come to mind. Writing of plunder, the underlying theme of this chapter, Taylor observed: "There are two modes of invading private property; the first, by which the poor plunder the rich, is sudden and violent; the second, by which the rich plunder the poor, slow and legal. . . . [Both] are equally an invasion of private property, and equally contrary to our constitutions" (Taylor 1814, 259).

Many conservative economists manage to turn a blind eye to this recent revolutionary confiscation. Worse yet, other economists even claim that these inequitable policies are necessary to create jobs or to make the economy more productive.

Capturing virtually all of the growth of wealth and income while shedding tax obligations may seem like cause for jubilation—at least within some circles—but, as I will show, when the chickens come home to roost this victory will turn out to be hollow, even for those who have captured the bulk of the plunder.

Setting the Stage

This book builds upon the understanding that a market economy is an inherently unstable system, with a built-in potential for periodic collapses. In the United States, crises had appeared every few decades, most famously in the Great Depression of the 1930s. In fact, over the last 300 years, devastating depressions regularly came every half century until the last half century.

That seemingly regular pattern of economic history suggested that another crisis was due by the early 1970s. At the time, the business press spent a great deal of time educating its readers about the dreaded Kondratieff cycle, named for the Russian economist who first identified the supposedly fifty-year pattern.

After a few years, the decade ended without an economic collapse and Ronald Reagan became president of the United States. Apprehension about the economic future gave way to an unwarranted optimism about the unlimited potential of markets.

Of course, Kondratieff never really explained the cause of the supposed regularity of the deep fifty-year business cycle, nor did anybody else for that matter. Just because the economy escaped the predicted crisis did not mean that it had actually dodged the bullet. In fact, confidence that grew in the wake of the failure of the timing of the Kondratieff prediction helped to sow the seeds of the impending economic collapse.

Cycles of confidence lie at the heart of normal boom and bust cycles, whether they be a massive Kondratieff cycle or the more common but less extreme variety. As the economy begins to prosper and business becomes more optimistic, optimism gives way to what economists now call irrational exuberance. Then, business casts caution to the wind, throwing money at projects that they would normally recognize as foolish.

At first, the cycle feeds on itself, because the illusion of prosperity initially stimulates demand, which seems to validate even fraudulent investments. Eventually, a few problems come to light, panic spreads, and the bust begins. Business remains timid, perhaps for many years, until a few brave souls begin to feel their oats. Their actions help to renew confidence and the cycle begins once again.

Each time the United States has increased income inequality disaster has followed. Here is the assessment from an influential book on income distribution, co-authored by the recent chair of the Harvard economics department:

> The period from 1860 to 1929 is thus best described as a high uneven plateau of wealth inequality. When did wealth inequality hit its historic peak? We do not yet know. We do know that there was a leveling across the 1860s. We also know that there was a leveling across the World War I decade (1912–1922), which was reversed largely or entirely by 1929. This leaves three likely candidates for the dubious distinction of being the era of greatest inequality in American personal wealth: c. 1860, c. 1914, and 1929. That each of these pinnacles was followed by a major upheaval—civil war and slave emancipation, world war, or unparalleled depression—suggests interesting hypotheses regarding the effects of these episodic events on wealth inequality (or perhaps even the impact of inequality on these episodic events). (Williamson and Lindert 1980, 51)

The best chance to avoid disaster is to try to maintain a balance. So, while radical policies favoring business may boost profits in the near-term, within a relatively short time virtually everybody—even the most favored business sectors—will have to pay a hefty price.

When the powerful grab too much too fast, the system is almost certainly headed for a disaster. Extra pressures build up, usually because the rich and the powerful have pushed their advantage too far. Then, the stage is set. Some seemingly minor event triggers the crisis. The balances that normally cushion the typical business cycle cease to function.

Although market economies require balance to avoid disaster, right-wing revolutionaries, intent on victory, not balance, remade the economy in the last three decades.

As the economy faltered in the late 1960s, capitalists believed that the only way for business to recover the advantages it enjoyed before the Great Depression was to take aggressive measures against the rest of society. In this quest, balance was out of the question. Instead, a certain amount of shortsighted meanness appeared to be a necessity.

Under the watch of the right wing, the distribution of income became skewed toward the rich in a way unseen since the 1920s. Increased inequality is not only a serious problem in itself, but is also a symptom of a whole array of equally dangerous tendencies. The right wing has engineered breakneck deregulation, increased incarceration, dangerous militarization, rapid deindustrialization, unchecked financialization, and the evisceration of the public sphere. Worse yet, this right-wing plague has contaminated much of the globe. Because international financial networks have become deeply engrained in virtually every country in the world, containing the crisis becomes almost impossible.

Throughout this book, I will use the expression "right-wing" to distinguish the current policies from traditional conservatism. Authentic conservatives want a minimal government with low taxes, but they display a certain degree of caution about the future consequences of their actions. Conservatives traditionally favor sound financial policies. They would never condone huge government deficits. Nor do authentic conservatives endorse military adventurism. Perhaps the quality that distinguishes the right wing from traditional conservatives is recklessness.

The reckless effort to commercialize and privatize every aspect of society creates an enormous gulf between rich and poor while destroying the environment. The problem with this conservative agenda is not just inequality or environmental damage, but a host of other policies that permeate society each of which will contribute to the self-destruction of the capitalist utopia conservatives hope to construct. For example, these policies have created disincentives to develop either labor-saving or environmentally friendly technologies, which are capable of giving domestic business a comparative advantage.

The following chapters will track the evolution of the right-wing revolution and elaborate on its destructive nature, as well as on economists' incapacity to deal with the severity of the problem.

Part 2

The Plot:
How the Right Wing
Captured America

Chapter 2

The End of the Golden Age of Capitalism

Background to the Golden Age

American business went through a series of dramatic changes during the first part of the twentieth century—none more traumatic than the Great Depression, which only ended when World War II revived the U.S. economy. The war not only revived prosperity but also paved the way for several decades in which the U.S. economy flourished as it never had before.

Because of the exceptional performance of the economy at the time, economists often refer to this period as the Golden Age. During the early Golden Age, everything seemed to be in place for an economy without depressions or recessions. Depression-year promises of a chicken in every pot gave way to an expectation of two cars in every garage. At the time, the strength of the economy seemed all the more dramatic considering that the U.S. economy had only recently emerged from the ashes of the Great Depression.

The striking dichotomy between the Depression and prosperity was not at all paradoxical. In reality, the Depression did much to pave the way for the postwar recovery. To begin with, the Great Depression set off a wave of intense competition that forced many firms to scrap outmoded plants and equipment. By 1939, U.S. firms had replaced one-half of all the manufacturing equipment that had existed in 1933 (Staehle 1955, 127). Although the total amount of investment during the Depression was relatively small, most of that investment was directed toward modernization rather than increasing capacity.

This modernization gave U.S. industry a level of efficiency far in advance of anything the world had ever seen before. University of Santa Clara economist, Alexander Field, makes a convincing case that the rate of productivity increase during the Depression years, 1929–41, was higher than any other period of the twentieth century—including the Golden Age (Field 2003).

During the war, business added still more modern equipment. This combination of modernization, together with the earlier elimination of old and outmoded capital goods left business with a stock of highly productive, modern capital that was the envy of the world. In fact, after the war, U.S. business was able to produce as much output as it had a decade before, even though it now used 15 percent less capital and 19 percent less labor (Staehle 1955, 133).

At the end of World War II, the United States held a seemingly unchallengeable economic position, in part due to the war. After all, the military production brought much new capital on line. The war sparked innovations that gave the United States the lead in much modern technology, including the development of the computer and the jet aircraft. At the same time, the war left the economies of potential U.S. competitors in ruins.

The state of consumer demand at the end of World War II also provided business with an exceptional opportunity. Many families had to defer their purchase of expensive consumer goods for an extended time. First, during the Depression many consumers were unable to afford cars and other expensive consumer goods. Later during the war, the government rationed production so factories that ordinarily produced consumer goods, such as automobiles, could build tanks and trucks. All the while, the existing stock of automobiles, as well as other consumer goods, was aging. This backlog of consumption was all the more powerful because many families liquidated their consumer debt and then accumulated considerable savings during the war. Consequently, a broad group of people had both the wherewithal and the desire to purchase expensive consumer goods, while business had more than ample productive capacity to meet their demands, setting the stage for a postwar boom.

In addition, financial conditions at end of World War II were almost ideal. Business was flush with cash. The Depression had unleashed a wave of bankruptcies, which had wiped out much of the previous U.S. corporate debt. The Depression had also frightened financial institutions, making them concentrate on high quality investments whenever possible. At the time, banks held many of their assets in the form of highly liquid U.S. government securities.

In terms of international finance, the position of the United States was just as enviable. By the end of World War II, about 70 percent of the world's monetary gold stock resided in U.S. vaults (Magdoff and Sweezy 1983, 9).

Psychological conditions following the war were also ideal. The harrowing experience of the Depression lowered expectations for the postwar economy. Many economists reasoned that since the war ended the Depression, ending the war would inevitably throw the economy back into a depression once again. An economic advisor to the Secretary of Commerce warned, "in the summer of 1946, unemployment may exceed 7 million, as rising civilian employment and reductions in working hours turn out to be insufficient to absorb the additions to the labor force consequent upon the rapid discharge of workers from the armed forces" (Bassie 1946, 126).

In June 1947, Joseph Livingston, a Philadelphia journalist surveying economists about their predictions, found that economists were expecting prices to fall 6.64 percent during the following year (Carlson 1977). Declines of this magnitude only occur during severe economic downturns. The public shared this bleak prognosis. In 1945, a Roper poll showed that less than 41 percent of the population of the United States believed that a postwar recession could be avoided (Wolfe 1981, 14).

A few economists at the time understood something new was afoot in the postwar period. James O'Leary was one of these exceptions. In a remarkable article, based on a paper that he delivered at the 1944 annual meeting of the American Economic Association, O'Leary gave a number of reasons why the postwar economy should prosper, but he emphasized the pent-up demand of consumers who were flush with a backlog of savings. Within a short period, O'Leary's interpretation of postwar conditions became commonplace, although it largely fell on deaf ears when he first made his views known (O'Leary 1945).

Initially, events seemed to confirm people's worst fears. At first, the economy did decline, so much so that one pair of economists later labeled the moment as the "Great Depression of 1946" (Vedder and Gallaway 1991). Unlike the real Great Depression, the setback of 1946 was very short-lived, so much so that few modern economists even know about it. Instead, the massive boom that followed dominates the memory of the postwar period.

While most economists predicted a depression, the economy proved them wrong. Prices did not fall at all. Instead, they rose at a rate of 8.09 percent, creating unfounded fears of a serious inflation (Carlson 1977). Robert J. Gordon of Northwestern University concluded, "Surely the greatest *economic* surprise of the first postwar decade was the failure of anything resembling a postwar depression to occur" (R. J. Gordon 1980, 115; emphasis original). Because the healthy economic conditions of the time were so unexpected, business responded even more enthusiastically than might have otherwise been the case.

The Great Depression also helped prepare the political as well as the economic climate in which the postwar prosperity blossomed. In the 1920s, the dominant political posture was to trust market forces to ensure continuing prosperity. The Coolidge administration faithfully reflected the *laissez-faire* temper of the middle class at the time. The Secretary of Commerce, Herbert Hoover, more realistically represented the interests of big business. Hoover understood that unregulated market forces by themselves would lead to certain disaster. Instead, Hoover advocated collusion through trade associations to moderate pure market forces, anticipating elements of the New Deal (Perelman 2006, chap. 7).

The Political Economy of the Golden Age

Once the Depression struck, much of the public quickly lost confidence in *laissez-faire*. This apprehension persisted during the early postwar period. After all, the experience of the Depression was still fresh in the minds of the American people, who could not forget that their ordeal had lasted more than a decade. They were intent on avoiding a repetition of the Great Depression at all costs. People realized that a multitude of smaller New Deal programs failed to get the economy rolling until the massive military build-up began.

During the early postwar period, many U.S. economists were coming under the spell of the recent theories of a brilliant British economist, John Maynard

Keynes (H. Stein 1969; Keynes 1936). Keynes exerted an enormous influence on economics even though he devoted a relatively small fraction of his time to economics proper. His other activities included work in business finance, government service, university management, and support for the arts, besides editing the prestigious *Economic Journal*. His ideas inspired the creation of both the International Monetary Fund and the World Bank.

Keynes was hardly a radical. He detested the socialist revolution in the USSR. Indeed, Keynes saw himself devising a strategy to save capitalism, believing that without some sort of government intervention the continuation of the Great Depression would doom the market economy.

The association between increased government spending during the war and the recovery from the Great Depression made a deep impression on the economics profession, especially in the United States. Given this mindset, the most common, albeit incorrect, interpretation of Keynes's work in the United States stressed that government spending was the most effective means of shoring up a weak economy (see Perelman 1989).

Many business leaders were sympathetic to this interpretation of Keynes. They actively lobbied for a continuation of a tame rendering of the new economic policy of the New Deal, recognizing its obvious economic benefits (H. Stein 1969; Neal 1981, 15–22). Nonetheless, once the Depression subsided, the right-wing hostility to government intervention openly took root in a substantial portion of the business community (R. Collins 1981). Many vehemently denounced both Keynes and Keynesian economics as socialistic.

In reality, Keynes's ideas were both complicated and vague. Even so, the idea took hold that the government could effectively prevent depressions by "scientifically" intervening in the economy to manage the level of economic activity, which would, in turn, boost productivity.

Although Keynes preferred productive investment, he facetiously suggested that the government could put people to work by hiring one group of people to bury old bottles filled with money while another group would dig for them (Keynes 1936, 129). In short, anything that could stimulate spending enough could get the economy back on its feet.

Keynes's theory seemed reasonable enough in many respects. If both the bottle buriers and bottle diggers received money for their superfluous services, both groups would spend their earnings on goods and services. The companies that sell to them would buy from other companies, eventually bringing life to all sectors of the economy. This notion that investment sets a cumulative process in motion lies at the heart of Keynesian policy, as it was practiced at the time. This simplistic reading of his work dovetailed with the experience of military spending lifting the economy out of the Great Depression.

Keynesian economics had another attraction. Unlike socialism, which advocated redistribution, Keynesian theory suggested that economic growth could benefit everybody. The research director of a business group, the Committee for Economic Development, asserted in 1947 that this strategy provided "a vitally needed lubricant to reduce class and group frictions. As long as we can get more by increasing the size of the pie there is not nearly so much temptation to try to get a bigger slice at the expense of others" (Maier 1987, 65).

Within this environment, some businesses found themselves compelled to compromise with labor. General Motors set the pattern for many large corporations by agreeing to give workers greater wages in return for labor's acquiescence to business's right to manage as it pleases. This arrangement, popularly known as the labor-management accord, worked relatively well as long as the economy continued to grow at a healthy pace. Within this agreement, the union abandoned its more far-reaching goals, opting instead to concentrate on a more limited objective of better wages. At the same time, business began to move factories to the Southern states where unions were less active.

Conservatives agreed with the goal of economic growth, but they insisted that nothing should interfere with the pursuit of profits. They warned that government involvement in the economy would hobble the natural dynamism of a capitalist economy and that preventing government interference in the economy would be the key to ensuring growth. According to this logic, by accepting the leadership of business, labor could benefit in the future once profits became strong enough to trickle down to the rest of society. Given the duration of the Great Depression, few poor people would be content to wait for an eventual trickle-down in the distant future.

Although some businesses may have appreciated the government's past efforts in fighting the Great Depression, by 1946 the urgency of depression conditions had subsided. A wave of strikes in the winter of 1945–46, described by one business writer as "nothing less than catastrophic civil war" frightened business leaders (Fones-Wolf 1994, 15). Charles F. Wilson, who temporarily left General Electric to become vice president of the War Production Board, declared in 1946, "The problems of the United States can be summed up: Russia abroad, labor at home" (Boyer and Morais 1955, 331). In other words, business must fight a domestic class war as vigorously as the ongoing cold war.

The first blow against the New Deal was the passage of the Taft-Hartley Act in June 1947 over President Truman's veto. This law severely limited union rights at a time when union support throughout much of the country was still strong. The Taft-Hartley Act also required unions to purge their ranks of communists, cutting organized labor off from its most effective organizers and the most articulate challengers of the status quo. Foreshadowing the right-wing onslaught a quarter century later, business launched an intensive campaign. The National Association of Manufacturers alone spent over $3 million on full-page ads in 287 daily newspapers in 193 key industrial centers in an effort to pass this legislation. Unions lacked the means to respond to the attack (see S. Rosenberg 2003, 70–74).

The Taft-Hartley Act was not the only arena of business activism. Even earlier, business interests gutted the proposed Full Employment Act of 1946 that would have given the government responsibility to fight unemployment. Initially, the act promised that "every American able to work and willing to work has the right to a useful and remunerative job."

Conservative political forces successfully whittled away at the bill. First Congress removed the word "Full" from the original title, renaming it The Employment

Act of 1946. In the final version of the law, the forces of moderation in the Congress reduced the requirement of full employment to a mere intention (Santoni 1986, 11–2). Instead of promising full employment, Congress inserted the reminder that "it is the policy of the United States to foster free competitive enterprise" to reassure business (Bailey 1950; see Wolfe 1981, 53). Robert Lekachman concluded: "Congress had carefully removed the political sting from S. 380's tail. The law merely asked the president only to prepare one more report. Congress was asked to do no more than study it" (Lekachman 1966, 174).

Despite the absence of any legislative requirement, the government still seemed to behave as if this meek rendering of the Employment Act actually constituted a modest commitment to the principle of low unemployment. Yes, recessions periodically infected the economy, but they were relatively mild. Each time the economy threatened to go into another deep slump, a moderate mix of fiscal and monetary stimuli managed to keep the economy afloat. As Milton Friedman noted, individuals and business became convinced that, "unless the recession is *exceedingly* minor, explicit action will be taken" (M. Friedman 1968; M. Friedman 1980, 79; emphasis original).

Indeed, during the first eight years after the passage of the Employment Act, the official unemployment rate averaged below 4 percent (*Monthly Review* 1983, 3). In reality, this enviable record owed little to a strong commitment to full employment on the part of the government. Instead, the economy was so healthy that quite minor efforts on the part of the government sufficed to keep the economy running strong.

Overconfidence

As the memories of the Great Depression receded into the hazy past, business and government leaders and many leading academic economists deluded themselves into believing that they had somehow mastered the art of managing the economy. When the economy temporarily slackened off during the Eisenhower years, followers of John Maynard Keynes assured the world that a renewed regimen of their policies would ignite another burst of prosperity. At the time, Paul Samuelson, perhaps the most influential of all American Keynesians, insisted that with proper fiscal and monetary policy the economy could have full employment and whatever rate of capital formation and growth it wanted (H. Stein 1969, 363).

In the words of economist Joseph Garbarino: "By 1955, the American economy had experienced ten years of fairly high level postwar prosperity and had weathered two minor recessions. The basis for concluding that a new economic era based on government's long-term commitment to stability and on industry's rationalized long range planning was at hand" (Garbarino 1962, 415). In light of the strong economic performance at the time, the tentative spirit of The Employment Act of 1946 gave way to an overarching confidence in the government's ability to control the economy. Walter Heller exuded the widespread air of certainty common at the time, writing: "[W]e now take for granted that the government must step in to provide the essential stability at high levels of employment and growth that the market mechanism, left alone, cannot deliver" (Heller 1966, 9).

Indeed, the economic successes of the Kennedy years redoubled the certainty in the powers of macroeconomic management. Confidence eventually gave way to overconfidence. Economists convinced themselves that their scientific training endowed them with the ability to fine tune the economy. For Arthur Okun, one of the most influential policy economists of the time: "More vigorous and more consistent application of the tools of economic policy contributed to the obsolescence of the business cycle pattern and refutation of the stagnation myths" (Okun 1970, 37; Okun 1980, 163).

Even the Council of Economic Advisors, caught up in the economic utopianism of the time, reported in 1965 that "both our increased understanding of the effectiveness of fiscal policy and the continued improvement of our economic information, strengthen the conviction that recessions can be increasingly avoided and ultimately wiped out" (Wolfe 1981, 69).

Indeed, the performance of the economy during the first decades of the postwar period seemed to justify the self-assurance of the Keynesians. In terms of "growth, price and distribution . . . the first two decades after World War II may well be a close approximation to the best that in practice can be obtained from a capitalist economy" (Minsky 1982, 376). Not surprisingly, promoters of the new economic policy became giddy with their early successes. They enthusiastically spread the gospel of perpetual prosperity, promising the faithful that they could manipulate the economy so deftly it could supposedly proceed forever untroubled by the periodic crises that plagued capitalism in the past.

This faith in the possibility of continuous prosperity became so ingrained that, by 1967, an international conference of influential economists convened in London to discuss whether the economists had actually vanquished the business cycle forever (Bronfenbrenner 1969a). Although most of the participants remained unconvinced of the ultimate demise of the business cycle, such skepticism was far from universal.

Most important, the business community largely accepted the notion that threat of a depression was a thing of the past. Investors who bet on the continuation of prosperity were more often than not being rewarded for their optimism at the time. Although successful investors could content themselves with the thought that they were sensible business people who recognized sound economic propositions, they typically based their expectations on the delusion that the inevitable downturn was unlikely, if not impossible.

Optimistic expectations seemed to be capable of fueling the postwar economic boom by stimulating a vigorous investment program, which would ensure that markets would be strong enough to sustain a high level of economic activity for decades on end. In this vein, Paul Samuelson assured the readers of his November 4, 1968, column in *Newsweek* that the new Keynesian economics works: "Wall Street knows it. Main Street, which has been enjoying 92 months of advancing sales, knows it" (DuBoff and Herman 1972).

A few economists warned that those who believed in the myth of perpetual prosperity were extrapolating from a mere two decades of experience in using their economic techniques (R. A. Gordon 1969, 4). This word of caution left most economists unfazed. Circles close to the center of the Democratic Party policy makers remained under sway of the idea that depressions were conquered once and for all (R. A. Gordon 1969, 4).

The overconfidence of the Keynesian economists paralleled a definite moderation in liberal expectations. Probably by the end of the war and certainly by the beginning of the cold war, liberals had largely abandoned their hopes of a serious restructuring of the economy. Instead, they merely called for more growth under the existing state of affairs, signaling that the liberals had run out of new ideas.

Keynesian economic management helped the economy do better than it might have done without any government intervention, but the market—even the guided market—is a system bedeviled with many complexities that defy simple solutions. As a result, markets fall far short of what a more organized, cooperative system could deliver.

Several problems plague the Keynesian scheme. The least noted of these is a subtle long-term problem. Suppose that government succeeds in preventing depressions or recessions for an extended period, just as the Keynesians suggested they could. During prosperous times, business has much less incentive to radically improve its technology. This problem explains why Alexander Field found that productivity improved so much during the Depression.

A more obvious problem is that investment depends upon anticipation about the future. When a business builds a factory, it does so with the expectation that it will find a ready market for the product. These expectations can fail for two reasons. First, the product may be inappropriate. For example, people purchased few slide rules after cheap calculators came on the market. When the product depends upon fashion rather than technology, future markets are even more uncertain.

An even deeper problem prevents markets from working at full efficiency. The productive potential of the economy far outstrips existing demand, especially when wealth and income are unequally distributed. Although inequality had eased during the New Deal and the war, insufficient demand still presented a barrier to full employment.

The American Keynesians were not worried about the long run threat to productivity. Instead, they turned their attention to the immediate future: what could be done to keep the economy humming? Here the Democrats ran into a political rather than an economic difficulty. They feared being tarred as socialists for promoting innovative government programs. They hit upon a solution, but it was not pretty. As we shall see, the bright and shiny economy of the Golden Age had a dark, ugly underside.

The Economists' Surrender

The stellar economic performance of the Golden Age owed much to an excessive reliance on military spending. When World War II ended, most influential policy makers feared that the natural course of the business cycle would return the U.S. economy to depression conditions without energetic government intervention.

At the same time, much of the business community had an ingrained distrust of government intrusion into the economy. As postwar prosperity took hold, more people began to feel that they did not need the government to ensure their prosperity. To some conservative ideologues and business interests in the United States, increased government spending and therefore Keynesianism had long smacked of socialism.

Virulent anticommunism was already a powerful political force in the postwar United States. Senator Joseph McCarthy, a now discredited politician, rose to prominence by making wildly overblown accusations of domestic communist conspiracies.

McCarthyism, of course, began well before McCarthy took center stage. Richard Nixon rose to national prominence with his own pre-McCarthy McCarthyism. However, this new wave of anticommunism was successfully blacklisting academics, government officials, entertainers, and just ordinary people.

Paul Samuelson, whom I mentioned earlier, became a prominent target. Samuelson's Keynesian-oriented book had become the most popular introductory book in the United States after the right wing succeeded in pressuring schools to withdraw support for Lorie Tarshis's earlier textbook. The Veritas Foundation was a leader in this effort (Leeson 1997, 125). A commentator in the right-wing *Educational Reviewer* asked: "Now if (1) Marx is communistic, (2) Keynes is partly Marxian, and (3) Samuelson is Keynesian, what does that make Samuelson and others like him? The answer is clear: Samuelson and the others are mostly part Marxian socialist or communist in their theories" (MacIver 1955, 128).

Later, long after becoming the first American to win the Nobel Prize for economics, Samuelson recalled, "having tasted blood in trying to root the Tarshis text out of colleges everywhere, some of the same people turned toward my effort" (Samuelson 1997, 158). Samuelson succeeded at defending his work, but at a serious cost. In a 1977 lecture, Samuelson described how he felt compelled to go to great lengths to make his book less controversial:

> if you were a teacher at many a school and the Board of Regents of your university was on your neck for using subversive textbooks, it was no laughing matter. Many months were involved in preparing mimeographed documentation of misquotations on the part of critics and so forth. Make no mistake about it, intimidation often did work in the short run. . . . My last wish was to have an intransigent formulation that would be read by no one. . . . As a result I followed an Aesopian policy of paying careful attention to every criticism of every line and word of my text. . . . In a sense this careful wording achieved its purpose: at least some of my critics were reduced to complaining that I played peek-a-boo with the reader and didn't come out and declare my true meaning. (Samuelson 1977, 870–72)

Ironically, Samuelson has a long history of antagonism to Marxian ideas, but tarring him with such labels was effective. Many of the leading Keynesian economists in the United States soon learned to shield themselves from the taint of socialism. Either because they succumbed to the anticommunist climate of the day or because they feared they had no chance of stimulating the economy through productive government spending. These avowed followers of Keynesian theory adopted a stunted version of their master's approach, often restricting their calls for increased spending to military programs, presumably intended to assist in the fight against communism—an approach that became known as military Keynesianism. In this sense, McCarthyism continued victoriously, long after the senator had faded from the scene.

In effect, then, the leading Keynesians in the United States proceeded as if they could ignore the relative merits of different kinds of spending. I have difficulty believing that Keynes himself would have sanctioned military Keynesianism. Although Keynes preferred that the government spend its funds on productive activities, his theory offered few specifics to dissuade the cold warriors who acted in his name (Perelman 1989).

Keynes himself failed to alert economists to the difference between military and civilian spending. After all, his *General Theory* blandly looked at the economy as a whole, paying no attention to the specifics of what was produced. To make matters worse, Keynes's followers took heart from his humorous aside about burying bottles, suggesting that society could disregard the question of who benefits from any particular program. Economists often fell back on saying that a rising tide supposedly lifts all ships. According to this line of thinking, spending of any kind—even wasteful military spending—stimulates the economy.

The Democratic Party followed a similar line of retreat, casting aside the occasional daring ideas that had bubbled up during the New Deal and the early postwar period. Instead, the party almost completely purged itself of leftist or even progressive influences, largely pinning its hopes on increased government spending—all too often military spending.

Military Keynesianism: NSC 68

During the Truman administration, Paul Nitze was heading a joint State Department and Defense Department task force. This group drafted an influential document, known as NSC 68, which became the clarion call for military Keynesianism (Etzold and Gaddis 1978). It proposed an intentional escalation of the cold war, in part, to stimulate the economy. This document ominously warned that "there are grounds for predicting that the United States and other free nations will within a period of a few years at most experience a decline in economic activity unless more positive governmental programs are developed than are now available" (United States National Security Council 1950, 410).

Given the risks of a renewed depression, NSC 68 called for a massive military buildup, which could simultaneously fight recession and communism. The authors explained:

> From the point of view of the economy as a whole, the program might not result in a real decrease in the standard of living, for the economic effects of the program might be to increase the gross national product by more than the amount being absorbed for additional military and foreign assistance. One of the most significant lessons of our World War II experience was that the American economy, when it operates at a level approaching full efficiency, can provide enormous resources

for purposes other than civilian consumption while providing for a high standard of living. (United States National Security Council 1950, 436–37)

According to the novelist Gore Vidal, Eisenhower's Secretary of State, John Foster Dulles, saw another purpose for NSC 68. Vidal heard Mr. Dulles predict that this policy would lead to an arms race that the Soviets were certain to lose because they were so much poorer. As a result, the Soviet economy would suffer irreparable harm trying to match U.S. military spending (Vidal 1992, 88). This idea circulated more openly during the Reagan years.

Military Keynesianism created risks of its own. In his widely praised, but largely unheeded Farewell Address, President Eisenhower warned of this unprecedented power of the military-industrial complex in American life: "In the councils of government, we must guard against the acquisition of unwarranted influence, whether sought or not, by the military-industrial complex. The potential for the disastrous rise of misplaced power exists and will persist." Eisenhower's warning was directed at the military Keynesianism of the Democratic Party, which had just alarmed the public about an imaginary missile gap *vis-à-vis* the Soviets during John F. Kennedy's presidential campaign.

Despite Eisenhower's warning, military Keynesianism won an official recognition that remained more or less unchallenged within the circles of power. In fact, people associated with this early military Keynesianism movement later became prominent among the neoconservatives who led the United States into the disastrous invasion of Iraq.

The Unbalanced Balance Sheet of Military Keynesianism

The purpose of military Keynesianism went beyond intending to increase the overall economic or political power of the United States. It was expected to shift the distribution of power within this society.

Obviously, military spending would ensure prosperity for the arms dealers and those who supply them. Military spending was also something that most business leaders could appreciate. Unlike some government activities that compete with the private sector—such as the provision of housing, transportation, or health care—military spending does not. In this sense, business appreciated the wastefulness of military spending.

Alan Wolfe used the housing sector to illustrate this attitude: "In 1940, when Congress passed the Lanham Act to provide 700,000 units of government housing for defense workers, the industry inserted a clause that these units would be destroyed when the war ended" (Wolfe 1981, 82). Similarly, he cited a Philadelphia realtor quoted in the *National Real Estate Journal*: "If I had to choose between seeing every old city in the country as an ash heap and seeing the government become landlord to its own citizens, I should prefer the ash heap" (Wolfe 1981, 82, citing Binns 1943; see also Gelfand 1975). In other words, with military spending, government purchases the means of destruction from private business without threatening existing markets the way that public housing would.

So Keynes's theory evolved into a strategy to float our ships on a rising tide of military spending in the name of the sacred creed of anticommunism. I can state here without equivocation that a rising tide does not lift all ships, as the economy of the 1990s clearly proved. Market economies develop unevenly. Any policy will hurt some group and help others. Military spending is no exception in this regard. Keynesian theory turned economists' attention from the specific impact of military spending to the beneficial impacts of an increase in government spending as a whole, regardless of its intended purpose.

Among the activities that military Keynesianism passed over was a concentrated effort to improve the civilian sector of the economy. Although military spending would provide employment for many workers, it would also undermine the government's ability to provide for other needs. Sadly, little thought was given to the wonderful opportunities that could have been possible if the largess of military budgets had been diverted to activities that could have improved the world.

Yet, military Keynesianism seemed to satisfy people of all stripes, except those without power. Liberals could satisfy themselves that the government was acting to maintain full employment. Business relished the military contracts, without the prospect of government doing anything to reduce their business opportunities. In addition, high military budgets also provided the excuse to reject popular demands for social programs, such as those that were initiated during the New Deal. Ultrapatriots could revel in the military superiority of United States. In addition, the economists would be free of any taint of socialism. The losers—those who could have benefited if the government had invested in the health, education, and welfare of the people—were not given a voice in the decision to embark on the path of military Keynesianism or even informed about the stakes.

In the end, military spending was unable to keep the Golden Age afloat. Business learned as much during the Vietnam War and then quickly forgot this lesson, while the government continued to squander its wealth through foolish and destructive ventures.

The Return of the Business Cycle

Despite the enormous wealth sunk into the military, by the late 1960s, the economy began to sink into a long period of decline. While perpetual prosperity seemed assured, few people—whether business leaders, elected officials, or economists—realized that the United States had spent the majority of its history enmeshed in either depressions, recessions, or wars. Time and time again, the economy would emerge from one of these periods of turmoil, then enjoy a period of prosperity, only to sink back once again. Never, however, was the boom period as successful as it was during the Golden Age.

In reality, the economic downturn should not be surprising. Markets have an intrinsic rhythm of boom and bust. After an economy runs at full throttle for a time, strains and pressures build up in the form of excessive speculation and imbalances due to inappropriate investments by overly optimistic firms. In addition, as Alexander Field's work on the Great Depression suggested, with depressions and recessions suppressed, business has less incentive to develop the kinds of efficiencies that allow for economic growth. Such is the nature of the capitalist economy that it requires periodic recessions or even depressions in order to steady itself (Perelman 1999).

As a result, as the Golden Age wore on, the rate of productivity growth began to experience a serious decline. So, even though wages stagnated, the rate of profit began to decline. This turn of events took business by surprise.

People rarely anticipate the sudden economic changes characteristic of a market economy. During the Golden Age, who would have guessed that for many of the citizens of the United States the fear of not even having a home, let alone a garage, would become a reality within a couple of decades? Who could have anticipated during the Golden Age that the United States would soon add such hideous words as homelessness, rust belt, and deindustrialization to its vocabulary?

Economists have never come to a consensus about what made the Golden Age so much better than the norm (Griliches 1988, 19). Business learned this lesson during the Vietnam War and then quickly forgot it, while the government continued to squander its wealth through foolish and destructive ventures.

These two differing events that characterized the period from 1930 through 1945 had one characteristic in common: both elicited strong government intervention that bequeathed extraordinarily healthy conditions to the economy that allowed for decades of almost uninterrupted increases in prosperity.

Just as the economy had used up the momentum that made the Golden Age possible, corporate leaders drew the opposite lesson from the experience—that government intervention was the cause of all of the ills of the economy; that only an unfettered market could ensure perpetual prosperity. With the slackening of economic growth, business could no longer afford to share the fruits of prosperity with labor. The stage was set for a more confrontational approach. Business was ready to hear Lewis Powell's message that will figure prominently in the next chapter.

Perhaps this outcome was predictable. The U.S. economy seemed to have a rhythm in which business gains a huge advantage every half-century or so. Each of these episodes seemed to end with an economic catastrophe during which business temporarily lost ground to the rest of society. This ebb and flow of power was not obvious at the time. Just as Tolstoy observed in the beginning of *Anna Karenina*, "each unhappy family is unhappy in its own way" (Tolstoy 1970, 1), the particulars of each of these cycles of disaster was still unique.

In the case of the late twentieth century, capital rebelled and carried out what was probably the greatest redistribution of wealth and income in the history of the world. At the same time, the right-wing revolution was unwittingly setting in motion a set of forces that threatens to undermine prosperity—even the prosperity of capital itself. As this cycle developed, the right wing convinced most of the economics profession to support its agenda.

Chapter 3

The Right Mobilizes

Business on the Ropes

The 1960s and early 1970s promised great change in the world. A vibrant job market gave workers and students the confidence to challenge the status quo, knowing that the economic consequence of incompliant behavior would not be very consequential. The majority of college students rejected the idea of a career in business, a choice made easier by the ease of getting by without climbing the career ladder (Vogel 1989, 54–57). Even more overtly, young people throughout the United States were flaunting their contempt for the status quo with the clothing they wore, the music they played, and the drugs they used.

Workers were in open rebellion on the shop floor. Just like the students, many young people on the assembly lines longed for more meaningful work. Merely toiling in repetitive jobs for more material goods did not seem to be an attractive enough future. A good number of these blue-collar workers identified with the counterculture. Some observers claimed that a visitor could not walk from one end of an automobile factory to another without feeling the effects of the pervasive marijuana smoke.

Perhaps most dramatically, Vietnam protests were sprouting like mushrooms. Along with the antiwar movement, the civil rights movement, the women's movement, the environmental movement, and virtually every imaginable challenge to the status quo, seemed to be gaining support. Even the consumers' movement became more militant. Perhaps most dramatically for the corporate world, people attacked places of business. Thirty-nine branches of the Bank of America experienced assaults, including one attack in 1970 that burned a branch in Santa Barbara, California to the ground (Vogel 1989, 57).

This ferment even affected the military—an institution with the means to enforce discipline with far more severity than the civilian sector. Yet a good number of soldiers, disgusted by the Vietnam War, rebelled against military discipline. Thousands deserted. Some soldiers even killed their officers, although much of the problems of military discipline did not appear in the mass media.

To a large extent, the government had to partially accommodate the popular anger at the status quo—so much so that Richard Nixon, no radical by any stretch of the imagination, left a legislative legacy far more radical than anything that was accomplished during the longer tenure of the supposedly liberal Bill

Clinton. One influential book concluded, "In retrospect, some would call the Nixon presidency the 'last liberal administration'" (Yergin and Stanislaw 1997, 64). Regarding the administration's regulatory record, Herbert Stein, Nixon's chief economic advisor and father of the television personality, Ben Stein, regretfully recalled, "Richard Nixon regarded himself as an opponent of government regulation of the economy. His economic advisers and most of his economic officials were even more strongly of that view. The outcome was disappointing. Probably more new regulation was imposed on the economy during the Nixon administration than in any other presidency since the New Deal, even if one excludes the temporary Nixon foray into price and wage controls" (H. Stein 1984, 190).

Nixon's legacy includes the Food Stamp program, creation of the Environmental Protection Agency, the Occupational Safety and Health Administration, Earned Income Tax Credits, and the Equal Employment Opportunity Commission, along with passage of the Freedom of Information Act and the Clean Water Act.

Nixon was not inclined to be a progressive. He went out of his way to fill positions with business-friendly people. As the Watergate scandal later revealed, he would stop at nothing to protect its power, and thereby the power of the powerful economic forces that his administration represented. Even more cynically than the Watergate affair, the first Nixon campaign secretly derailed peace talks with Vietnam to deny the Democratic candidate, Vice President Hubert Humphrey, any credit for extricating the government from a tragic military quagmire.

With all the turmoil on the streets and so many people challenging the system, this period merely represented an opportunity to move toward a more balanced society capable of curbing previous excesses. Nonetheless, the political climate during the Nixon administration terrified many conservatives, who worried about the prospect of a radical takeover of the state and the end of capitalism, as they knew it.

I remember chairing an environmental meeting in Chicago in 1970, when David Friedman—son of Milton Friedman, the leading conservative economist in the United States at the time and now a distinguished economist in his own right—spoke up in defense of an endangered species. He went on describing its decline in emotional terms until he finally came to his punch line—the species in question was none other than the American capitalist.

I did not realize it at that time, but David Friedman's remarks were not quite as original as I thought. While Friedman demonstrated good humor in making his case, others were less jocular in making the same point. A few years later at a meeting of elite corporate executives called by a well-connected business organization, The Conference Board, the businessmen expressed horror as a series of disasters, scandals, and injustices shook public confidence in business. One displayed proper gallows humor, lamenting: "At this rate business can expect support from the environmentalists. We can get them to put the corporation on the endangered species list" (Vogel and Silk 1976, 71).

Others expressed their fears in a more straightforward manner, exclaiming, "The American capitalist system is confronting its darkest hour" (Vogel and Silk 1976, 71). The participants voiced their skepticism for democratic solutions. One executive warned that "the dolts have taken over the power structure and the capacity of the nation in the US" (Vogel and Silk 1976, 189). Another asked, "Can we still afford one man, one vote? We are tumbling on the brink." Still another warned: "One man, one vote has undermined the power of business in all capitalist countries since World War II" (Vogel and Silk 1976, 75). Ominously, a number of the assembled executives spoke vaguely of the need for "war-time discipline" and "a more controlled society" (Vogel and Silk 1976, 76).

The Trilateral Commission, an organization of elites in the United States, Europe, and Japan commissioned a volume entitled, *The Crisis of Democracy: Report on the Governability of Democracies*. The author of the contribution on the United States, Samuel P. Huntington, an influential professor at Harvard, complained, "The vigor of democracy in the United States in the 1960s thus contributed to a democratic distemper, involving the expansion of governmental activity, on the one hand, and the reduction of governmental authority, on the other" (Huntington 1975, 102).

According to Huntington, "Some of the problems of governance in the United States today stem from an excess of democracy . . . the effective operation of a democratic political system usually requires some measure of apathy and noninvolvement on the part of some individuals and groups (Huntington 1975, 114). So, for Huntington, if only people would become more apathetic and uninvolved in the political process, a stunted democracy would work to the satisfaction of conservatives.

Although the executives vented their frustration at the environmentalists and other social activists, they probably realized that the real threat they faced was something far more dangerous: the economy was rapidly deteriorating. This weakening of the economy in the late 1960s came as a complete shock. People had been taking prosperity for granted. Now, with its enviable conditions rapidly eroding, business was unlikely to sit by for long, especially while it faced severe challenges to its privileges and power.

Attacking social movements and policies might have given some satisfaction to business executives, but the social movements in themselves did not directly threaten business, except to the extent that they indirectly undermined the ability to discipline workers. The underlying problem was the built-in tendency for market economies to fall into deep recessions or even depressions.

In any case, business launched an aggressive offensive in an effort to regain control of the situation. Control remained illusive, but at least business could shore up its profits by curtailing wages, regulations, and taxes. In this respect, business was successful. The redistribution of income toward the rich reflects the extent of their success, although their policies have already proven destructive for the majority of society and will ultimately even harm the interests that business executives hold most dear.

Business Mobilizes

In the tense environment of the 1960s, business was not about to stand by and allow democratic forces to challenge its power. Perhaps the most effective battle cry came in 1971 from what now appears to be a most unlikely source—soon to be Supreme Court Justice Lewis Powell. Today, the world largely remembers Powell as a moderate Southern justice who was willing to make some accommodations to the civil rights movement.

Powell's contribution to the right-wing revolution occurred behind the scenes. At the time, he was a high-level corporate lawyer who strongly identified with his clients, so much so that he took up smoking because he was representing Philip Morris (Jeffries 1994, 189). Powell was also chairing the Richmond City School Board and the Virginia State Board of Education.

Eugene B. Snydor, Jr., a neighbor and friend, was a director of the U.S. Chamber of Commerce and chair of the Chamber's Education Committee. Snydor asked Powell to prepare a report on what the Chamber later called "ways to provide the public a more balanced view of the country's economic system" (Media Transparency. n.d.). Powell's report, dated August 23, 1971, a mere two months before his nomination to the court, was called "Attack on American Free Enterprise System." A more appropriate title would have been "The Attack of American Free Enterprise System."

Powell's memo is largely forgotten today. A lengthy biography of almost 700 pages filled with detail about Powell's life never even mentioned the memorandum (Jeffries 1994), yet this short piece set off a movement that changed the face of the world. The memo also seems to have energized the Chamber. Although the Chamber is perhaps one of the most powerful lobbies in Washington today, its influence had dwindled by that time. Michael Pertschuk, chair of the Federal Trade Commission during the late 1970s, no doubt exaggerated when he described the Chamber of that period "as a feeble and discredited vestigial organ." Pertschuk credits the reinvigorated Chamber as a prime mover in rolling back regulation:

> The communications arsenal of the Chamber of Commerce includes a biweekly newsletter, *Washington Report*; A monthly magazine, *Nation's Business*; a telephone "hotline" that, it is claimed, can generate 12,000 phone calls to legislators within twenty-four hours; radio programs; and a television show, "It's Your Business," syndicated to 137 television stations. In April 1982 the Chamber inaugurated a nationwide satellite television network, the American Business Network (Biznet), unabashedly calling it "the most effective tool ever devised to influence legislation." (Pertschuk 1982, 57n)

More recently, Mark Blyth observed:

> Capitalizing on the Congressional reforms in 1974 that wrested power away from incumbent committee chairs and senior senators, the ACC [American Chamber of Commerce] began to mobilize more from the grass roots up, on the assumption that direct influence at the district level would have a higher payoff as power in

Congress was now more diffuse. By 1980, the ACC had set up twenty-seven hundred Congressional Action Committees in member districts. These institutional reorganizations were so successful that "within a week [the ACC] could carry out research on the impact of a bill on each legislator's district and through its local branches mobilize a 'grassroots campaign' on the issue in time to affect the outcome of a vote." (Blyth 2002, 153n)

Despite its massive influence, Powell's memo displayed virtually no interest in coming to grips with the issues that motivated the social movements. Despite the memo's call for a vigorous ideological challenge to the left, Powell gave no indication that he had even bothered to read much about the issues of the day, let alone anything that the left had to say. Instead, he merely expressed his dismay that people disagreed with the conservative view of the world that Powell and his clients shared.

The manifesto included only a handful of references from the popular press, made up of three items from his local Richmond papers, along with single nods to *Newsweek*, *Fortune*, the *Washington Post*, the *Wall Street Journal*, and *Barron's*. He mentioned only one now forgotten book entitled *The Ideological War against Western Society*—not even the book itself but just an introduction by Milton Friedman.

John Calvin Jeffries, Powell's former clerk and his biographer, described Powell as a man who held dear the old Southern way of life. He "venerated the traditional connectedness of home, church, and school. He feared the rootlessness, the anonymity, the impersonality of life in modern cities." In a Prayer Breakfast Speech to the American Bar Association in 1972, Powell lamented that Americans were being "cut adrift from the type of humanizing authority which in the past shaped the character of our people." Teachers, parents, neighbors, ministers, employers—these were the "personal authorities [that] once gave direction to our lives." Relationships with them "were something larger than ourselves, but never so large as to be remote, impersonal, or indifferent. We gained from them an inner strength, a sense of belonging, as well as of responsibility to others." After recounting Powell's expressions of his values, his biographer concluded, "Here was Powell the true conservative" (Jeffries 1994, 297).

Many of the protesters on the streets shared some of Powell's lofty sentiments, calling for more humanized personal relationships, but Powell's vision of a good society sharply differed from theirs. Although Powell was not an archsegregationist, he was far from friendly to the civil rights movement. For example, writing in *US News and World Report*, Powell condemned civil disobedience. "This heresy," he wrote, "was dramatically associated with the civil rights movement by the famous letter of Martin Luther King [Jr.] from a Birmingham jail. As rationalized by Dr. King, some laws are 'just' and others 'unjust'; each person may determine for himself which laws are 'unjust'; and each is free—indeed even morally bound—to violate the 'unjust' laws." Powell rejected such views as a precursor of "organized lawlessness and even rebellion" (Powell 1967, 238).

Could Powell's biographer also have noted in this context: "Here was Powell the true conservative"? After all, Powell's leadership in supporting Nixon's first Supreme Court nominee, Clement Haynsworth, Jr., a very conservative Southerner who was identified with segregation, seems to have been what sparked his own nomination. The nomination failed because of Haynsworth's financial irregularities rather than his civil rights record, but it signaled Nixon's Southern Strategy—a successful appeal to the racist Southern electorate to abandon its traditional Democratic leanings.

I should add that Powell's expression of disgust with civil disobedience is ironic. As a corporate lawyer, he knew corporate civil disobedience was commonplace. In fact, some federal judges even believe that corporations have an overriding obligation to their stockholders to increase profits, even if their actions are illegal (Easterbrook and Fischel 1982).

Powell's manifesto was a militant call to arms rather than a serious analysis of reality. Powell declared: "political power is necessary; that such power must be assiduously [sic] cultivated; and that when necessary, it must be used aggressively and with determination." He called upon business to mount an aggressive ideological war. He pointed to the campuses as his first line of attack. He warned that business should not directly challenge academic freedom as such, but rather it should demand "openness," "fairness" and "balance"—by which he meant the business perspective.

Powell exhorted business to apply every conceivable kind of pressure to change the educational system, the political system, the legal system, and the media—all of which had failed, in his eyes, to adequately protect business interests. According to the memo, "[t]he most disquieting voices joining the chorus of criticism come from perfectly respectable elements of society: from the college campus, the pulpit, the media, the intellectual and literary journals, the arts and sciences, and from politicians. In most of these groups the movement against the system is participated in only by minorities. Yet, these often are the most articulate, the most vocal, the most prolific in their writing and speaking."

Powell decried every sort of challenge to business, even the questioning of tax loopholes: "It is dismaying that many politicians make the same argument that tax measures of this kind benefit only 'business,' without benefit to 'the poor.' The fact that this is either political demagoguery or economic illiteracy is of slight comfort. This setting of the 'rich' against the 'poor,' of business against the people, is the cheapest and most dangerous kind of politics."

Like the executives that assembled at the Conference Board meeting, Powell warned that the very survival of the free enterprise system was at stake. Even so, he complained that business leaders "have shown little stomach for hard-nose contest with their critics and little skill in effective intellectual and philosophical debate."

Powell gave few specifics about the enemies who threatened what Powell called, "the free enterprise system," but the one person to whom he gave the most attention was Ralph Nader. This choice was ironic. Nader was an earnest, uncharismatic, quiet young man of Lebanese descent, very much unlike the protesters who infuriated Powell. In fact, Nader was actually a very strong advocate for the free enterprise system that Powell espoused.

Like Powell, Nader favored stronger law enforcement, but his targets were the mammoth corporations—some of the same corporations that Powell represented—that were able to abuse their power to prevent the sort of fair play that markets are supposed to provide.

For example, Nader first came to public attention a few years earlier in 1965 with a book entitled *Unsafe at Any Speed*, which detailed the reluctance of the automobile industry to produce safe cars. He singled out General Motors' Chevrolet Corvair, which had a suspension that made it liable to roll over. In the words of Nader's biographer, "[w]orried about litigation challenging the Corvair's safety, GM hired private detectives to tail Nader in an attempt to dig up information that might discredit him, and even had women accost him in an apparent seduction/blackmail scheme. Instead, journalist James Ridgeway broke the story about GM's snooping and dirty tricks in *The New Republic*" (Bollier 1991).

Nader sued General Motors and won $425,000. He used the settlement to start the first Public Interest Research Group in Washington, DC, and then dozens of other public interest organizations, including Capitol Hill News Service, Center for Auto Safety, Center for Justice and Democracy, Center for Science in the Public Interest, Clean Water Action Project, Corporate Accountability Research Group, Disability Rights Center, Foundation for Taxpayers and Consumer Rights, National Coalition for Universities in the Public Interest, Pension Rights Center, Public Citizen, Critical Mass Energy Project, Global Trade Watch, Tax Reform Research Group, and the Telecommunications Research and Action Center.

Largely because of Nader's initiatives, Congress passed the 1966 National Traffic and Motor Vehicle Safety Act, which was only the beginning. One writer, while decrying Nader's 2004 presidential campaign, admitted:

> More than any other single person, Ralph Nader is responsible for the existence of automobiles that have seat belts, padded dashboards, air bags, non-impaling steering columns, and gas tanks that don't readily explode when the car gets rear-ended. He is therefore responsible for the existence of some millions of drivers and passengers who would otherwise be dead. Because of Nader, baby foods are no longer spiked with MSG, kids' pajamas no longer catch fire, tap water is safer to drink than it used to be, diseased meat can no longer be sold with impunity, and dental patients getting their teeth x-rayed wear lead aprons to protect their bodies from dangerous zaps. It is Nader's doing, more than anyone else's, that the federal bureaucracy includes an Environmental Protection Agency, an Occupational Safety and Health Administration, and a Consumer Product Safety Commission, all of which have done valuable work in the past and, with luck, may be allowed to do such work again someday. He is the man to thank for the fact that the Freedom of Information Act is a powerful instrument of democratic transparency and accountability. He is the founder of an amazing array of agile, sharp-elbowed research and lobbying organizations that have prodded governments at all levels toward constructive action in areas ranging from insurance rates to nuclear safety. (Hertzberg 2004, 25)

This list, while extensive, is far from complete. Nader's operation was especially impressive because nothing of the sort existed before, but his efforts were trivial compared to the massive organizations that business established in response to the Powell memo. At the same time, as I will discuss later, Nader personified a new thrust for the Democratic Party, which remained blind to working-class disaffection.

In itself, Powell's memo was not particularly impressive. What gave the memo its force was the fact that the Chamber of Commerce circulated it among the rich and powerful, who were receptive to its message. Although Powell's memo emboldened business to launch its counterattack to the 1960s, business had tenaciously fought to push its own interests long before Lewis Powell was even born.

Even during the early 1930s, when the majority of the business community probably supported Roosevelt in his effort to save capitalism, some people associated with leading business organizations, such as J. P. Morgan and DuPont, tried to enlist retired general Smedley Butler to lead a fascist coup against the government of the United States (see Archer 1973; Colby 1974, 292–98).

What made the business offensive following the Powell manifesto unique was the massive commitment to a systematic assault on virtually every institution that had any influence on society. In the words of Mark Blyth, "[b]usiness was learning to spend as a class" (Blyth 2002, 155).

Powell's Call to Arms

Given the alarming state of affairs that he saw, Powell called for a far more aggressive stance on the part of business. He asserted, "We in America already have moved very far indeed toward some aspects of state socialism." He ended his manifesto with the dire warning: "business and the enterprise system are in deep trouble, and the hour is late."

The program that Powell laid out included efforts to make sure that business would oppose politicians who support antibusiness agendas, such as favoring consumerism or the environment. His memo challenged the Chamber of Commerce to establish a staff of scholars and speakers. He wanted these people to evaluate textbooks to demand "balance" in the name of academic freedom. These Chamber of Commerce representatives should also demand equal time to speak on campus. The Chamber should also use its influence to ensure that people with a probusiness perspective should be hired. He insisted that business must bring its message to the public school system as well.

Powell also called for the monitoring of television for antibusiness messages. He advised the Chamber to develop scholarly journals, publish books, and advertise extensively in order to get its message across. Finally, Powell advocated that business mobilize for legal action.

Powell may have seen himself as leading a mission. Given the importance that Powell gave to Ralph Nader, General Motors would seem to be a likely ally. Less than a month after the date of his memo, he followed up with a letter to a law school friend, Ross L. Malone, general counsel of the General Motors Corporation, asking for help. This letter echoed his manifesto. Powell hoped to alert "top management" of the company to the "contentious time in which we live" and the "plight of the [free] enterprise system." A massive propaganda campaign, he wrote, was being waged against business. "[M]anagement has been unwilling to make a massive effort to protect itself and the system it represents." Unless the business community acted, Powell warned, the capitalist system was "not likely to survive" (Landay 2002).

Powell's manifesto displayed a tough resolution to build a long-term movement just as business was ready to receive his message. As the crisis of the 1970s hit, big business changed its mind about government. The regulatory system that had once seemed reliably business-friendly was now operating too frequently in the public interest rather than protecting business.

More crucially, the comfortable economic arrangement that had been so profitable was unraveling. The first reaction of business was one of panic. The resolve expressed in the Powell memo and the cynical political strategy of Richard Nixon were perfectly timed to ignite the revolution to remake the country in a more business-friendly way.

Within a few decades, the Chamber of Commerce became the largest employer of lobbyists in the United States, spending $193 million on lobbyists between 1998 and early 2005 (Knott 2005). Since then, business executives closely followed Powell's blueprint. Thomas Edsall summed up the aftermath, "During the 1970s, business refined its ability to act as a class, submerging competitive instincts in favor of joint, cooperative action in the legislative arena. Rather than individual companies seeking only special favor [sic] . . . the dominant theme in the political strategy of business became a shared interest in the defeat of bills such as consumer protection and labor law reform, and in the enactment of favorable tax, regulatory and antitrust legislation" (Edsall 1984, 128–29). Later, I will describe the extent of the subsequent one-sided class war that changed the economic, social, and political landscape in the United States.

Before I turn to the outcome of the revolution that Powell helped to ignite, let me say a word about terminology. The ensuing outcome had much in common with conservatism. The new political environment was sympathetic toward business and hostile toward labor, but it also differed starkly from traditional conservative values. Conservatives embrace balanced budgets and support individual liberties. They resist the temptation to rush into wars.

We lack an adequate vocabulary to describe the current state of affairs. People often refer to the foreign policy of the George W. Bush administration as neo-conservative, because many of its leading proponents were previously liberals. In a similar reversal of language, people often refer to the extreme reliance on market solutions as neoliberal, meaning that this position harkens back to classical liberalism, which meant *laissez-faire*, rather than the current American expression, liberalism, which means reliance on the government to correct the defects of the market.

Anti-Vietnam War Protests

Powell was appalled at the apparent social disintegration of the 1960s. Traditional relations of authority were unraveling—in the family, at work, between the races, and in the community at large. For the most part, the business leaders seemed to be aware of only part of this disintegration. While the left was fervently protesting a society filled with injustices—including inequality, racism, and an imperialist agenda capped by a brutal war in Vietnam—an emerging right-wing movement had a different, but equally passionate view of the world.

Even so, the fears that Powell and the corporate executives expressed about the dangerous influence of consumer groups and environmentalists were wildly overblown. After all, Richard Nixon was sitting in the White House and was about to win a landslide reelection within little more than a year after the Powell memo. While business leaders watched in horror as the protest movements gathered strength, these executives seemed unaware of the growing power of the emerging conservative ferment.

The antiwar protestors, of course, did have some slight influence on policy, but their actions in no way threatened business in general. In fact, a sizeable portion of the business community eventually became sympathetic to the antiwar movement. I was working in a corporate office at the time. Most of the high-level employees initially supported the war. As the value of the company stock began to fall, I began to explain the connection between the war and their investments in the stock market. They were surprisingly receptive.

I did not know it at the time, but many executives were already coming to recognize the damage that the war was causing the economy. According to Alfred C. Neal, who for 20 years was president of the influential business organization, the Committee for Economic Development, some leading executives had been skeptical about the war for some time. He recounts, "At a meeting in the fall of 1966, a concerned group of executives heard reports that only the secretary of defense and the president knew what was in the defense budget and its current status; the director of the budget did not. . . . While students rioted . . . the executives in the CED [Committee for Economic Development] at least read the fiscal riot act to the country's political leaders" (Neal 1981, 42).

With more business opposition to the War, antiwar protests became more "respectable." In this environment, the media became more willing to supply critical information, lending further support to the movement. Dissatisfaction within the military was an even more critical factor in ending the war. Of course, most important of all was the will of the Vietnamese people to fight against the most powerful military power in the world.

Nonetheless, business faced a far more ominous threat than the unruly social movements: the momentum of postwar prosperity was fast disappearing. American dominance in the world economy was fading as Japanese and European competitors were challenging U.S. business, even on American turf.

Although the war in Vietnam was part of the problem facing business, it strengthened business's position in one important respect, although I am not sure if anybody noticed this consequence at the time. The war indicated how far the U.S. government would go to protect its interests abroad. If the United States would expend so much in a land where its economic interests were marginal at best, just think how far the government would go to protect U.S. investments in more strategic parts of the world. As a result, Vietnam became a powerful symbol of the willingness of the government to protect corporate interests around the globe, in effect offering business an implicit guarantee that the United States would stand behind its investments abroad.

This posture encouraged business to move manufacturing offshore. Even more crucially, given the threat to move abroad, this stance gave business enormous leverage to force workers to accept lower wages and fewer benefits.

Social Ferment on the Right

The conservative grassroots countermovement began in earnest following the defeat of Arizona senator Barry Goldwater in 1964. The bulk of these activists were unenthusiastic about carrying water for the great corporations. Instead, they saw themselves as part of a great battle to wrest the Republican Party away from the corporate-friendly wing often associated with the name of Nelson Rockefeller. These insurgents regarded the Rockefeller Republicans as being completely out of touch with the common people, more beholden to corporate interests than what they saw as true Republican principles. These conservatives were appalled that the Rockefeller Republicans sometimes made loose strategic alliances with some of the progressive forces in the nation.

The owners of small businesses that flocked to this movement knew that government regulations affected their businesses much more than the large corporations. Because large corporations have the means to fend off government oversight, regulators shift their attention to weaker companies, putting the weaker companies at a competitive disadvantage. In addition, large corporations enjoy economies of scale in meeting regulations. For example, the cost of filling out a new form relative to total business revenues is much less for a giant multinational than for a small business. The large corporations also have better access to government contracts, the courts, and the politicians.

A pervasive anger fueled these new conservative activists, who had a right to be angry on a purely political level. President Johnson had won reelection by portraying their candidate, Barry Goldwater, as a maniacal warmonger. Goldwater did favor a relatively belligerent foreign policy, but his most damning statement came on October 24, 1963, more than a year before the election, in response to a question regarding former president Eisenhower's recent statement that the United States could reduce its six NATO divisions in Europe to one. Goldwater responded that if NATO commanders in Europe had the power to use tactical nuclear weapons on their own initiative, then indeed six divisions could probably then be cut down to one. Nelson Rockefeller's campaign for the Republican nomination used this remark to discredit Goldwater as reckless. Then during the general election, the Johnson campaign picked up where Rockefeller left off, and he did so with a vengeance. The presidential campaign hammered the public with the message that Johnson was some sort of "peace candidate," despite his planned escalation of the Vietnam conflict. Although Johnson's ploy displayed a callous cynicism, it proved to be an effective electoral strategy (White 1965, 311–12). Not only did the Democrats win the presidency but also by 1964 the Republicans held only 33 seats in the Senate.

Issues far afield from those that Lewis Powell raised were also igniting passions. Discontent had begun to bubble up in the South following the Supreme Court's *Brown v. Board of Education* decision that mandated school desegregation (see Perlstein 2001, chap. 1).

For many, the very authority of God was being called into question. Earlier, in 1962, the Supreme Court's *Engel v. Vitale* decision prohibited state-mandated prayer in public school classrooms. Perhaps no cause stirred up this new movement more than abortion. The 1973 *Roe v. Wade* decision, which Powell himself affirmed as a member of the Supreme Court, dramatically intensified the fervor of the Right.

Over and above these sources of resentment, the New Right was not pleased to see young people flaunting traditional sexual mores. Many were just as offended to see blacks and women claiming more prominent positions in the workplace.

This business divide also had a geographical dimension. The new conservative activists initially tended to be more sympathetic to the emerging wealth of the western part of the country as opposed to the old wealth of the east coast. Some commentators even referred to this tension as a struggle between the Cowboys and the Yankees (see Oglesby 1976).

This picture of the social divide at the time is obviously oversimplified. Some people on the Left supported some issues dear to the Right, while some on the Right sympathized with some of the goals of the Left. Strictly speaking, many people were on neither side. For the most part, however, the perception of the gulf between Left and Right both within the Republican Party and within society as a whole was certainly both wide and deep.

The country was unanimous in one respect: nobody seemed to be satisfied with the situation. For some, change was intolerably slow; for others, any change was intolerable. Traditional liberals seemed to lack a capacity for decisive action. Conservatives—especially those with this new conservative movement—certainly did not.

The decision of the corporate sector to throw its lot in with radical conservatism was the key to the right-wing revolution. Corporate leaders were never really worried about "dolts" gaining power. Certainly, the threat of socialism was not a realistic possibility. During the Depression and World War II, the Soviet Union still had some popular support but not by 1970. Even the legacy of the New Deal had already faded quite a bit by the time. By the 1970s, both the Democratic and the Republican parties were firmly in the business camp. Even the leadership of the union movement was openly hostile to most of the social movements.

Despite the dramatic displays on the streets of the United States, the real crisis of the time for business was economic. The healthy rate of growth that the United States had enjoyed throughout the post World War II period was rapidly disappearing. The economy was slipping into a period of stagflation, a word coined at the time to reflect the simultaneous scourges of economic stagnation and inflation that were plaguing the economy. In this environment, economists became receptive to the idea that the government was the problem and a freer market, the solution.

Chapter 4

Richard Nixon's Class War

Nixon's Revolution

Given the rapidly deteriorating economic situation and the apparent militancy of workers and other progressive organizations, seizing political control was an obvious strategy. Following the lead of Lewis Powell, business mobilized enormous resources in its successful offensive, but this action could not have succeeded without the willing collaboration of politicians.

No politician was better suited for the task than Richard Nixon, who later put Powell on the Supreme Court, but deep tensions existed between the corporate executives and Richard Nixon. Some of the business executives saw the Nixon administration as virtually surrendering the country to socialism.

Nixon was hardly admiring of the executives. He felt that business leaders lacked backbone. H. R. Haldeman, Nixon's Chief of Staff recorded in his diary, "When crisis hit, Nixon concluded, business and academic leaders simply 'painted their asses white and ran like antelopes.' The 'so-called managers' were not what the country needed—the historical moment beckoned for what he called the 'two-fisted' types" (Cowie 2002, 257).

Haldeman called the president's analysis "leadership decadence theory," which Nixon expounded on in August 1971, less than two weeks before Powell published his call to arms. While dining on the presidential yacht Sequoia with the Reverend Billy Graham, Henry Kissinger, and several close aides, Nixon explained that "our real problem in this country is not the youth, not the people who have fallen away, but rather our leadership class, the ministers (except for the Billy Graham-type fundamentalists), the college professors and other teachers . . . the business leadership class, etc., where . . . they have all really let down and become soft" (Haldeman 1994, 338). By the end of the decade, Jerry Falwell began to organize a so-called Moral Majority, successfully bringing fundamentalists into the Republican fold.

While the business leaders supposedly panicked in the face of the dangerous situation of the time—a combination of the expression of enormous dissatisfaction with the existing social conditions together with the underlying deterioration of the economy—Richard Nixon recognized that the conditions represented an opportunity as well as a threat. He clearly understood that the liberal establishment failed to connect with the people it claimed to represent.

Certainly, the liberals associated with the Democratic Party offered little or no leadership at the time. To the extent that the Democrats addressed pressing social issues, they did so belatedly, only in response to the clamor from the social movements. Worse yet, the Democrats did nothing to speak to the deeper issues that troubled ordinary people.

The exceptional rise in the standard of living that began during the depths of the Great Depression and continued through the first decades of the post–World War II period had not really satisfied the deeper desires of the working class. Once the economy seriously faltered, throwing economic and social insecurity into the mix, the dissatisfaction began to mutate into anger.

The genius of the Nixon administration was its ability to harness the festering resentments that plagued American society, while drawing upon the grassroots organizations that grew up in the wake of the unsuccessful Goldwater campaign. A key part of the Nixon formula was to successfully define liberals—the self-proclaimed inheritors of the New Deal—as elitist enemies of the common people. In a sense, Nixon was merely polishing the crude rhetoric of the racist presidential campaign of Governor George Wallace of Alabama, but Nixon did so more successfully. By following this strategy, the same Nixon administration that the corporate executives denounced as presiding over the decline of capitalism, cunningly laid the basic groundwork for the capitalist offensive that eventually transformed the U.S. economy and society.

Richard Nixon won the presidency of the United States in 1968, just as the bloom was wearing off the economy. The onset of an economic decline almost inevitably prevents a successful reelection campaign, especially if it occurs during an unpopular war with no prospect of victory. Yet Nixon won an overwhelming victory in his quest for a second term in 1968. Nixon owed his reelection in part to divisions within both the Democratic Party and its base of support, but Nixon himself helped to create the conditions that divided the opposition. Nixon also had the chair of the Federal Reserve Board, Arthur F. Burns, whom we will encounter later, provide temporary economic stimulation to obscure the underlying problems.

Nixon's New Class Warfare

Nixon devised a strategy to move the center of gravity of the Republican Party from country-club Republicans. Instead, he chose to make the party appeal to working-class people as well as the angry voices of the New Right, often tapping in to its virulent racism. In his insightful article about Nixon's tactic, Jefferson Cowie, concluded, "[h]e struggled to find ways of bringing the 'Southern Strategy' to the urban North and to drive the 'silent majority' wedge between organized labor and the Democratic Party" (Cowie 2002, 258). In this way,

> Richard Nixon recast the "labor question" for the 1970s. "When you have to call on the nation to be strong—on such things as drugs, crime, defense, our basic national position—the educated people and the leader class no longer have any character, and you can't count on them," Nixon explained to his closest advisors

gathered to discuss the administration's "blue-collar strategy." His search for a constituency with the "character and guts" to meet the many crises of the early 1970s
led him to conclude, "when we need support on tough problems, the uneducated
are the ones that are with us." (Cowie 2002, 257)

Of course, Nixon was not intending to support the economic interests of labor
against those of business:

> In Nixon's thinking about workers, he focused [on] making workers' economic
> interests secondary to an appeal to their allegedly superior moral backbone and
> patriotic rectitude. He also sought to mobilize their whiteness and their machismo
> in the face of the inter-related threats of social decay, racial unrest, and faltering
> national purpose. His cultural formulation of workers' interests meant he was not
> going to break new legislative ground in the name of the working class, but as it
> became clear, he was also not going to launch an open offensive against organized
> labor or the key institutions of collective bargaining in the United States. (Cowie
> 2002, 258)

With a sinister genius, Nixon flattered the hard hat workers, assuring them
that they were the heart and soul of the nation, unlike the wayward blacks, braless women, and hippies, whom conservatives regarded as non-producers. Kevin
Phillips, who is generally credited with developing Nixon's Southern Strategy,
explained what was happening to Gary Wills, a perceptive political observer:
"'The clamor in the past has been from the urban or rural proletariat,' he said.
'But now 'populism' is of the middle class, which feels exploited by the Establishment. Almost everyone in the productive segment of society considers himself middle-class now, and resents the exploitation of society's producers. This is
not a movement in favor of *laissez faire* or any ideology; it is opposed to welfare
and the Establishment'" (Wills 1971, 266).

In other words, the workers and farmers whom Phillips lumped together as
populists historically regarded powerful business interests to be their enemies.

The success of Nixon's blue-collar strategy may have owed something to his
own deep-seated prejudices against blacks, Jews, and members of the counterculture. Yet somehow Nixon sensed that traditional blue-collar workers wanted
a dignity that society denied them. These workers did not encounter powerful
corporate executives in their normal lives, but they did come face to face with
professionals who seemed to look down on them. Much of the counterculture
was rejecting, even mocking, ideals that many of these people were expressing
through their work ethic (Sennett and Cobb 1972).

For many of these workers, frustration had turned to anger. Not knowing
how to direct their anger in constructive ways left them vulnerable to manipulation. Since the days of Nixon, the right wing has been masterful in misdirecting
such blue-collar anger into ways that helped conservatives attack their real economic interests.

Nixon and the Right may have been conning these workers, but at least they
acknowledged some part of the feelings of working-class people. In contrast, the
Democrats failed to respond either to the workers' deeper concerns or to Nixon's

blue-collar strategy. By playing on widespread fears, resentments, and insecurities, the Nixon administration successfully made working people feel that their problem was cultural. The Nixon administration validated a feeling of victimhood that many of these blue-collar workers felt. These people knew that they worked hard. The Nixon administration created the impression that if only everyone had the same work ethic—or even the same cultural values—working-class people would be respected and would enjoy an improved quality of life.

By successfully framing the situation in this way rather than in terms of economic power, many workers were unable to understand the root of their conditions. In reality, with profits under pressure, business needed to squeeze society from all sides in order to stave off the slumping rate of profit. Business was particularly intent on draining as much as they could from the same workers whom the Nixon administration was successfully courting. By focusing workers' attention on wedge issues unrelated to the economy, the workers were unaware of the trap that was laid for them.

Nixon found confirmation that his strategy was working in May 1970, when a contingent of blue-collar construction workers launched a sometimes violent protest in New York in response to a city directive to fly American flags at half-mast to honor the deaths of four student antiwar protesters shot by members of the Ohio National Guard at Kent State University (Cowie 2002, 264). Based on his detailed research, Tom Wells puts this demonstration in context:

> With support from the CIA and Jay Lovestone, an AFL-CIO intelligence operative, it [the White House] helped Peter Brennan and other New York union officers organize a supportive demonstration of nearly a hundred thousand people in Manhattan. The union leaders didn't need much help though. "This group required very little encouragement," Colson informed Nixon afterward. Union officials told workers they would lose their pay for the day if they failed to attend the demonstration. Probably with White House assistance, Brennan got union leaders in other cities to stage additional pro-administration rallies. Nixon later appointed Brennan secretary of labor. (T. Wells 1994, 447)

Of course, the Republicans never became the party of the working class, but the party only needed to get a portion of blue-collar workers to cast aside their traditional Democratic leanings and vote for the Republicans. Later during the elections that year, this blue-collar swing vote proved decisive in many districts. Where the Republicans were able to lure enough blue-collar voters, they tended to win.

The Democrats foolishly made Nixon's strategy even more effective. Following Nixon's landslide victory over George McGovern in 1972, the Democratic Party took measures to make sure that grassroots organizations would be unable to exert significant power within the party. The Democrats' post-Watergate congressional victory in 1974 included a number of seats that the Democrats took in previously solid Republican districts. The Democrats drew the wrong lesson from this experience, deciding that their best strategy would be to continue to chip away in Republican suburbs, rather than to work as strongly on behalf of their once solid working-class constituencies.

Nixon and the Race Card

Race has always been a very sensitive issue in the United States. Nixon enthusiastically tapped into the toxic pool of distrust and dissatisfaction, cleverly linking it with the preexisting racial tensions. Although playing the race card made excellent sense as a political strategy, any reasonable person would have to know that to do so would impose a serious cost on the country. For example, Barry Goldwater, often seen at the time as the epitome of the emerging right wing, displayed an unusual degree of integrity during his campaign against Lyndon Johnson. Goldwater made an agreement in 1964 with Lyndon Johnson to keep race out of the Presidential contest between them: "'If we attacked each other,' Goldwater explained, 'the country would be divided into different camps and we could witness bloodshed.' Sensitive to the charge hurled 'again and again . . . that I was a racist,' he stuck to his word even in the campaign's last desperate days when fringe advisor F. Clifton White produced a documentary film intended to exacerbate white fears of black urban violence. Goldwater condemned the film and ordered it suppressed" (O'Reilly 1995, 251).

Nixon felt no such compunction. Running for the nomination in 1968 against Ronald Reagan, the favorite candidate of the Goldwater wing of the party, Nixon needed to undercut his rival's support in the South. In so doing, Nixon played the race card masterfully and went on to win the nomination. Once he captured the nomination, he perfected his so-called Southern Strategy, identifying the Democratic Party in the South as the party of blacks. This tactic was so successful that the Republican Party now enjoys nearly complete control of that previously Democratic stronghold (O'Reilly 1995, 282–86).

By 1970, the Nixon administration tentatively began to foster affirmative action. Perhaps the most notable example was the proposed Philadelphia Plan. The ostensible object of the plan was to raise the percentage of minority group members working in six Philadelphia area construction trades (see U.S. Senate 1970).

What drove Richard Nixon to spearhead this first policy of affirmative action? Certainly, Nixon was no heady reformer. Indeed, he had some practical goals in mind. First, he could contain some of the demands for reform by offering affirmative action without threatening the powerful corporate interests that he represented. Even better, he could integrate African-Americans into the labor force more quickly, hoping that this increased supply of employable labor would relieve the pressure for higher wages. Perhaps best of all, the Philadelphia Plan offered the prospect of splitting two of the most powerful voices for reform. Nixon could attack the unions in the name of racial justice, thereby discrediting the unions in the eyes of liberals.

Even more important, the Philadelphia Plan served to threaten both working-class and middle-class whites that African-American progress would come at their expense. This attitude made many working-class whites resentful of both people and organizations that were advocating progress for black society.

Once the public forgot this obscure program, racial animosity continued to fester, allowing Nixon to continue to enjoy the fruits of his Southern Strategy.

Finally, tension between the races would lead discontented workers in the North to embrace the Republican Party.

Similarly, I am convinced that the government was as receptive as it was to the women's movement for equally cynical reasons. As in the case of the movement for African-American civil rights, the women's movement had a long and proud history well before the dawning of affirmative action policies. Affirmative action for women conveniently relieved labor market pressure while setting group against group.

An objective observer might also have expected that the alienated workers might have seen that they were suffering many of the same conditions that fueled many of the protest movements at the time. The Nixon administration, however, was playing on emotion, not objective reason.

This tactic of setting one group against another took a more ominous turn with the Federal Bureau of Investigation's COINTELPRO. According to a U.S. Senate investigation:

> COINTELPRO is the FBI acronym for a series of covert action programs directed against domestic groups. In these programs, the Bureau went beyond the collection of intelligence to secret action designed to "disrupt" and "neutralize" target groups and individuals. The techniques were adopted wholesale from wartime counterintelligence, and ranged from the trivial (mailing reprints of Reader's Digest articles to college administrators) to the degrading (sending anonymous poison-pen letters intended to break up marriages) and the dangerous (encouraging gang warfare and falsely labeling members of a violent group as police informers). (U.S. Senate 1976)

By sowing distrust and hatred, this vicious program led to a number of deaths.

In summary, the Nixon administration carefully fostered the notion that privileged white elitists working on behalf of blacks were responsible for most of the problems of working-class people. Alienating much of the white working-class from both working-class blacks and from progressive white professionals successfully fragmented the traditional New Deal coalition. Keying in on the anger and resentment of the white working-class, Nixon was able to deflect the attention of many of them from their economic conditions to emotional issues. By using wedge issues to create confusion, the Nixon administration managed to get many workers to vote against their own self-interest as well as against the interest of the country as a whole.

Nixon's War on Drugs

The Nixon administration declared a war on crime, but crime served as a code word for blacks and other people who disagreed with the administration. The famous war on drugs is a case in point. Dan Baum interviewed many of the founding fathers of this ill-conceived "war" (D. Baum 1996). Some of them freely admitted that the war on drugs had little to do with either public health or safety. Instead, they saw the stereotypical drug user as either an antiwar activist or an urban black. Not without reason, neither group had much affection for the

Nixon administration. Attacking these "enemies" seemed to be a tempting opportunity to further the political agenda of the party in power. In Baum's words, "[In the 1968 primaries] Nixon looked at 'his people' and found them quaking with rage and fear: not at Vietnam, but at the lawless wreckers of their own quiet lives—an unholy amalgam of stoned hippies, braless women, homicidal Negroes, larcenous junkies, and treasonous priests. Nixon's genius was in hammering these images together into a rhetorical sword. People steal, burn, and use drugs not because of "root causes," he said, but because they are bad people. They should be punished, not coddled" (D. Baum 1996, 12).

According to his close advisor, H. R. Haldeman, Nixon "emphasized that you have to face the fact that the whole problem is really the blacks. The key is to devise a system that recognizes this while not appearing to" (D. Baum 1996, 13, citing Haldeman 1994, 53).

The war on drugs had another attractive feature: it deflected blame from a sagging economy, destructive business practices, or society at large, holding individual behavior responsible. For example, the war on drugs played an important role in framing matters of workplace safety. The ostensible purpose of the Occupational Safety and Health Administration (OSHA) was to attempt to prevent business from exposing workers to unhealthy and unsafe conditions. The rhetoric associated with the war on drugs allowed opponents of workplace safety regulations to blame the workers themselves for their own misfortunes. Symptomatic of this attitude was an article that *Government Executive* published in 1982, entitled, "White House Stop-Using-Drugs Program—Why the Emphasis Is on Marijuana." According to this article, "[w]hile OSHA was created [in itself, a result, in part, of political pressure in Washington by anti-Big Business activists] and gushing regulations having to do with workplace machines and procedures, corporations themselves began attacking a major part of the problem where it really was—in alcohol and drug use by employees" (D. Baum 1996, 188).

The rhetoric associated with the war on drugs also provided an easy answer to those who saw poverty as a sign of injustice. Defenders of the status quo could respond that poverty was a result of personal deficiencies, as evidenced by widespread use of narcotics.

In the 2000 presidential election campaign, the world discovered another unintended right-wing benefit of the war on drugs. Many Southern states have felony disenfranchisement laws. Draconian drug laws account for much of the swelling prison population. The enforcement of these drug laws falls disproportionately upon the poor, especially poor blacks. Ira Glasser observed: "According to federal statistics gathered by the Sentencing Project, only 13 percent of monthly drug users of all illegal drugs—defined as those who use a drug at least once a month on a regular basis—are black, about their proportion of the population. But 37 percent of drug-offense arrests are black; 53 percent of convictions are black; and 67 percent of all people imprisoned for drug offenses are black" (Glasser 2006).

So, largely because of the war on drugs, criminal convictions removed more than four million people from the voter lists (Abramsky 2006). Because the poor and the minorities, who make up a disproportionate number of the prison population, are likely to vote Democratic, their disenfranchisement was the decisive factor in the presidential election of 2000. For example, the state of Florida, where Bush won by a mere 537 votes, disenfranchised 200,000 black Floridians.

The right wing receives a further electoral boost from the increased population of prisoners, over and above disenfranchisement. The Census Bureau counts incarcerated prisoners as part of the districts where the state houses them rather than in one of the districts that supply many of the prisoners. As a result, not only does imprisonment deny people the right to vote, it gives an extra weight to voters in the Republican-dominated rural districts where many prisons are located.

This Census Bureau policy distorts the balance of power just as counting the nonvoting slaves as three-fifths of a person helped the planter class in the antebellum South. For example, the state of New York tends to vote Democratic, although the less-populous upstate region is mostly Republican. Despite their lesser numbers, Republicans still control the state senate. If prisoners were counted as part of the district where they last resided, as many as seven upstate districts might have to be redrawn, with the downstate Democrats picking up some seats (Roberts 2006).

In conclusion, because of the harsh drug laws along with the racial and class biases of the judicial system, Nixon's war on drugs continues to reinforce the Republican advantage.

Right-Wing Momentum

Nixon's political instincts, along with his personal animosity toward various racial and ethnic groupings, helped him in devising various wedge issues to divide traditional Democratic supporters, but Nixon did not seem to have a particularly strong ideological commitment. For example, he seemed perfectly willing to go along with the expansion of regulation as long as the policy would strengthen his administration or at least quiet his enemies. By chipping away at working-class support for the Democrats and winning the southern states, the Republicans further demolished the once solid New Deal coalition.

Although Nixon laid the political groundwork for the right-wing revolution, business regarded his administration as a failure. The economy was not prospering. New regulatory agencies were springing up.

Nixon's achievement, though destructive, was certainly remarkable. An objective observer at the time would have expected that the alienated workers, who were feeling the first effects of the economic slowdown, would have found a natural ally in the Democratic Party. Instead, the Democrats more or less took workers for granted, assuming that the Republican Party would have no appeal for them. After more than three decades, the Democrats have still not discovered a way to win back the lost blue-collar voters.

Because of the Watergate scandal, Nixon resigned from office before his second term ended. After a relatively short interlude with Gerald Ford as the caretaker for the remainder of Nixon's second term, Jimmy Carter won the presidency.

Carter ran as a relatively conservative Southern governor. A coterie of fellow Georgians were at the center of his administration, but his lack of belligerency allowed Republicans to portray him as a typical wobbly liberal. Two factors doomed his presidency. First, Henry Kissinger and a handful of other Republican Party faithfuls convinced Carter to admit the exiled Shah of Iran to the United States for cancer treatment. This decision created a fury in Iran, culminating in the takeover of the U.S. Embassy. The resulting hostage crisis made Carter seem weak in the public eye. Carter's reelection faltered further with Ronald Reagan's strong performance in the presidential debates.

In addition, an oil shock slowed economies around the world. Long lines at gas stations further infuriated voters. More subtly, many of the economic distortions that the Vietnam War created were finally taking a toll on the economy at the time. The public was ready to hear Ronald Reagan's simplistic message that markets rather than Democratic elites could create the sort of prosperity that the Golden Age had led people to expect.

These economic conditions were more damning for the Democrats. The Keynesians had promised perpetual prosperity, yet the United States faced a perfect storm of high interest rates, inflation, and sluggish economic activity.

Carter's lack of belligerence in international affairs alienated an elite group of cold war Democrats. This group abandoned the Democratic Party and reinvented themselves as neoconservatives. Although neither they nor their policies ever had much popular support they eventually became a powerful force in the emerging Republican coalition.

Reagan built upon Richard Nixon's earlier insight into working-class resentment, especially white working-class resentment. In fact, he scheduled the first speech of his successful presidential campaign in Philadelphia—not Philadelphia, Pennsylvania, with its strong roots in the early history of the republic, but Philadelphia, Mississippi, mostly known as the site of a ghastly murder of three civil rights workers. The signal was unmistakable.

The Republicans triumphantly returned to the White House with Reagan's election. By this time, the Republican Party shifted far to the right; the Democrats had also followed the same trajectory.

With little opposition, the Reagan administration created a corporate lovefest. Using its mastery over the media, the Reagan White House was free to relentlessly pursue its objectives without even the pretension of concessions to the movements that had been striking fear into the corporate executives of the Nixon era. He announced his intentions in his First Inaugural Address: "government is not the solution to our problem; government is the problem." Under the first Bush presidency, the administration smoothed some of the harsh edges of the Reagan policy, but the results were largely the same.

When Bill Clinton took over the White House, the procorporate atmosphere continued. Clinton offered a few symbolic victories for progressives, but little more. Only weeks after winning the presidency, Clinton acknowledged that "We're Eisenhower Republicans here. . . . We stand for lower deficits, free trade, and the bond market. Isn't that great?" Clinton even conceded that with his new policy focus "we help the bond market and we hurt the people who voted us in"

(Pollin 2003, 21; Woodward 1994, 91, 165). Later, in words that would have resonated with Ronald Reagan, Clinton declared in his 1996 State of the Union Address that "the age of big government is over."

For the most part, Clinton followed a strategy of triangulation, placing himself midway between the positions of Republican and Democratic parties, all the while embracing many of the Republican causes as his own. Accordingly, Clinton managed to manipulate Congress into passing legislation, such as welfare "reform" and the North American Free Trade Agreement that Democrats would have continued to block under a Republican presidency. Joseph Stiglitz, Clinton's Nobel Prize-winning chief economic advisor summarized the effect of the administration: "We did manage to tighten the belts of the poor as we loosened those on the rich" (Stiglitz 2004, 108).

By this time, the right wing had effectively undermined the idea that the government could do anything to make the economy work better for ordinary people. Many potential voters abstained, no longer believing that they could use the ballot to promote economic justice. As a result, conservatives were largely free to do as they wished, especially because of the absence of an effective opposition party with a different vision. As a result, with the younger Bush in office, the procorporate agenda began with a vengeance—without a pretense of evenhandedness.

To be fair, Reagan and his successors enjoyed a great advantage over Nixon. With the Vietnam War raging, Nixon had to contend with a succession of protest movements that rattled him. By the time Reagan took office, the economy was weak—so much so that workers feared for their jobs to a degree that had not been felt since the Great Depression. Within this environment, the already-weakened labor movement was subdued.

Reagan made unions even weaker soon after taking office by firing the striking air traffic controllers. Ironically, their union was the only one that endorsed Reagan's bid for office. This stance signaled to business that the government would support employers who took a hard line against unions, emboldening business to oppose unions at every turn, realizing that the government would not be likely to punish business from taking measures that were prohibited by law.

In addition, both Reagan and Clinton, unlike the awkward Nixon, were remarkably adept at public relations, allowing them to pursue policies that a lesser politician could not have dared to propose. Clinton, however, applied his talents to enacting a good part of the Republican agenda, claiming it as his own. As a result, the right-wing, procorporate activist organizations flourished in ways that Lewis Powell could not have imagined.

Considering the fears of corporate America in the 1960s, the transformation from the protest movements of the time to the probusiness political environment that followed is breathtaking to say the least! The administrations of Reagan, Clinton, and the Bushes administered what must have seemed unimaginable business victories.

Scorched Earth Economics

Monetary policy was an important weapon in the right-wing arsenal. The Vietnam War, along with sharp spikes in oil prices in 1973 and 1979, had created enormous strains on the economy. In 1979, Carter's last year in office, inflation reached 11.3 percent. By 1980, inflation increased even more to 13.5 percent. Although none of this was desirable for business, it laid the groundwork for one of the most effective monetary offensives in modern history.

Because of inflation, interest rates were soaring. To make matters worse, the economy was slowing down, giving rise to the term stagflation, meaning a deadening combination of stagnation and inflation. Inflation offered a convenient target for the Republicans, even though they had administered its buildup.

Carter was left to cope with the economy he inherited. Under great pressure "to do something," Carter "fired" the head of the Federal Reserve Board by appointing him Secretary of the Treasury, replacing him with Paul Volcker, a longtime Fed official. Soon thereafter the Federal Reserve used its powers to tighten credit in 1979, intentionally engineering a recession. Actually, the Fed had done so five times before since the end of the war and the middle of the 1970s (Romer and Romer 1989, 135).

Business leaders appreciated that this downturn would work to their advantage, believing that profits could only be preserved by reducing wages. By creating unemployment, labor would fear the threat of termination. Under such conditions, business would be in a good position to reassert its authority both at the bargaining table and on the shop floor.

Certainly, Paul Volcker echoed these sentiments in explaining his motives for making credit scarce. He lectured the Joint Economic Committee of the Congress on October 17, 1979, "The standard of living of the average American has to decline." "I don't think you can escape that" (Rattner 1979). Listening to Paul Volcker at the time of the 1980 recession, one would imagine that labor was doing quite well. In truth, the real hourly wage was already about 50 cents lower than it had been in 1973.

Monetary policy is a particularly attractive a tool for conducting class warfare because it gives the impression of a neutral matter rather than a direct attack on anybody. Joan Robinson, a magnificent British economist, explained, "There is in some quarters a great affection for credit policy because it seems the least selective and somehow lives up to the ideal of a single overall neutral regulation of the economy [and] it conceals the problems of political choice under an apparently impersonal mechanism" (Robinson 1962, 99–100).

Presumably, the leadership of the Fed believed that a short recession would tame labor and then allow healthy economic growth to resume. Such was not the case. The economy had become more fragile. Consequently, the downturn was far more ferocious than anybody had imagined—the most massive economic downturn since the Great Depression.

Even as the recession took on more terrifying proportions, Volcker still insisted on holding the course. In further congressional testimony in July of 1981, he complained, "So far, only small and inconclusive signs of a moderation in wage pressures have appeared. Understandably, wages respond to higher prices. But in the economy as a whole, labor accounts for the bulk of all costs, and those rising costs in turn maintain the momentum of the inflationary process" (Volcker 1981, 614).

As late as January 1982, Volcker was still unwilling to relent, telling another congressional committee:

> No successful program to restore price stability can rest on persistently high unemployment. . . . The obvious challenge is to shape our policies in a way that can permit and encourage recovery to proceed while maintaining the progress we are seeing toward greater price stability. . . . But in an economy like ours, with wages and salaries accounting for two-thirds of all costs, sustaining progress will need to be reflected in the moderation of growth of *nominal* wages. The general indexes of worker compensation still show relatively little improvement, and prices of many services with a high labor content continue to show high rates of increase. (Volcker 1982, 89)

Although the press saw Volcker as an almost saintly figure, untainted with the self-interest that contaminated most political figures, his recession was a disaster for the country in general and for labor in particular. Rebecca Blank and Alan Blinder, later vice chair at the Fed, estimated that the substandard economic performance of the 1973–83 decade reduced the income share of the lowest fifth of the population by almost 1 percentage point and raised the poverty count by 4.5 percentage points (Blank and Blinder 1986, 207).

Of course, we cannot ascribe the recession to a single individual. Although Paul Volcker was cruelly insensitive to the hardship of unemployment, he was no more so than most business and political leaders. Certainly, business had been clamoring for the sort of policies Volcker carried out. Also, economists were lavish in their praise for Volcker.

The official civilian unemployment rate reached nearly 10 percent. The actual unemployment rate was considerably higher, probably about 15 percent. Still, the Federal Reserve refused to let up the pressure. At this point, the recession threatened to turn into a full-scale financial panic.

Recessions are an imperfect instrument for disciplining labor. Although business initially enjoys saving on wage costs as a result of mounting unemployment, recessionary conditions eventually prove counterproductive for business as well. Once business begins to feel pain of the recession, it demands that steps be taken to get the economy moving once again.

The disastrous economic consequences of the Volcker recession helped Ronald Reagan win the presidency from Carter in 1980. The economy reached the point where the recession became counterproductive in the eyes of many business leaders. Volcker, however, saw the world from the perspective of the financial sector, which takes a more draconian view of inflation than the rest of the business community. Only when the crisis threatened the values of the loans that the major banks had made to Mexico did business demand something be done to stimulate the economy. Paul Krugman puts the situation in perspective, writing, "By late summer of 1982, the US inflation was subsiding, but the recession seemed in danger of spiraling out of control. The sudden emergence of the Third World debt crisis raised fears of financial chaos" (Krugman 1990, 84).

Immediately thereafter, in order to finally bring the economy out of the tailspin of which Volcker was so proud, the Federal Reserve Board began to loosen the monetary reins and the Reagan administration resorted to deficit spending of unparalleled proportions to boost the economy. The damage to labor was done. Business had gained a firm upper hand. The economy was in the hands of Ronald Reagan.

Setting the Stage for the Capitalist Offensive

Three distinct strands of thought make up the right wing—libertarians, cultural conservatives, and conservative class-warriors representing the interest of big business. Of course, individuals may feel an affinity to more than one of them. Not everybody fits into these simple classifications. In any case, these forces began to converge in the 1970s to form the triumphant right wing.

The *Roe v. Wade* decision and the flaunting of social mores roused religious conservatives. The falling rate of profit together with the political successes of Ralph Nader gave conservative class-warriors a sense of urgency in its crusade to turn back the clock on regulation and taxes. The libertarians opposed increased regulation.

Sincere cultural conservatives are relatively indifferent about economic management, although their present leaders closely follow Republican talking points more closely than the Scriptures. Conservative class-warriors are equally indifferent to theological matters. Libertarians consistently oppose what they consider to be excessive government. Because of their divergent interests, these groups form a rather uneasy alliance.

For the most part, the various elements of the right wing have managed to coexist by carefully downplaying their differences, while providing valuable support for one another at crucial junctures. For example, these cultural conservatives mesmerized working-class voters by diverting their attention to noneconomic issues, such as gun control or abortion, allowing the economic class-warriors to capture control of the reins of government. Once in power, the economic class-warriors took strong stands in favor of issues of importance for the cultural conservatives. Libertarians gained the least from the alliance. Although they applauded deregulation of economic affairs, they silently watched increasing government intrusion into personal behavior and an escalation of corporate welfare.

Before the right-wing revolution, big business had been quite comfortable with the regulatory state. Although business demands that the government avoid regulatory interference in business affairs, it expects government to underwrite business's own activities through subsidies, tax write-offs, and protection from competition. Especially while Democrats controlled the major committees in Congress, breaking with the leadership posed serious political risks for them. The large corporations had profited from labor peace. Unlike many small companies, they had been able to absorb the costs of regulations and the power of strong unions. This situation provided big business with a competitive edge relative to its smaller challengers.

For all their talk about the wonders of the market, the aim of these conservative class-warriors is to make sure that government continues to serve the interest of the corporations and the super rich. Alan Murray, a columnist for the *Wall Street Journal* and by no means unsympathetic to the corporate world, once blurted out what any objective observer of business already knows: "Capitalists, for the most part, don't care much for capitalism. Their goal is to make money. And if they can do it without messy competition, so much the better" (Murray 2004).

Much of the small-business community that fueled a significant portion of the early Goldwater activism might have more in common with the cultural conservatives, although they shared a distaste of taxes and regulation with the conservative class-warriors. Yet these same people had good reason to be suspicious of the large corporations.

Historically, religious fundamentalists were no more enamored by the corporate plutocrats than were the libertarians (Armstrong 2001, 170–71). Rural fundamentalists had been instinctually anti-Wall Street for over a century, whether they were rallying under the left-wing banner of William Jennings Bryan or the right-wing banner of Joseph McCarthy. More educated urbanites whose religion guided their politics were likely to follow the Social Gospel or even call themselves Christian socialists. Although Christian socialists were not really socialists, they called upon the state to help the poor rise up in society.

Today, religious fundamentalists call upon the government to regulate personal behavior in matters, such as abortion or homosexual activity, and in corporate behavior such as indecency in the media. They also welcome government subsidies in the form of "faith-based initiatives" or as vouchers for education in their schools.

Principled libertarians were most likely to stray from the fold, opposing foreign adventures, state intervention in personal affairs, and government giveaways to the corporations and super rich—the latter being the bread and butter of the conservative class-warriors. Libertarians emphasize either the defense of personal liberties or of property. Those libertarians who emphasize the defense of property rather than personal liberties often turn a blind eye to corporate welfare and other government abuses. Not infrequently, conservative class-warriors take up the rhetoric of property libertarianism to advance their own agenda.

Liberals also played an important role in setting the stage for the Powell memo. By the 1960s, the liberal establishment had run out of big ideas. They set their sights on smaller targets. Conservatives had long favored deregulation, insisting that regulation represented an unwarranted intrusion into business management. By the time of the Carter administration, many liberals joined conservatives in opposing regulation. While conservatives saw regulation as opposed to business interests, these liberals complained that regulation had long been excessively friendly to business. In particular, liberals charged that regulation was penalizing consumers by preventing competition from lowering prices.

Powell's nemesis, Ralph Nader, became one of the most vocal advocates of the liberal demand for deregulation. Senator Edward Kennedy of Massachusetts, often regarded as an icon of political liberalism, also joined in. Topping off the pressure for deregulation, in 1967 the Ford Foundation—often incorrectly seen as a progressive foundation—began a $1.8 million grant to the Brookings Institution that ran until 1975 for a program of studies in the regulation of economic activity. This effort resulted directly or indirectly in twenty-two books and monographs, sixty-five journal articles, and thirty-eight doctoral dissertations (Derthick and Quirk 1985, 35–37).

The first big break in deregulation came in the transportation industry, where Kennedy and Nader took the lead. This liberal pressure for deregulation had two important consequences. First of all, regulation of transportation originally began in the nineteenth century because strong competition led to repeated bankruptcies. The underlying problem was that the cost of carrying another passenger or another ton of freight is very small, while the capital costs for planes or track are huge. As I will discuss in more detail later, competition drives prices down toward these small costs, leaving the carrier unable to cover its fixed costs. A cost structure like transportation inevitably leads to repeated bankruptcies, like those that plagued the railroads in the nineteenth century before regulation and the modern airline industry after deregulation (see Perelman 1999; 2006).

More important for the course of the right-wing revolution, the liberal call for deregulation made it a respectable liberal policy. In fact, no prominent liberal economist spoke up to explain why the blanket indictment of regulation—even though it was limited to some specific industries—was ill-advised. The liberal stance on regulation opened up the way for the right wing to call for wholesale deregulation, especially those regulations designed to protect the public rather than industry.

Chapter 5

Remaking the World
for Business

Business's Revenge

In their wildest dreams, business executives of the 1960s could have never imagined what transpired in recent decades. Political leaders no longer concern themselves with the remote possibility of a drift in the direction of socialism; instead, they now see themselves as remaking the whole world in the image of their right-wing ideals. Political leaders no longer have to concern themselves with protestors on the streets; instead, they stop at nothing to curry the favor of business. Taxes, whether levied on the wealthy or on corporations, have literally melted away, while the burden of government falls increasingly on the backs of the middle class. In fact, the first administration of George W. Bush brazenly called for tax cuts and deregulation as the answers to virtually all problems, except for those problems, real and imagined, which the administration invoked in its demands for greater monitoring and regulation of people's personal and political behavior.

As the right wing gained power, it developed a sophisticated rhetorical style that managed to capture the spirit of class antagonism. Speaker of the House Newt Gingrich was a master of this mode of communication. In 1990, four years before Gingrich ascended to his leadership position, his organization, GOPAC, circulated a memo instructing Republicans about the most effective method of communication in the political arena. The memo recommended that his fellow travelers adopt a vocabulary built upon confrontational words, such as "decay, sick, unionized bureaucracy, greed, corruption, radical, permissive, and bizarre" to make their opponents seem unappealing (Gingrich 1990; see also Oreskes 1990). When the memo became public, there was a brief apology for recommending that Republican zealots attack the character of those who disagreed with them by calling them traitors. The apology was soon forgotten.

Instead, party stalwarts continued to follow the spirit of the memo, poisoning political dialogue with hate-filled rhetoric. Sadly, this form of communication proved to be remarkably effective. Perhaps we should not be surprised. Lord Acton, an icon of traditional conservative thought once observed: "If hostile interests have wrought much injury, false ideas have wrought still more" (Dalberg-Acton 1877, 2).

But the right wing drew upon false emotions even more effectively than false ideas, effectively expressing the wounded feelings of less advantaged parts of society, pretending that conservatives were in the same situation as the dissatisfied workers. Both were supposedly the unfortunate victims of a mythical liberal conspiracy. Both suffered under the sway of evil liberal power—a power wielded by professionals, such as government administrators, who occupy a station in life above those of the working class. Corporate power was nowhere to be found in the right-wing message, except as a benign force that promised jobs and prosperity.

This message was so convincing that many lower- and middle-class people were moved to vote for politicians whose economic policies seriously injured them year after year. Even after the Republicans captured the White House, the Congress, as well as most of the judiciary in 2002, the right wing continued to act like sore winners, whining about how the all-powerful liberal establishment abused them. For example, under the heading, "Who We Are; Who Our Opponents Are," Newt Gingrich wrote, "Since the 1960's, the conservative majority has been intimidated, manipulated and bullied by the liberal minority. The liberal elites who dominate academia, the courts, the press and much of the government bureaucracy share an essentially European secular-socialist value system. Yet they have set the terms of the debate, which is why 'politics as usual' is a losing proposition for Americans" (Gingrich 2005, xii–xiii).

Grover Norquist, who began as a student working closely under the tutelage of Newt Gingrich and who perhaps has since become the premier political theoretician and organizer of the right wing, explained the reason behind this form of communication, "We are trying to change the tones in the state capitals—and turn them toward bitter nastiness and partisanship" (Kilgore 2003, 9). During the 2000 presidential campaign, conservative activist David Horowitz published a pamphlet entitled *The Art of Political War: How Republicans Can Fight to Win*. Like Norquist, Horowitz was an admirer of what he understood to be the tactics of Vladimir Lenin. According to Horowitz, "Politics is war conducted by other means. In political warfare you do not fight just to prevail in an argument, but to destroy the enemy's fighting ability. . . . In political wars, the aggressor usually prevails" (Rampton and Stauber 2004, 3).

Both the disgraced Representative Tom DeLay, arguably the most powerful Republican in Congress at the time, and the Heritage Foundation widely distributed this venomous work (Rampton and Stauber 2004, 3).

The right-wing anger resonated with much of the working class, especially as the economy faltered and workers' economic conditions became increasingly insecure. If workers' jobs were at risk, the fault lay with regulations or with taxes. Corporate power was always blameless.

As of this writing, the hapless Democrats still seem at a loss to figure out a way to respond to the hyper-aggressive tactics of the Republicans. Unwilling to challenge corporate power, the Democrats merely offer bland explanations of their policies without making any attempt to address people's real concerns. The cold Democratic response only confirms their distance from the working class.

This ineptitude first helped Gingrich capture the House of Representatives for the Republicans and later allowed the right wing to capture all three branches of government, until the Democrats regained the legislative branch in 2006.

Despite its rhetorical skills, the degree of success of the procorporate offensive is surprising, to say the least. After all, the corporate-driven economy never managed to produce anything like the prosperity that the United States experienced during the first decades of the post–World War II economy, even during the final few years of the Clinton administration. Despite the economic failures of this corporate-driven economy, the right wing still managed to perpetuate the idea that the solution to all social and economic ills was to rely even more heavily on the purported marketplace efficiency. Corporate executives even became among the most widely admired people in the country—at least until a wave of scandals in the early years of the new millennium revealed something of the way corporations actually worked.

In this period, as the social safety net disintegrated, privatization and deregulation became the watchwords of efficiency. In 1978, airline deregulation finally took place. Although fares on competitive trunk lines fell and more flights were available on some routes, the experiment was far from a success. In fact, problems abounded. Safety and service deteriorated. Passengers faced long delays and fewer connections, often on overbooked flights. Although the established airlines welcomed deregulation as an opportunity to earn great profits, they either failed altogether or faced repeated bankruptcies.

The Republicans used this brief flurry of deregulation to push for a different kind of deregulation—one that would free business from health, safety, and environmental regulations. Successive administrations and the courts shredded environmental and safety regulations with abandon. Each time one of these initiatives resulted in a bad outcome—and most of them did—the inevitable response was that the market had not been given enough free play. For example, even after the disastrous deregulation of energy markets created havoc, the right wing demanded even more deregulation of utilities.

This right-wing revolution exceeded even the dreams of Adam Smith, who limited the role of government to the provision of education, justice, national defense, and public works (A. Smith 1776, Book V, chap. 1, Part 1).

Today, the right wing has moved well beyond Smith, privatizing even these activities. Private highways supported by tolls are becoming more common. The government has turned to corporations to run prisons. By 2002, the United States housed more than 93,000 prisoners in private jails and prisons (U.S. Department of Justice 2003, Table 6.26, 499). The 2002 No Child Left Behind Act seems to have been designed to set the country on the road to privatized education, which would turn the clock back by a more than a century. Perhaps most surprising of all, private contractors' share of all defense-related jobs rose from 36 percent in 1972 to 50 percent in 2000 (Markusen 2003, 474).

All the while, the quality of life for most citizens of the United States has deteriorated, despite the enormous technological advancements that should have ensured universal improvements. Yet almost nowhere could one hear anybody, either within the halls of Congress or in the media, question whether the country was headed in the wrong direction.

I will now turn to the question of why critical voices went largely unheard.

The Power of Money

The transformation of the U.S. social and economic system that occurred during the New Deal and World War II represented an emergency response to the destabilizing sequence of first a collapse in the economy and then the need for military mobilization. For the most part, the public at large seemed to recognize the need to take action. In contrast, the successful business counterattack was the handiwork of a very small number of very wealthy individuals and powerful corporations that refashioned the socioeconomic landscape to suit their purposes. Echoing Powell without mentioning his name, William Simon, former Secretary of the Treasury insisted that "[f]unds generated by business . . . must rush by the multimillions to the aid of liberty . . . to funnel desperately needed funds to scholars, social scientists, writers and journalists who understand the relationship between political and economic liberty. [Business must] cease the mindless subsidizing of colleges and universities whose departments of economy, government, politics and history are hostile to capitalism" (Simon 1978, 230–31).

After leaving the Treasury Department, Simon became president of the John M. Olin Foundation, one of the biggest funders to the new generation of rightwing think tanks. Altogether, the top twenty think tanks are estimated to have received more than $1 billion during the 1990s (Callahan 1999).

With more than generous funding, a host of well-financed think tanks and organizations sprung up almost overnight, ready to fight for everything Powell had recommended and much, much more. By the new millennium, these think tanks formed part of a vast international network of organizations spread throughout the industrialized world (see McGann and Weaver 2002).

Well-placed intellectuals began to act as "idea brokers" for these powerful foundations, which were prepared to throw money at people who could further their agenda. Nobody was more successful in this regard than Irving Kristol, editor of *The Public Interest* and a professor of social thought at New York University, whom the *New York Times Magazine* once dubbed the "Patron Saint of the New Right" (Goodman 1981). Certainly one of the great movers and shakers of the right-wing movement, "Kristol made AEI [the American Enterprise Institute] his Washington base of operations. . . . Kristol, in particular, serve[d] as broker between conservative funding sources and the Washington-based research organizations, [and] supplied new arguments—if they were really needed—for supporting AEI and similar research endeavors" (Smith 1991, 180).

No single source has adequately covered Kristol's influence. For example, Kristol was also instrumental in obtaining the initial funding for the Federalist Society, which I will discuss later. With money from Rupert Murdoch, he founded *The Weekly Standard*. His position as an editorial page writer for the *Wall Street Journal* gave him another outlet to push his right-wing agenda.

He also used that venue to publicize the value of his services. For example, in a series of editorials, he wrote:

> So the corporation today is largely defenseless: a nice big fat juicy target for every ambitious politician and a most convenient scapegoat for every variety of discontent. (Kristol 1978a, 147)
>
> The sad truth is that the business community has never thought seriously about its philanthropy, and doesn't know how. . . . How can we identify such people, and discriminate intelligently among them?" corporate executives always inquire plaintively. Well, if you decide to go exploring for oil, you find a competent geologist. Similarly, if you wish to make a productive investment in the intellectual and educational worlds, you find competent intellectuals and scholars—"dissident" members as it were, of the "new class"—to offer guidance. Yet few corporations seek any such advice on their philanthropy. How many large corporations make use of academic advisory committees for this purpose? Almost none, so far as I can determine. . . . Businessmen who cannot even persuade their own children that business is a morally legitimate activity are not going to succeed, on their own, in persuading the world of it. You can only beat an idea with another idea, and the war of ideas and ideologies will be won or lost within the "new class," not against it. Business certainly has a stake in this war, but for the most part seems blithely unaware of it. (Kristol 1978b, 144–45)

Lewis Lapham, editor of *Harper's Magazine*, offered a rare glimpse into the way Kristol worked behind the scenes. At the suggestion of Irving Kristol, Lapham met with the executive director of the Olin Foundation in the late seventies, Michael Joyce, who offered Lapham a position as editor of a new journal of cultural opinion meant to rebut *The New York Review of Books*. The annual salary was to be $200,000, to be paid for life, even in the event of his resignation or early retirement. Lapham declined the offer. The publication *The New Criterion* appeared in 1982 (Lapham 2004, 37).

A concerted right-wing effort to bully institutions to fall in line was wildly successful. Even institutions that had been closely aligned with the power structure succumbed to a wave of blistering attacks from the Right. For example, the *New York Times*, *Washington Post*, the Ford Foundation, and the Brookings Institution, which had been aligned with a relatively centrist Democratic perspective, suddenly replaced their management with people much more receptive to the conservative view of the world (Judis 2000, 168).

The Heritage Foundation

No right-wing think tank has been as effective in pushing the right-wing agenda as the Heritage Foundation. Like so many well-funded conservative operations that sprouted up in the 1970s, the Heritage Foundation owed a great debt to Lewis Powell. Two young Republican congressional staff members, Paul M. Weyrich and Edwin J. Feulner, Jr., were outraged that the American Enterprise Institute (AEI) was insufficiently partisan in supporting a bill that these activists were promoting. The AEI, long identified with the Republican Party, was keeping a low profile at the time because of an ongoing Internal Revenue Service (IRS) investigation of both the supposedly nonpartisan organization and its president, William Baroody, for organizing a "brain trust" for Goldwater's 1964 presidential campaign (Edwards 1997, 4–5; Judis 2000, 123).

The two activists approached beer magnate Joseph Coors, who willingly provided funding for their proposed organization. The semiofficial biography of the Heritage Foundation reported, "Coors' decision to commit his company to a prominent role in public affairs was reinforced when he read a confidential 5,000-word memorandum by Lewis E. Powell, a prominent Democratic attorney in Richmond, Virginia. . . . Coors recalled that the Powell memorandum 'stirred' him up and convinced him that American business was 'ignoring' a crisis. He wondered why business leaders and organizations weren't speaking out more forcefully against President Nixon's 'new economic policy'" (Edwards 1997, 9).

Conservative think tanks were nothing new. The Foundation for Economic Education, begun in 1946, claims to be the oldest research organization promoting individual freedom, private property, limited government, and free trade. Corporations generously showered funds on this organization. Former Senator Lee Metcalf, in his exposé of the utility companies, reprinted internal documents to show how from its earliest days, this organization curried favor with the power industry, successfully enough that 34 of the major utilities donated money to the foundation in 1964. The *Reader's Digest* reprinted its articles. However, the Foundation for Economic Education more or less addressed the true believers (Metcalf and Reinemer 1967; see also Beder 2003, 73).

What distinguished this new generation of think tanks was their formula for success. The earlier generations of think tanks did original research or engaged in ideological analysis to address sympathetic audiences. In contrast, the Heritage Foundation, the leading right-wing think tank, which became a model for much of the right wing, produces shorter, less technical reports addressing more topical subjects, directing their attention to the mass media (J. Smith 1989, 189).

Perhaps most distinctively, this new generation of think tanks displayed a degree of aggressive partisanship far beyond anything that had ever existed before. Even those earlier conservative think tanks, such as the AEI, which were trying to promote Republican causes, did so with a modest pretense of respectable even-handedness. In contrast, this new generation of think tanks adopted a take-no-prisoners attitude.

To influence the public more effectively, the Heritage Foundation devotes one-third of its budget to marketing. Edwin Feulner, who now heads up Heritage, gladly accepts the characterization of his operation as a "marketing machine" (Feulner 2002, pp. 77–78).

The Heritage Foundation's marketing success greatly exceeded the expectations of its founders. In its 2002 Annual Report, the Heritage Foundation legitimately boasted of its work as "conservatism's megaphone" (Heritage Foundation 2003, 26; see also Landay 2004). Feulner offered an even more telling metaphor for the foundation's strategy: using the foundation to saturate the intellectual market with studies and "expert" opinion supporting the proper policy conclusions the same way that Procter & Gamble does in selling soap (Herman 1993,

44). As this approach proved its effectiveness, older, established organizations began to adopt its methods.

Since the early 1970s, 43 of these major conservative activist organizations have received at a minimum $2.5 to $3 billion in funding (Landay 2004). Such funding is continuing to grow. For example, the Walton family announced in early 2004 that it would be moving $20 billion "into the Walton's private philanthropy, most of it earmarked for education 'reform'—the euphemism for school privatization" (Ford and Gamble 2004, 22). Later, I will explain why school privatization represents such an attractive wedge issue for conservatives, with the potential of splitting minorities from unions.

Key to the success of the Heritage Foundation is its unprecedented influence over the media. According to the foundation's Annual Report, "During 2002, the ideas, proposals, scholarship and views of Heritage's analysts and executives were featured in more than 600 national and international television broadcasts, more than 1,000 national and "major market" radio broadcasts, and some 8,000 newspaper and magazine articles and editorials. In short, when Washington listens, it frequently hears the voice of The Heritage Foundation" (Heritage Foundation 2003, 33).

The Heritage Foundation won much influence over the news media by "assisting" overworked and understaffed newsrooms, although the foundation innocuously represents this activity as just helping "reporters better understand the facts." According to Heritage's Annual Report,

> [n]o single initiative has been more effective in this regard than the Center for Media and Public Policy's Computer-Assisted Research and Reporting (CARR) program.... [T]he CARR program offers journalists training in a cutting-edge discipline: data analysis.... During 2002, [Heritage] provided training and assistance to dozens of reporters and news researchers—becoming "part of the newsroom team" on a variety of high-impact stories.
>
> As *The Washington Post* noted in a feature on the CARR program, on April 19, 2002, "All Washington think tanks are in the business of supplying journalists—as well as legislators and other decision-makers—with their take on policies and issues, most often in the form of briefings, papers, or books. But Heritage is taking this relationship to a new level by providing reporters with raw data and showing them how to analyze it, essentially offering to serve as a news-room's own research department." (Heritage Foundation 2003, 31; see also Deane 2002)

To be sure, the elimination of the Fairness Doctrine in 1988, which allowed the broadcast media the freedom to deliver one-sided, corporate-friendly stories, helped Heritage's megaphone get a better hearing. In addition, the partial defunding of public broadcasting made sure that noncommercial media would not dare to challenge the right-wing message.

Despite these advantages, Heritage still deserves enormous credit for running a very effective megaphone. For example, before the Reagan administration took office, the Heritage Foundation laid out a blueprint entitled *Mandate for Leadership: Turning Ideas into Action*. "Eighty percent of its recommendations were deemed accomplished by the end of the Reagan era" (Landay 2004).

Heritage's success prodded other right-wing think tanks to become more aggressive. For example, the once-stodgy AEI became a major force in pushing the United States into the invasion of Iraq.

Ironically, despite the enormous success of the Heritage Foundation and the other right-wing think tanks in shaping the perception of the world, these organizations flood the media with conservative commentators who never cease to complain about the imaginary dominance of the liberal media. At the same time, leading conservative ideologues privately denigrate liberal journalists as wimps. For example, consider the evaluation of Grover Norquist, who told a liberal journalist "that the most significant difference between liberal journalists and conservative journalists is that the former are journalists first while the latter are conservatives first [if journalists at all]" (Alterman 2004, 26).

I do not want to give the impression that the Heritage Foundation is guided solely by its ideological preconceptions. For example, the foundation had been very harsh on the government of Malaysia, but after the Malaysians displayed the good sense to get representation from Belle Haven Consultants, a firm cofounded by Edwin J. Feulner, Heritage's president and that retains his wife as "senior adviser," the organization suddenly became very supportive of Malaysia (Esdall 2005).

The Aftermath: Reshaping the Legal System

Among the first signs of the new business offensive was the creation of organizations intended to protect business interests in the courts. On the national level, the Chamber of Commerce Web site credited Powell's memo with inspiring the creation of its National Chamber Litigation Center (U.S. Chamber of Commerce 2007) In the spirit of Lewis Powell, this legal arm of the Chamber successfully challenged a host of environmental and labor regulations.

Even more influential are the regional law firms. In 1973, within two years of the appearance of the Powell memo, the California Chamber of Commerce proposed what would later become the high-powered Pacific Legal Foundation, a nonprofit set up in Sacramento, California, from seed money raised by J. Simon Fluor of the Fluor Corporation. Fluor, at the time a major contractor of the Alaskan pipeline, was incensed that environmental litigation had caused significant delays on the pipeline, as well as some other projects, including off-shore drilling (Houck 1984, 1460). According to *Barron's* the founding mission of the Pacific Legal Foundation was to "stem the rampage" of environmentalists and "clever poverty lawyers suing to obtain welfare checks for people regardless of need at the taxpayers expense" (Thomas 1976). Not surprisingly, the first annual report of the Pacific Legal Foundation cited the Powell memo (Weinstein 1975, 43).

In 1975, business interests formed the National Legal Center for the Public Interest (NLCPI) "to assist in the establishment of independent regional litigation foundations dedicated to a balanced view of the role of law in achieving economic and social progress" (Houck 1984, 1475). This organization spawned a number of new regional, business-friendly, nonprofit law firms.

Joseph Burris, former Pacific Legal Foundation Chairman, reminded corpo-rate attorneys in 1979 of the strategic importance of these new law firms: "Because of our special position, and because many of you prefer to maintain a low profile where direct confrontation with government agencies is concerned, we are the logical spearhead to do the job" (Alliance for Justice 1993, 10).

Normally, a public interest designation suggests service to underrepresented elements of society, rather than the welfare of powerful corporations. Even so, the government accepted the claims that these law firms are public interest organizations. As a result, the IRS allows donations to these operations to be treated as tax-deductible. By 2005, the Pacific Legal Foundation had already accumu-lated more than $5 million dollars in contributions (Media Transparency, n.d.).

Of course, corporations could directly hire their own legal representation, but these supposedly public interest law firms provide valuable cover. As Mr. Burris indicated, representing the corporate interests under the guise of public interest is much more effective than doing so directly.

Conservative, corporate-friendly foundations also have gone to great expense in courting prospective conservative lawyers, while they are still in school. Three conservative, second-year law students, David McIntosh, Lee Liberman at Chicago, and Steven Calabresi at Yale, began a small group that eventually became the Federalist Society, with the immodest mission to "reorder priorities within the legal system," according to a society pamphlet (Kendall and Lord 1998, 21). Spurred on by the ubiquitous William Kristol, the Institute for Educa-tional Affairs along with the Olin Foundation, both associated with William Simon, provided generous funding to help "fund travel expenses for sixty law students and twenty legal scholars to attend the first nationwide symposium on federalism at Yale Law School in 1982. This conference drew two hundred and featured keynote speaker Judge Robert Bork. Given this easy access to money, within three years the Federalist Society expanded to thirty chapters, many located at the top law schools. A symposium appears each year in the *Harvard Journal of Law and Public Policy* (Stefancic and Delgado 1996, 110–11). By early 2004, the organization's Web site claimed that its Student Division had more than 5,000 law students and chapters at 170 of 182 ABA-accredited law schools, including all of the top 20 law schools.

No wonder. Membership in the Federalist Society puts students in a powerful network that is extraordinarily effective in placing young lawyers in strategic positions, especially because the Reagan administration began its practice of ide-ologically screening all federal judges: "During Reagan's second term in office, Assistant Attorney General Stephen Markman, who chaired the Washington Chapter of the Federalist Society, oversaw [Attorney General] Meese's judicial appointment process, with assistance from Society cofounders Liberman and Calabresi" (Kendall and Lord 1998, 21). This Federalist Society influence has grown far stronger over the intervening years.

Powerful conservative foundations have also effectively used their wealth to influence judges. For example, by 1993 the generously funded George Mason University Law and Economics Center had provided training to over 40 percent of the federal judiciary (Alliance for Justice 1993, 46). This institution holds seminars that take place in plush resorts. A *Wall Street Journal* report describes one of these seminars at the Sundial Beach Resort in Sanibel, Florida, "Nearly all of the judges' expenses, about $5,000, for the two weeks, are paid by some 90 major corporations, law firms and foundations. A Koch foundation contributes the most, about $1,000 toward each judge's tab. . . . Tax returns show that two Koch-controlled family foundations have contributed at least $1.3 million toward the seminars" (Fialka 1999; Marcus 1998, A20).

This generosity comes into perspective once you realize that Koch businesses have repeatedly found themselves charged with violations of the law. The *Wall Street Journal* report reminded its readers, "Koch Industries has settled some of the most expensive environmental lawsuits in the country, including cases in Minnesota and Texas where huge oil spills have cost it over $6.9 million in civil penalties and $50 million for damages and cleanup costs" (Fialka 1999, A20).

Just what does this law and economics movement advocate? A *Wall Street Journal* writer offered a glimpse into this ideology by describing one of its leading lights, "Judge Richard A. Posner has little use for words like fairness and justice. 'Terms which have no content,' he calls them. What America's lawyers and judges need, he says, is a healthy dose of free-market thinking. From the bench of the U.S. Court of Appeals for the Seventh Circuit here, Judge Posner applies a standard of economic efficiency in cases where many others fail to see markets at play. He calibrates social costs and benefits on questions of religious expression and privacy" (Barrett 1986).

Not everybody is enamored with Posner's work, despite his prolific output and its wide-ranging scope. According to one skeptic's evaluation:

> Posner's arguments are composed of speculative and implausible assumptions, overbroad generalizations, and superficial descriptions of and quotations from cases that misstate or ignore facts, language, rationales, and holdings that are inconsistent with his argument. None of the cases discussed by Posner support his thesis. Instead, the reasoning and results in these cases employ varying standards of care, depending on the rights and relationships among the parties, that are inconsistent with the aggregate-risk-utility test but consistent with the principles of justice. (R. Wright 2003)

Despite any lingering questions about the quality of his work, Posner certainly knows how to capture attention. He famously advocated the purchase and sale of babies:

> [The baby] shortage appears to be an artifact of government regulation, in particular the uniform state policy forbidding the sale of babies. That there are many people who are capable of bearing children but who do not want to raise them, and many other people who cannot produce their own children but want to raise children in their homes, suggests the possibility of a thriving market in babies, especially since the costs of production by the natural parents are typically much lower than the value that many childless people attach to the possession of children. There is, in fact, a black market in babies, with prices as high as $25,000 reported recently, but its necessarily clandestine mode of operation imposes heavy information costs on the market participants, as well as significant expected punishment

costs on the middlemen (typically lawyers and obstetricians). The result is higher prices and smaller quantities sold than would be likely in a legal market. (Posner 1977, 113)

Major corporations are less interested in baby markets than avoiding expensive judgments. The attraction of the law and economics movement lies more in its insistence that all regulations should be narrowly decided on questions of economic costs and benefits.

One critical study summed up this approach to regulation: "Cancer deaths avoided, wilderness and whales saved, illnesses and anxieties prevented—all these and many other benefits must be reduced to dollar values to ensure that we are spending just enough on them, but not too much" (Ackerman and Heinzerling 2004, 39).

More often than not, much of the data upon which such decisions rest will come from the corporations themselves, which consistently exaggerate regulatory costs, while the benefits often defy measurement. Grateful jurists have been very open to the corporate perspective on costs and benefits of regulation.

As for recalcitrant judges who must be elected, corporations sponsor "citizens" groups to rank them publicly according to their attitude toward business. Judges who display excessive sympathy for consumers or the public at large earn bad rankings, which can make reelection difficult, especially in light of massive corporate donations to corporate-friendly challengers.

Perhaps the most effective part of the corporate onslaught on the legal system has been in changing the law itself. Through massive campaign donations, conservative interest groups assured themselves of the election of compliant legislatures at the local, state, and national levels. The proliferation of tort reform throughout the United States is symbolic of the ease with which this control of the political process allowed the corporate sector to change the law.

Tort Reform

Corporations and corporate-friendly foundations have generously contributed millions of dollars to the so-called tort reform movement, which aims at curtailing suits that hold corporations liable for their actions (Alliance for Justice 1993, 52–69). Such suits are especially important because the government has largely abdicated its duty to protect the public from corporate abuses. In addition, the suits often give plaintiffs the right of discovery, opening the innards of the corporations to public scrutiny.

A major think tank, the Manhattan Institute, cast some light on the manner in which the corporate sector manipulates the political process to reshape society in a manner friendlier to corporate power. The Institute solicited contributions from corporations that could profit from the organization's ability to shape the debate to limit liability for big corporations by influencing judges to adopt the corporate perspective:

The think tank claimed to make "the rhetoric of liability reform incorporate transcending concepts like consumer choice, fairness and equity"; and ensure that the "terms of debate remain favorable" by paying scholars to write books that articulate the corporate position and are then read by judges, commentators, and talk-show hosts. The think tank boasted, "Journalists need copy, and it's an established fact that over time they'll 'bend' in the direction in which it flows. If, sometime during the present decade, a consensus emerges in favor of serious judicial reform, it will be because millions of minds have been changed, and only one institution is powerful enough to bring that about. . . . We feel that the funds made available will yield a tremendous return at this point—perhaps the 'highest return on investment' available in the philanthropic field today." (Court 2003, 42–43)

This corporate tort reform movement brilliantly uses expensive but misleading and sometimes even fictitious examples to argue against an individual's right to sue corporations. In fact, individuals rarely win their cases when they sue corporations. Even when juries award the well-publicized huge verdicts, the plaintiffs rarely see nearly as much money as the jury decides. Even the *Wall Street Journal* reported that appeals or prior agreements between opposing lawyers generally reduce the actual payment (Hallinan 2004).

Two senior fellows at the Manhattan Institute, Peter Huber and Walter Olsen, have been especially prominent in the campaign for tort reform. According to Huber, trial lawyers cost the economy more than an astounding $300 billion a year in indirect costs—equivalent to almost $500 billion in current dollars (Huber 1988). How could Huber come up with such a number? It was easy:

From a single sentence spoken by corporate executive Robert Malott in a 1986 roundtable discussion of product liability, Huber, in his 1988 book *Liability: The Legal Revolution and Its Consequences*, adopted an unsubstantiated estimate that the direct costs of the U.S. tort system are at least $80 billion a year—a number far higher than the estimates in careful and systematic studies of these costs. Huber then multiplied Malott's surmise by 3.5 and rounded it up to $300 billion—and called that the indirect cost of the tort system. The 3.5 multiplier came from a reference in a medical journal editorial concerning the effects on doctors' practices of increases in their malpractice insurance premiums. Huber's book contained no discussion of the applicability of this multiplier. It would appear that Huber, who has recently taken to lecturing on the dangers of "junk science," certainly knows whereof he speaks. (Galanter 1992, 84)

In public, corporate executives complain loudly about the cost of liability suits, even though they tell potential investors that such costs are inconsequential. For example, Frank Popoff, CEO of Dow Chemical, warned the public that product liability costs are "a killer for our global competitiveness." Yet in Dow's annual report to its investors it blandly declares, "It is the opinion of the company's management that the possibility that litigation of these [product liability] claims would materially impact the company's consolidated financial statements is remote." Similarly, Monsanto's vice president for government affairs has charged that liability litigation "clogs our courts, curtails American innovation and creativity, drives up the costs of consumer products, and prevents some valuable products and services from ever coming to market." Yet in Monsanto's report to shareholders, the company reported that "while the results of litigation cannot be predicted with certainty, Monsanto does not believe these matters or their ultimate disposition will have a material adverse effect on Monsanto's financial position" (Stefancic and Delgado 1996, 107, citing Nader 1995).

Despite such duplicitous claims by the corporations and shoddy research in one of the key documents in their campaign, corporations and the think tanks that represent their interests have been remarkably successful in promoting their one-sided version of tort reform. For example, even before the Republican takeover of Congress in 2002, the American Tort Reform Association listed some of their numerous victories: "Since 1986, 45 states and the District of Columbia have enacted ATRA-supported tort reforms into law. Thirty states have modified the law of punitive damages; Thirty-three states have modified the law of joint and several liability; Twenty-one states have modified the collateral source rule; Twenty-nine states have penalized parties who bring frivolous lawsuits; seven states have enacted comprehensive product liability reforms; Medical liability reforms have also been enacted in most states" (http://www.atra.org).

President George W. Bush repeatedly interjected the statement in his reelection campaign, "Frivolous lawsuits drive up the cost of health care, and they therefore affect the Federal budget. Medical liability reform is a national issue that requires a national solution," as if frivolous malpractice suits are a major problem in the health care crisis that plagues the United States today (Bush 2004). Soon after he was sworn in, Congress passed legislation to limit class action suits—perhaps the most effective legal avenue for holding corporations in check—and to move them from the state courts to the already overburdened federal courts, which are expected to be less sympathetic to plaintiffs and more likely to dismiss the cases without trial.

The tort reform movement has won victories that are even more significant. For example, in 2003, the Supreme Court in *State Farm Mutual Automobile Insurance Co. v. Campbell et al.* limited punitive damages on the grounds of the Fourteenth Amendment—a constitutional provision enacted at the end of the Civil War to protect the rights of the freed slaves.

This decision will strongly limit corporate liability in the future. One conservative supporter of the decision reported: "The effect of State Farm v. Campbell on these blockbuster punitive damage awards was almost immediate" (Viscusi 2004, 16). The fact that in the same session the Supreme Court would uphold California's three strikes law, which allows life sentences for shoplifting, while making large punitive awards from corporations more difficult is indicative of the imbalance between corporate rights and human rights in the United States today.

Corporations are increasingly developing their own tort reform by having their customers, often unwittingly, sign away their right to sue. Instead, any grievance goes to an arbitration board. All too often, the corporations themselves get to select the arbitrators.

Takings

Perhaps the greatest victory of the right-wing legal onslaught has been the rein-terpretation of a fairly straightforward clause of the Fifth Amendment that reads: "Nor shall private property be taken for public use, without just compensa-tion." The meaning of these words was fairly clear. The government has the obliga-tion to compensate property owners as in cases of eminent domain when the government physically takes control of property, for example, to build a road.

Richard Epstein, a University of Chicago law professor, who now holds the exalted title, James Parker Hall Distinguished Service Professor of Law at the University of Chicago, and Peter and Kirsten Bedford, Senior Fellows at the Hoover Institution, extended the meaning of this clause far beyond what any-body else had dared to imagine. He proposed to include any regulation that reduced the value of any property as a taking.

Epstein singled out "zoning, rent control, workers' compensation laws, trans-fer payments, [and] progressive taxation" (R. Epstein 1985, x). In the last few years, several states have passed referenda that enact versions of Epstein's theory.

While Epstein opposed any government policy that might redistribute in the direction of the poor, to my knowledge he was silent about what we may call Givings—the reverse Robin Hood redistribution in which the government pre-sides over the transfer of wealth and income in the direction of the rich and pow-erful. Since Professor Epstein's book appeared, Givings have proceeded at breakneck speed.

The students who created the Federalist Society enthusiastically embraced Epstein's reinterpretation of the Constitution. These students, however, were in a distinct minority. The leading legal minds in the country dismissed Epstein's theory. Even conservative luminaries, who sympathized with Epstein's politics, rejected his legal analysis. For example, Robert Bork, whose failed nomination to the Supreme Court made him an icon within conservative legal circles, wrote: "My difficulty is not that Epstein's constitution would repeal much of the New Deal and the modern regulatory-welfare state but rather that these conclusions are not plausibly related to the original understanding of the takings clause" (Bork 1990, 230; cited in Kendall and Lord 1998, 7).

Similarly, Charles Fried, the solicitor general in the Reagan administration, recalled:

> Attorney General Meese and his young advisers—many drawn from the ranks of the then fledgling Federalist Societies and often devotees of the extreme libertarian views of Chicago law professor Richard Epstein—had a specific, aggressive, and it seemed to me, quite radical project in mind: to use the takings clause of the Fifth Amendment as a severe brake on federal and state regulation of business and prop-erty. The grand plan was to make government pay compensation as for a taking of property every time its regulation impinged too severely on a property right—limiting the possible uses for a parcel of land or restricting or tying up a business in regulatory red tape. If the government labored under so severe an obligation, there would be, to say the least, much less regulation. . . .

It made me very nervous. I would readily ignore [my reservations] if I had been sure the argument was correct on its merits. . . . It was the merits that bothered me. (Fried 1991, 183–84; cited in Kendall and Lord 1998, 67)

Other less conservative legal scholars were far less generous in their evaluations of Epstein's theory. A participant in a symposium devoted to Epstein's book concluded:

Takings belongs with the output of the constitutional lunatic fringe, the effusions of gold bugs, tax protestors, and gun-toting survivalists. . . .
Takings is a travesty of constitutional scholarship. It is clearly written and systematic, but it displays these undoubted virtues in the deployment of a mass of assertion that is riddled with self-contradiction and backed by very little in the way of serious argument. Epstein fails to confront most of the obvious objections to his position. What persuasive force the book has derives from its author's previous scholarly reputation, his considerable rhetorical facility, and his tone of absolute conviction. (Grey 1986, 23–25)

President Reagan's Attorney General during his second term sided with the students who founded the Federalist Society. Ed Meese first came to the public notice as a deputy district attorney of Alameda County, California, which included Berkeley and its University of California campus. Meese became famous for his energetic prosecution of Berkeley radicals. Soon afterwards, Governor Ronald Reagan appointed him to be secretary of legal affairs. Later, when Reagan became president, he brought Meese to Washington to serve first as counselor (1981–85) and then as Attorney General (1985–88). As Attorney General, Meese began the process of screening judges for conservative purity. He strongly criticized liberal Supreme Court rulings for straying from the "original intent" of the founders.

The term, original intent, was one of the many absolutist expressions that the right wing used to indicate that those who disagree with them were violating the spirit of the Constitution, which only true conservatives were capable of interpreting. Despite this public demand for purity insofar as the Constitution was concerned, at a conference on economic liberties that he convened at the Justice Department in 1986, Meese was not above inviting fellow conservatives to "join us in what we would describe as a little 'constitutional calisthenics'" (Kendall and Lord 1998). That year Meese was involved in a different sort of constitutional calisthenics in trying to cover up the government's efforts to illegally finance terrorists who were trying to overthrow the government of Nicaragua (see L. Walsh 1993).

Within the Takings Clause, Meese argued, "a revolution in, or perhaps more accurately, a revisiting and restoration of economic liberty is a prospect" (Kendall and Lord 1998, 20). Meese's calisthenic exercise first bore fruit in *Nollan v. California Coastal Commission* (1987), in which the Pacific Legal Foundation convinced the Supreme Court to adopt much of Professor Epstein's outlandish view of the Takings Clause. The efforts of Meese and his circle to reshape the judiciary by screening judges before their appointments gave the movement the power to gut the regulatory structure.

In 1982, the Federal Courts Improvement Act established both the Federal Circuit Court of Appeals and the Court of Federal Claims, giving them exclusive jurisdiction to hear takings claims against the federal government. The Act also eliminated the former Court of Claims and Court of Custom and Patent Appeals, creating Court of Appeals for the Federal Circuit as a central patent appeals court. This new court contributed a great deal to the unwarranted strengthening of intellectual property rights in a way that is undermining the vitality of the U.S. economy (see Perelman 2002, 35).

The attack on regulation continued on other fronts as well. David McIntosh, one of the three founders of the Federalist Society, used his position, first within the office of Vice President Quayle and then as a congressional representative, to head up the crusade against regulation. One famous case symbolized the recklessness of the campaign:

> David appeared at a news conference to kick off the House debate. He brought along a three-foot-high stack of newly proposed federal rules, bound in scarlet ribbon, to symbolize red tape, and a bucket with holes in it, leaking confetti. The leaky bucket was there to demonstrate the absurdity of federal bureaucrats. The Consumer Product Safety Commission, he said, had proposed a rule requiring that "all buckets have a hole in the bottom of them, so that they can allow water to go through and avoid the danger of somebody falling face down into the bucket and drowning: The leaky bucket regulation.
>
> It was a great story, a favorite of Republicans and talk radio that season. Too bad it wasn't quite true. In response to the deaths of an estimated forty babies each year who fall into five-gallon buckets full of water, the agency had examined ways to prevent these toddler drownings. One bucket manufacturer pointed out that some industrial buckets used for dry materials have holes, and this was mentioned in an advance notice of rule-making. But, as the agency chief wrote in a letter to McIntosh, the commission never seriously considered proposing it. Moreover, the CPSC had already reached a voluntary agreement with bucket manufacturers to place warning labels on their product. (Easton 2002, 295)

No matter. The talk radio hosts continued to repeat the story. So did McIntosh, first on the Op-Ed page of the *Indianapolis Star*. Weeks later, he again reiterated the "leaky bucket" canard in testimony before the Senate Judiciary Committee (Bleifuss 1995). Such disinformation is a legitimate political tool. After all, victory is far more important than truth.

The right-wing revolution reinforced its victories in the legal sphere by using its financial resources to remake the media, the academic world, and the political environment to its liking. So successful has this capitalist restoration been that today most of the United States, as well as a good part of the rest of the planet, see the world through corporate eyes. The same handful of right-wing think tanks is even financing an Institute on Religion and Democracy to use the same hardball pressure tactics to intimidate church groups from accommodating liberal ideals (Goodstein and Kirkpatrick 2004).

In my own field, economics, these tactics have succeeded in changing the entire framework of the discipline. Leftists have been purged; liberals have been marginalized, while those friendly to the corporations have been generously subsidized. I cannot think of a single economics department in an elite university with a decidedly liberal tilt. Indeed, most economics departments are overwhelmingly conservative.

Privatizing Education

Education is essential for economic progress, yet in recent decades, the right wing has consistently been unfriendly to public education. For example, the Walton family's donation of $20 billion to help conservative causes was weighted toward the privatization of public education. The right wing expresses a number of objections to public education. Some religious conservatives protest that public education collides with their most cherished theological beliefs. The most public examples are sex education and scientific explanations of evolution and the big bang, which they find threatening to their belief about God's creation of the world.

The financial community looked forward to the establishment of Educational Maintenance Organizations, so named to suggest that profit-oriented schools would prosper in an education market, much like the Health Maintenance Organizations that have taken over much of the medical care in the United States. Given the abominable reputation of the HMOs, the publicists for privatized education, with their eye on skeptical public opinion, strategically renamed their dream as Educational Management Organizations, a relabeling that the George W. Bush administration endorsed.

Public education makes an inviting target for politicians, who enthusiastically scored points with their constituents by expressing deep concern for the children left behind. The same business and political leaders who cynically decry the sorry state of public education are largely responsible for the problem that they now call upon private education to solve. They callously starved public education of needed support. Some do so with glee.

For urban blacks, the appeal of the privatization of education is understandable. Although segregation is unconstitutional, it remains embarrassingly common in the schools. This separation is more economic than racial. Public schools largely depend upon local property taxation. Because schools that serve the poor are generally located in areas with low property values, poor children rarely get the same educational opportunities as children from more affluent families (Carnoy 1994, 134–35).

For example, Jonathan Kozol reported that in 1989, Chicago spent about $5,500 for each student in its secondary schools, compared to about $8,500 to $9,000 for each high school student in the highest-spending suburbs to the north. In New York during 1986–87, funding per student was $11,300 in the upper-middle-class Long Island suburbs of Manhasset, Jericho, and Great Neck; $6,400 in the largely working-class suburb of Mount Vernon; and $5,600 in the high-minority New York City public schools. Three years later, the figures were $15,000, $9,000, and $7,300 respectively. Although the proportionate change was equal, the absolute changes favored the already rich districts (Kozol 1991, 54, 237). A little more than a decade later, Kozol found the same disparities between rich and poor school districts (Kozol 2005, 321–24).

Even if poor, urban schools within a particular school district were to receive nearly equal funding, they would still have to spend their resources differently. Schools that service poor students have more need for special education, counseling, security, and so on. To make matters worse, because teaching in poor schools is frequently more challenging than teaching in more affluent settings, many more experienced teachers prefer to teach in suburban schools, leaving impoverished schools with a greater proportion of less qualified instructors (see Boyd, Lankford, Loeb, and Wyckoff 2005). For example, teachers in schools with a large share of minority students are less likely to have a master's degree. Higher salaries could attract more qualified teachers to those schools, but such funding is nowhere on the horizon (Bracey 1998).

Suburban schools are generally newer, while inner city and, to a lesser extent, rural schools are often in a state of disrepair. As a result, the poorer school districts face higher costs of operating their physical plant than the more affluent suburban schools. For example, a General Accounting Office report to Congress noted that "one third of the nation's 80,000 public schools are in such poor repair that the fourteen million children who attend them are being housed in unsuitable or unsafe conditions" (U.S. General Accounting Office 1996). Jonathan Kozol described a rather extreme instance: the Martin Luther King Junior High School in East St. Louis, Illinois, where sewage repeatedly backed up into the school, including the food preparation area (Kozol 1991, 21).

Lewis Powell, often portrayed as a moderate on the Supreme Court, wrote a key decision about educational equity in a 1973 case, *San Antonio Independent School District v. Rodriguez*. Powell determined that education is not "a fundamental interest" inasmuch as education "is not among the rights afforded explicit protection under our Federal Constitution." Nor, he wrote, was "absolute deprivation" at stake. "The argument here," he said, "is not that the children in districts having relatively low assessable property values are receiving no public education; rather, it is that they are receiving a poorer quality education than that available to children in districts having more assessable wealth." In cases where wealth is involved, he said, "the Equal Protection Clause does not require absolute equality" (Kozol 2005, 242).

In California, a state often equated with perpetual prosperity, many poor students have appallingly limited educational opportunities. The American Civil Liberties Union filed a suit, *Williams et al., v. State of California* (1999), which charged that "[m]any students lack textbooks of any kind. Other students must rely on illegible or incomplete photocopies provided by teachers when and if teachers have time and the individual resources to make the copies. . . . Sometimes three or four students to a book with no opportunity to take the book home and study for homework. . . . Sometimes as few as 13 percent of the teachers have full nonemergency teaching credentials. . . . Some California public schools . . . simply do not provide enough basic supplies, such as pencils, crayons, paper, and scissors."

Inequities in funding and poor school performance reinforce each other in innumerable ways. For example, schools strapped for money turn to junk food companies as a way to find cash. According to many experts, eating such food interferes with children's ability to pay attention. Even worse, David Satcher, George W. Bush's surgeon general, reported in May 2000 that more than a third of poor children have untreated dental cavities. Even if junk food does not obstruct students' performance, certainly toothaches will (Rothstein 2001). To add insult to injury, companies such as McDonald's and Coke provide educational materials on nutrition to impoverished schools reinforcing their hold over children's diets.

Educational inequalities are inexcusable. Rather than immediately addressing these inequities, California wasted scarce resources in fighting the suit for years. Eventually, the plaintiffs settled for a pittance. American Civil Liberties Union lawyer, Catherine Lhamon, explained to Jonathan Kozol that "sufficient textbooks" became "one book for every child to use at school without sharing and to be able to bring home" and "good repair of school facilities" became nothing more than a mandate to "unlock the bathrooms" and "a classroom seat for every child." She despaired, "I couldn't believe at first we were fighting so hard and so long to win so little. But we felt these students are so far behind that we needed to get everybody to a floor beneath which no school can fall, and then begin to have another conversation on what children actually need" (Kozol 2005, 376).

Conservatives rarely acknowledge the gross inequities of school funding, even though the rich and famous go to great lengths to get their children into elite schools and even preschools (Nelson and Cohen 2002; Kozol 2005, 135–39). Instead, the opponents of more spending on education insist that throwing more money at education will serve no good purpose. President George W. Bush, himself a product of an extremely expensive system of private education, callously compared more educational spending to "pumping more gas into a flooded engine" (Bruni 2001).

The right wing insists that the educational system is responsible for its own problems. Conservatives berate the educational system for a lack of accountability and bloated administrative structures that do little to promote education. The same critics never mention that a never-ending flow of mandates accounts for a good part of this administrative bureaucracy.

The conservatives' response to the deficiencies in public education was the cynically named No Child Left Behind Act, which requires that schools spend inordinate amounts of money for testing. The estimated annual direct costs of testing are $400 million (Danitz 2001). In a world in which corporations can outsource their labor around the globe, can anyone believe that rote training will prepare students to compete?

Because of the penalties that schools face for poor test performance, school systems have little choice but to spend even more money for services that are supposed to improve test results. The money spent on these tests of dubious value could easily be spent on more productive activities.

States are responding to the high costs of testing by switching into multiple choice tests "that merely require students to recall and restate facts," according to Thomas Toch, codirector of a new research group. To make matters, worse, in 2006 the testing industry was beset with an embarrassing rash of errors—although not for the No Child Left Behind tests (Winerip 2006).

However, from another perspective, this diversion of funds into nonproductive channels is welcome since it furthers the ultimate conservative objective. By deflecting schools from real education, the emphasis on testing undermines public education and further fuels calls for outright privatization.

Given the disastrous conditions of public education for the poor, conservatives piously call for the privatization of education without committing themselves to following up their victory with tax increases sufficient to give the new system a chance to work. Instead, these politicians pretend that the imagined savings supposedly made possible by supreme managerial efficiency of private business will be more than enough to finance the improvement of education—promises similar to those once made by advocates of Health Maintenance Organizations.

Other promoters of privatized education relish a tactical opportunity to create a divide between blacks and teachers' unions, whose members reliably vote Democratic. In an answer to the question, "What do you look for in an issue to go after or to recommend to the Republican Party to pursue?" Grover Norquist, mentioned earlier as head of Americans for Tax Reform and one of the most influential Republican strategists in Washington, responded, "Does it divide the left? School choice reaches right into the heart of the Democratic coalition and takes people out of it. It divides the left because the teachers' unions are on one side and all the parents of poor children are on the other and it makes Bill Clinton choose between poor parents and teachers' unions" (Berlau 1998).

Barbara Miner cited a number of other right-wing leaders and organizations who echoed Norquist's sentiments, including Terry Moe, a senior fellow at the conservative Hoover Institution and coauthor of the book, *Politics, Markets, and America's Schools*:

> [The issue comes down to] a matter of power.... [The National Educational Association and American Federation of Teachers] have a lot of money for campaign contributions and for lobbying.... They also have a lot of electoral clout because they have many activists out in the trenches in every political district.... No other group can claim this kind of geographically uniform political activity. They are everywhere. [School vouchers are a way to diminish that power.] School choice allows children and money to leave the system, and that means there will be fewer public teacher jobs, lower union membership, and lower dues. (Miner 2004, 22–23)

Conservatives have also begun to fund rival teacher's organizations, such as the Alabama Conference of Educators. Not surprisingly, "conservative foundations also support taxpayer-funded vouchers for private-school students and charter schools operated independently of traditional school-district supervision" (D. Golden 2004). The right wing insists that school vouchers for the purchase of education on the private market will eliminate the inequities in education. Certainly, privatization will add to the profits for some of the same corporations that fund the right wing while, as Grover Norquist and Terry Moe noted, dividing those who suffer most under the current system from the teachers unions.

However, if the right wing succeeds in financing education through vouchers, the debate will quickly shift. The first step will be to make vouchers means-tested, meaning that people earning above a certain income will no longer be eligible. In the process, education will become redefined an entitlement, like other welfare programs. Soon, taxpayers will protest having to subsidize the undeserving; they will demand that schools eliminate their "frills." Programs for the poor inevitably become poor programs. The outcome will be that the politicians will relieve the rich of much of the tax obligation of supporting education, while the poor will see their educational opportunities degrade even further.

Teachers' unions oppose privatization of education on several grounds. They question that the state will be able to monitor and control the quality of private education. Private providers will have the advantage of being able to cherry-pick by excluding difficult students or students with special needs. Because public schools will still have to service most of the physically and emotionally disabled students, they will have difficulty matching the results of the private providers, unless the latter prove to be absolutely incompetent. Finally, even though school-teachers are already underpaid, private providers will be freed from union contracts and will be able to make employment conditions much less favorable. For service workers, such as custodians, the switch to private employers will be even harsher.

When teachers' unions highlight how teachers will suffer economically with these changes, the right wing portrays teachers as just another special interest group, who put their own selfish needs ahead of those of the poor, especially black, students in their care. Teachers, of course, bear little responsibility for the inequities of the public school system, but the right wing has been very effective in portraying teachers unions as public enemies. The rhetoric has become so heated that on February 23, 2004, Secretary of Education Rod Paige actually went so far as to call the teachers' National Education Association a "terrorist organization."

Lost in these debates is the sad fact that no major political party seems ready to come to the aid of public education, which has long been a mainstay of the U.S. economy. The economic effects of privatization will not be felt immediately. Over time, however, as a larger share of the workforce suffers the handicap of inferior education, the negative effect on all aspects of society will become unmistakable.

Part 3

Retribution:
How the Takeover
Undermines the Economy

Chapter 6

Economists Justifying the Plot

Nonsense on Stilts

Late in the eighteenth century, the conservative legal philosopher and economic ideologue, Jeremy Bentham, railed against the rhetoric of the French Revolution, denouncing it as "rhetorical nonsense—nonsense upon stilts" (Bentham 1962, 501). While I don't subscribe to Bentham's politics, his expression exquisitely expresses the way the right wing won control of the economy, spouting nonsense while being lifted up on the powerful stilts of money and influence. Of course, no account of this transformation can neglect to mention how the Democrats' timidity contributed to the success of the right wing.

Right-wing zealots no doubt can take great satisfaction in the extent of their victories. We need look no further than the enormous transfer of wealth and income to the super-rich in the last few decades to get a sense of the magnitude of what they have accomplished. Almost unnoticed among the slew of right-wing political victories is an uncomfortable fact: these right-wing policies have set in motion destructive forces that threaten national prosperity.

Relatively few people seem to understand the self-defeating nature of the right-wing revolution. The destructive power of the revolution should be obvious to its first direct victims. They must feel the toll that right-wing policies have already taken on their lives, but the right wing has sown so much confusion that quite a few of the victims of the right-wing juggernaut are unable to identify the cause of their woes. Consequently, in many recent elections, the right wing has possibly even managed to win the support of the majority of voters harmed by their policies. Winning public assent for such policies is an incomparable political feat.

Conservatives may feel that they have good reason to gloat over their victories, but the super-rich and the corporate sector—the intended beneficiaries of the right-wing revolution—should also be concerned about a Pyrrhic victory. Although the right-wing policies have not yet wrought much of their inevitable damage, ultimate victims will not just be the poor and working classes; eventually even those occupying the privileged positions in society will pay a steep price for their greed.

Here is a suggestive tidbit pointing to the gap between right-wing ideology and economic reality: the stock market actually performs better under Democratic administrations than under Republican leadership, despite the Democrats' supposed hostility toward business:

> [S]ince 1900, Democratic presidents have produced a 12.3 percent annual total return on the S&P [Standard and Poors] 500, but Republicans only an 8 percent return. In 2000, the Stock Trader's Almanac, which slices and dices Wall Street performance figures like baseball stats, came up with nearly the same numbers (13.4 percent versus 8.1 percent) by measuring Dow price appreciation. (Most of the 20th century's bear markets, incidentally, have been Republican bear markets: the Crash of '29, the early '70s oil shock, the '87 correction, and the current stall occurred under GOP presidents.). (Vinzant 2002)

A more technical study, appearing in the *Journal of Finance*, reached a similar conclusion for the period beginning in 1927. This article compared how much investors in the stock market would earn over and above the Treasury bill rate during Democratic administrations with the amount they would earn during Republican administrations. Subtracting the Treasury bill rate eliminates any distortion that inflation might cause. The authors find that returns on the stock market exceeded the rate on a Treasury bill by "2 percent under Republican and 11 percent under Democratic presidents—a striking difference of 9 percent per year!" (Santa-Clara and Valkanov 2003, 1841).

The *Journal of Finance* article reported that this difference between the rates of return on Treasury bills and the stock market was far greater for investments in small firms than for large firms. Under Democratic administrations, stock in the largest firms earned a still significant 7 percent greater return under Democratic administrations than under Republican administrations; for the smallest firms, the difference rose to an astounding 22 percent.

The authors regarded this differential between large and small firms as a puzzle. The solution to this "puzzle" may be relatively simple: politicians respond to influence. Large established firms often rely more on political influence than on their productive capacity. Because politicians rely on campaign finance and appreciate the lure of lucrative future employment in the corporate sector after they leave government, both parties cater to the whims of the largest corporations.

Small firms, in contrast, must depend more on their own productive advantages. In a vibrant economy, many small firms can grow and prosper, sometimes even to the extent that they can eventually become able to challenge larger firms. In a more stagnant economy, smaller firms are more likely to languish or even fail, leading to the seeming puzzling differential.

This relationship between Democratic administrations and either the stock market or the GDP is far from conclusive evidence of a right-wing threat to prosperity. I mentioned this relationship about the stock market here mostly because it is so counterintuitive.

The significantly greater growth of the economy during Democratic administrations, measured by the Gross Domestic Product (GDP), is more pertinent than the differential in stock market returns. Since 1930, the growth rate has been 5.4 percent for Democratic administrations, compared to an anemic 1.6 percent for Republican administrations (Vinzant 2002).

I should add that these striking differences between Republican and Democratic administrations severely underestimate what is at stake with the right-wing revolution. After all, the right wing has successfully moved both parties in the direction that it favors. So, a better base line to get a handle on the right-wing revolution would be the level of growth that would occur under the sort of policies that the Democrats would have pursued before the right-wing revolution began.

Now, I want to examine the ominous forces that are at work undermining future prosperity of the U.S. economy.

A Stampede of Tax Cuts for the Wealthy

Grover Norquist cut his political teeth in 1978 while working on California's infamous Proposition 13, which set off the national tax cutting frenzy. Since then, tax cuts have remained high on the right-wing agenda. Massive tax cuts promise immediate benefits for the rich and powerful.

Despite the obvious attractiveness, the economy, which rewards the wealthy so handsomely, heavily depends on the government. For example, looking back on the history of the United States, the government financed much of the railroad construction. This investment was fundamental in the creation of a modern economy. Railroads permitted the extension of agriculture to land that could not have been farmed profitably if farmers had to deliver their produce using traditional transportation methods. Railroads also provided demand that made modern industry possible in the United States. For example, in 1830, before the railroad boom, one year's wear and tear for horseshoes and other farm implements was 100,000 tons of pig iron, which represented half of the total U.S. consumption of pig iron (Lebergott 1984, 131). Railroads were responsible for the development of economies of scale that permitted the application of advanced technologies.

Railroads first developed the modern management practices that became the model for large businesses. Railroads were also responsible for the creation of modern financial markets in the United States. In short, virtually everything that people today identify with the success of the U.S. economy has roots in the government-financed railroads.

Government also finances public education, subsidizes basic science, and adjudicates contracts making complex business ventures possible. Government investment made possible the computer, the Internet, satellite telecommunications, and a host of other modern technologies. What the right wing calls "free enterprise" still depends heavily upon the government, even if we ignore the billions of dollars that such free enterprises take in unproductive government handouts and subsidies.

Those who benefit most from tax cuts rarely acknowledge that government programs make important contributions to their own prosperity. Almost a century ago, Supreme Court Justice Oliver Wendell Holmes wrote in a dissenting opinion, "Taxes are what we pay for civilized society" (Holmes 1927)—but Holmes's decision represented a minority view both on the court and among the rich.

Holmes could have gone much further. In the long run, a weakened government sector will also be less capable of promoting business interests. Such costs will not appear immediately. For example, even if the entire education system were to disappear today, business would not feel the brunt of the effects until the cumulative losses became pressing. Once the negative consequences become obvious, considerable time will be required to remedy the situation.

Unfortunately, ideological blinders prevent most people of influence from recognizing the contributions of the government sector. Peter Lindert, one of the coauthors of the book on income distribution mentioned earlier, concluded the first volume of his wonderful international survey of the relationship between social spending and economic growth with an observation about the tenacity of the ideology of minimal government involvement:

> If high-budget welfare states have achieved much the same growth with greater equality, why haven't the lower-spending countries crossed over [and taken up the same policies]? The shorthand answer is "history and ideology." Recent surveys confirm what we have long known. The separate historical paths followed by the low-budget countries of the English-speaking world and by Switzerland have shaped a political ideology that will remain firmly opposed to a universalist welfare state for the foreseeable future. . . . [T]he opposite is also true: There is no compelling economic reason to expect any great retreat from the welfare state. (Lindert 2004, 307)

Sadly, the prediction in the last part of his conclusion may fall victim to the force of the right wing. I am afraid that even European social democracies are beginning to follow much the same path as the United States in dismantling their social supports.

Starve the Beast

Two highly respected liberal economists, William Gale and Peter Orszag, recently appointed to head the Congressional Budget Office, predict that the fiscal policies of the right-wing tax cuts are a recipe for disaster. Because the tax cuts create deficits, the federal government must borrow more money to make up the difference between tax receipts and government spending. The increasing competition for borrowed money raises interest rates. Investment and consumer demand will fall as interest rates increase, cutting into potential growth, imposing an estimated annual cost for the average household $1,500 to $3,000 per year (see Gale and Orszag 2004; and Gale and Orszag forthcoming).

These estimates seem excessive. Besides, the problem is not the size of the deficit but the policy changes that the right wing can engineer by stoking fears about the disaster that deficits can create. The idea is that with the government facing seemingly unmanageable deficits, the public will be stampeded into a wholesale slashing of government spending.

As a result, regulatory policies that inconvenience the corporate sector as well as social programs that might benefit ordinary people will disappear. The right wing gleefully refers to this situation as the starve-the-beast strategy—by depriving the government of adequate revenue, its regulatory powers will necessarily shrink.

Traditionally, Republicans represented themselves as the party of fiscal sobriety, insisting that balanced budgets were essential to solid economic performance. In the 1980s, a new strategy began to emerge. Conservatives began to welcome huge deficits.

For example, in 2001, President George W. Bush expressed his support for this tactic, reporting that the government's fast-dwindling surplus (created by his own tax cuts) was "incredibly positive news" because it will create "a fiscal straitjacket for Congress" (Sanger 2001). Similarly, California Governor Arnold Schwarzenegger said that he wanted to use his budget plan to "starve the public sector" without raising taxes, "because we don't want to feed the monster" (Delsohn 2005).

Nobody has been more adamant about pursuing this strategy than our old friend, Grover Norquist, who told an interviewer: "I don't want to abolish government. I simply want to reduce it to the size where I can drag it into the bathroom and drown it in the bathtub" (Norquist 2001). Conservative economists, such as Milton Friedman, agree, although in less colorful terms. They applaud growing federal budget deficits created by tax cuts, which will eventually create pressure to cut social programs and regulation (M. Friedman 1988; M. Friedman 2003).

In reality, all except a handful of principled libertarians have no interest whatsoever in thoroughly starving the beast. To the extent that government subsidizes and protects business, conservative class-warriors welcome the governments' engagement with open arms. Only when the government lends support to the poor and disadvantaged does the right wing regard state spending as an abomination.

The conservative class-warriors are just as opportunistic in their attitude toward regulation. The regulatory system in the United States is hardly the fierce beast that business pretends it to be. For example, popular protests by farmers who felt cheated by the railroads led to the creation of the Interstate Commerce Commission, one of the first regulatory agencies in the country. Yet the railroads privately welcomed the Interstate Commerce Commission, realizing that only people from within the industry would have the expertise to regulate it. Besides, the commission would diffuse popular anger toward the railroads.

Since then, industry has perfected the practice of hiring regulators soon after they leave government. In this way, regulators understand that they will harm their career path if they behave in a way that upsets industry.

The Republicans invented another technique to undermine inconvenient regulation. Agencies, such as the Patent and Trademark Office and the Food and Drug Administration, now fund much of their operations from fees paid by those whom they regulate. This arrangement leads them to view those whom they regulate as clients, even though their real client should be the public at large. Rather than subjecting drugs or patents to careful scrutiny, these agencies put pressure on their staff to process applications as quickly as possible in order to generate more revenue.

For programs that directly serve the general population, such as education or public transportation, inadequate resources prevent them from operating satisfactorily. The resulting dissatisfaction with these programs strengthens the case for privatization.

In short, the right-wing strategy is to intentionally create a crisis of financial disorder with the expectation that a sense of urgency will panic the public into acquiescing to the preferred remedies of the conservatives. A measured discussion of the real issues would certainly be more likely to lead to a healthy economy, but a rational dialogue would probably not result in the one-sided outcome that the right wing desires.

In Praise of Inequality?

Conservative economists typically attribute the poverty of the poor to natural market forces; the less fortunate do not deserve to earn more than what they can earn in the market. If the poor want more income, they should just work harder or smarter. Government policies to reduce income inequality or to help the poor enjoy a larger portion of society's wealth and income are confidently denounced as destructive, at least according to this ideology.

Conservative economists conveniently ignore the perverse political and social influences that reinforce inequality. Questions of race, class, or gender do not enter into their discussion of inequality. Nor do many economists acknowledge that the forces that maintain inequality limit the potentially valuable contributions of those held back down by inequality.

This ideological predisposition makes economists extremely critical of any thought of redistribution of wealth or income. Consider the words of Nobel Laureate Robert Lucas. After noting the differential growth rates among countries, he writes: "Is there some action a government of India could take that would lead the Indian Economy to grow like Indonesia's or Egypt's?.... The consequences for human welfare involved in questions like these are simply staggering: Once one starts to think about them it is hard to think of anything else" (Lucas 1988, 5).

Not only was Lucas willing not to think of anything else, he wanted others to do likewise:

> Of the tendencies that are harmful to sound economics, the most seductive, and in my opinion the most poisonous, is to focus on questions of distribution. In this very minute, a child is being born to an American family and another child, equally valued by God, is being born to a family in India. The resources of all kinds that will be at the disposal of this new American will be on the order of 15 times the resources available to his Indian brother. This seems to us a terrible wrong, justifying direct corrective action, and perhaps some actions of this kind can and should be taken. But of the vast increase in the well-being of hundreds of millions of people that has occurred in the 200-year course of the industrial revolution to date, virtually none of it can be attributed to the direct redistribution of resources from rich to poor. The potential for improving the lives of poor people by finding

different ways of distributing current production is nothing compared to the apparently limitless potential of increasing production. (Lucas 2003)

According to this theory, markets appropriately reward the rich and powerful because of their superior productivity. Consequently, they deserve every bit of what they earn. Supposedly, the best cure for poverty is to allow natural economic forces to follow their course. These economists are unapologetic about their stance. For example, when Finis Welch, who gave his prestigious Richard T. Ely lecture at the 1999 meeting of the American Economic Association, he provocatively titled his talk, "In Defense of Inequality." There, Welch proclaimed, "I believe inequality is an economic 'good' that has received too much bad press. . . . Wages play many roles in our economy; along with time worked, they determine labor income, but they also signal relative scarcity and abundance, and with malleable skills, wages provide incentives to render the services that are most highly valued. . . . Increasing dispersion can offer increased opportunities for specialization and increased opportunities to mesh skills and activities" (Welch 1999, 1 and 15).

Ludwig von Mises, an Austrian economist and one of the leading icons of libertarian economics, went even further than Welch, proclaiming: "Inequality of wealth and incomes is the cause of the masses' well-being, not the cause of anybody's distress. Where there is a 'lower degree of inequality', there is necessarily a lower standard of living of the masses" (von Mises 1955). Does inequality really get too much bad press, as Finis Welch suggests?

The Imaginary Trickle Down

Supposedly, the opportunity for more income will drive both rich and poor to work harder, causing the economy to grow faster. Over time, virtually everybody in society will be better off as affluence trickles down, even into the poorest citizens.

The trickle down just does not work. Despite the significant economic growth of the last three decades, as we have seen, relatively few people have benefited very much. However, economists—even highly skilled economists—were unprepared to understand the situation that the right-wing revolution created. Consider the experience of Rebecca Blank, a very talented economist, who was working as a senior staff economist for the Council of Economic Advisers for the George H. W. Bush administration in the fall of 1989:

> One of our responsibilities was to produce short memos for the White House when major economic statistics were released, summarizing the implications of these data. In October, the Census Bureau released its annual report on income and poverty for 1988, which happened to be a year of very strong economic growth and rising average personal incomes. Oddly, however, the poverty rate fell by an insignificant amount that year. I wrote up my summary and brought it to my boss for approval. He read it through, handed it back to me, and said, "Add a paragraph explaining why poverty didn't fall last year." I dutifully went back to my desk, sat down at my computer, stared at it a while, and realized I had no explanation to offer. . . . Rising poverty occurring alongside of economic expansion is particularly

troubling because of the long-cherished belief that economic growth is a sure way to reduce need. (Blank 1997, 53–54)

Looking back, Blank realized that the problem was the absence of the wage growth that usually accompanies economic expansion. Recall that the income share of the bottom 90 percent of the population fell just as real hourly wages peaked. Economists' most popular explanation of stagnant wages today is that workers lack the proper skills. But where do such skills originate? Are workers expected to develop technological skills while they are unemployed or flipping burgers? Are workers responsible because society does not adequately support education? Warren Buffett knows better.

Should we blame workers because they did not have the income or the connections to be able to study at elite universities? Why is the education of a CEO about the same as a poorly paid school teacher (Krugman 1996)? And what about the many highly educated people who still cannot find work commensurate with their training? Economists also have a ready answer for this question: workers must also be flexible in order to meet the changing demands of the job market.

For example, consider the attitude of W. Michael Cox, chief economist for the Federal Reserve Bank of Dallas, one of the most prominent cheerleaders for markets, who always finds a way to describe markets in the best possible light. When faced with the quandary about essential workers, such as firemen having to work two jobs to be able to afford to live in New York, Dr. Cox pontificated: "I think it's great. . . . It gives you portfolio diversification in your income" (Scott 2006).

Here Dr. Cox has outdone himself, justifying the unjustifiable, while implicitly financializing the job market. Just as investors should do well to diversify their portfolios, workers would be well advised to hold more than one job. Of course, sophisticated investors divide their funds among many, even hundreds of different stocks. If only the poor, benighted workers would figure out how to extend the day beyond 24 hours, they could do the same. I wonder how Dr. Cox would feel however if groggy firefighters who are supposed to save his house were already exhausted from their other job.

A central thread of this book is that inequality hinders, rather than promotes economic growth. To make matters worse, once inequality reaches a tipping point, it sets off powerful destructive forces, especially after people begin to perceive that the existing level of inequality is excessive. Now that the distribution of income in the United States is coming to resemble, or perhaps even surpass, conditions in 1929, we may benefit from taking a longer perspective in evaluating what has transpired since the Powell memo.

Inequality and Racism

One of the most glaring omissions in Welch's analysis of inequality was racism. If poor people fall behind and if many of those poor are nonwhite, conservative economists disregard race and explain that the market is justifiably paying a premium for "unobserved" skills that these people lack.

Of course, racism—like many of the problems identified in this book—did not suddenly begin in the 1970s, although the right-wing strategy certainly relied heavily on nurturing underlying racist sentiments. Without such encouragement, racial animosity might eventually expire.

Consider the experience of the Irish in the United States. A century and a half earlier, many people in the United States regarded the Irish as an inferior "race." People attributed to the Irish many of the negative stereotypes still associated with blacks today. British immigrants transplanted some of this antagonism toward the Irish from their native land, where "scientists" attempted to "prove" the racial links between the Irish and blacks. For example, John Beddoe, the President of the Anthropological Society of London in 1870, developed a well-known "Index of Nigrescence" that might be applied to the "Africanoid Celts" to measure how close the physical attributes of the Irish and Africans were. Cartoons showing Irish people as apelike commonly circulated in both the English and the U.S. press (Beddoe 1885, 5; Levy and Peart 2002; L. Curtis 1997, 20–21).

A good deal of the hostility to the Irish occurred because employers took advantage of their poverty and desperation, paying them horribly low wages to supplant native-born workers who had higher wage expectations. Many workers blamed the Irish rather than their employers for the downward pressure on wages. Over time, the stigma associated with Irish heritage gradually dissipated.

Similarly, overt anti-Semitism has largely disappeared from most of the United States. In contrast, racist politics still pay positive dividends. The social and economic costs of this corrosive strategy have been enormous—not just for the blacks themselves, but for the poor and the working class as a whole.

For example, two Harvard professors, Alberto Alesina and Edward Glaeser, studied the causes of the differences between welfare programs in the United States and elsewhere in the world. They identified racial diversity as one of the key factors in determining the kind of economic policy found in a country. They found convincing evidence that countries with more homogeneous populations had considerably more generous welfare programs (Alesina and Glaeser 2004, 140–41). Within the United States, the welfare policies displayed a similar pattern: states with more homogeneous populations were more generous; other states, less so (Alesina and Glaeser 2004, 146–49).

Of course, race is not the only factor in determining the nature of welfare policies. Political arrangements are also extremely important. Alesina and Glaeser insisted that proportional representation, which is common in Europe, rather than a winner-take-all arrangement that the United States uses, makes a big difference. Also, the existence of a strong labor movement is important (Alesina and Glaeser 2004, 107–19). Finally, the authors showed that ideological biases influence the outcomes. For example, people in the United States believe that people move out of poverty far more easily than they actually do, significantly reducing the perceived justification for a stronger welfare system (Alesina and Glaeser 2004, 4).

Where the Harvard study falls short is in its inadequate attention to the potential for change. The authors did not go so far as to suppose that these three factors—racial makeup, political arrangements, and labor movement—deterministically set the welfare system. They acknowledged that ideology can play an important role. They described how the strength of the labor movement affects the political arrangements. They even offered a fairly solid account of how conservatives responded to the growing Populist movement in the late nineteenth-century United States, playing the race card, splitting the Populists, and then leaving them in oblivion (Alesina and Glaeser 2004, 155–61). But these academic nuances cannot do justice to the way in which the right wing cynically mobilized political forces to fan the flames of racial disharmony in an effort to distract the majority of people from their own economic interests.

The Natural Trickle-Down Elimination of Inequality

Economists' glaring lack of concern about the level of inequality owes a great deal to Simon Kuznets, a Nobel Laureate and brother of my adviser in graduate school. In his presidential address to the American Economic Association in late 1954, Kuznets laid out what came to be the prevailing view about the natural course of inequality. Seeing a trend toward economic equality by the end of the 1940s based on his analysis of data from United States, England, and Germany, Kuznets proposed that economic inequality naturally follows an inverted U-shaped curve. According to Kuznets, when poor countries first began to develop, inequality increased until the economy became more sophisticated, which then set in motion a trend toward more equality.

Kuznets, who won his Nobel Prize for his careful analysis of economic data, was understandably modest about this suggestion, referring to his lecture "as a collection of hunches" rather than the sort of painstaking analysis for which he was justifiably famous (Kuznets 1955, 26). Kuznets's followers were far less modest than Kuznets, recasting his casual observation almost as a natural law of market economies.

The evidence that markets are a benign arrangement with a built-in tendency toward equality is not particularly convincing. A longer view of the developed market economies over the last century and a half suggests a different pattern.

Market economies have a tendency toward inequality. Kuznets himself suggests that the tendency of the wealthy to have more savings tends to lead to an increasing concentration of wealth and income (Kuznets 1955, 7). As I suggested earlier, at some point inequality of income becomes so extreme it sets off an economic crisis. In the wake of such catastrophes, new institutional arrangements arise, which temporarily moderate inequality. In fact, first among the causes that offset the tendency toward inequality Kuznets lists "legislative interference" and "political" decisions (Kuznets 1955, 9).

Writing at a time when the momentum of the New Deal had not entirely dissipated, Kuznets did not acknowledge that such egalitarian policies depended on political support. After a short time, the rich and powerful seem to be able to regroup and assert their powers. As a result, the institutional support for a more equitable income distribution frays and the tendency toward inequality begins anew.

Economists embraced Kuznets's hunch so enthusiastically because it had such comforting implications. Coming in the midst of the cold war, Kuznets's hunch had an even more urgent message: unfettered markets could naturally accomplish what socialism could only promise.

So, political leaders should just let business promote economic growth rather than even thinking about directly redistributing resources to help the poor, the message Lucas later echoed. Markets are not just the best means of creating widespread prosperity, but also a sure route to equality.

Unfortunately, Kuznets's idea proved to be overly optimistic. By the late 1940s, just as Kuznets was about to launch his theory, the forces that were promoting equality had already lost much of their momentum. Looking back from 1980, Jeffrey Williamson and Peter Lindert, authors of a classic book on inequality of income in the United States, speculated, "By almost any yardstick, inequality has changed little since the late 1940s. If there has been any trend, it is toward slightly more inequality in pre-fisc [pre-tax] income and toward slightly less inequality in post-fisc income. This stability has been extraordinary even by twentieth-century standards" (Williamson and Lindert 1980, 92).

Even the more modest appraisal of Lindert and Williamson turned out to be overly optimistic. In retrospect, instead of stability, a powerful trend toward inequality had already begun to take hold by the time they published their book. What appeared to be stability in 1980 was only a temporary pause. The right wing had already launched its renewed offensive to restore the sort of inequality that existed just before the Great Depression. As the Soviet government receded into history, pretenses of egalitarianism no longer had any political value.

By this time, anything that threatened to inconvenience corporate balance sheets had to be vigorously attacked. Are wages too high? Then, attack labor. Reagan's firing of the air traffic controllers union set the stage for a widespread attack on labor.

Are regulations bothersome? Then, eliminate them. Within a few decades, the corporate sector was supreme, unburdened of a good part of the regulatory structure that had been in place at the end of the 1960s.

The new economic climate freed business from much of its obligation to pay either decent wages or taxes. Despite following the recipe of the mainstream economic cookbook, the miraculous trickle down never materialized.

Chapter 7

A Touch of Reality

The Natural Trickle-Up Nurturing of Inequality

Let us return to the relationship between inequality and the personal use of corporate jets. To add insult to injury, over and above the non-collection of taxes, government policies subsidize corporate jets to the tune of billions of dollars (Stiglitz 2004, 108).

The Federal Aviation Administration (FAA) annually collects $10 billion in taxes and fees to support and refurbish the Air Traffic Control System. Although business jets account for more than 18 percent of all flights, they only pay 5 percent of money that the FAA collects. The airlines are asking for rule changes that would require business aircraft to pay their fair share, amounting to a share of up to $2 billion dollars (Meckler 2006; Palmieri 2006).

Because the FAA charges passengers fees, they help to pay for the executive abuse of corporate jets. Because of the increased congestion of air traffic, passengers also face more delays and a greater safety risk.

Airlines also pay greater taxes to support corporate jets. In addition, they lose customers because of the greater inconvenience of travel. As the airline industry scrambles to save money, its first target is labor. Pilots, mechanics, and flight attendants have experienced dramatic cuts in wages and benefits, especially pensions and medical care, making another contribution to the growing inequality in the United States. Even these dramatic reductions in cost are usually insufficient to prevent bankruptcy, causing the public to have to cover part of the companies' pension obligations.

Nobody could claim that executive golfing excursions are a major cause of the slash-and-burn labor-management practices of the airlines. But this example does serve to illustrate how one corporate abuse leads to another, creating a spiral of inequality.

The Social Engineering of Inequality

What has really changed is the relationship between workers and employers. With the balance of power tipped decisively in the direction of employers, workers have limited ability to demand wage increases.

Earlier, Richard Nixon used affirmative action to undermine labor's bargaining position at a time of low unemployment. Nixon, at least, had to go through the motions of courting labor in order to appeal to blue-collar workers. By the time of Ronald Reagan, no such display was necessary. Instead, Reagan began his administration by firing the air traffic controllers. For labor, it has been all downhill since then.

Between 1948 and 2003, the share of unionized workers in the private sector has fallen from almost 35 percent to a little more than 8 percent. Declining employment in manufacturing explains some of this loss, but the hostile atmosphere resulting from unfriendly actions by government and the courts was also a major factor.

Welfare reform added to the unfavorable mix. Lawrence Mead, a prominent advocate for conservative welfare reform, explained that "there are good grounds to think that work, at least 'dirty' low-wage jobs, can no longer be left solely to the initiative of those who labor" (Mead 1986, 13). At the time, the right wing was not yet strong enough to push through such legislation.

By 1995, the political tide had moved in favor of welfare reform. The president of the U.S. Chamber of Commerce, the same organization that promoted Powell's manifesto worked tirelessly promoting the cause of welfare reform, made clear the purpose of pushing women off the welfare rolls: "Well, there are lots of jobs. Anytime there's high unemployment, there's also [nonetheless] the long list of jobs that go a-begging. The fact of the matter is everyone wants to start in the middle or upper middle, and now you're going to be driven to start at the bottom and begin to work your way up" (Pimpare 2004).

Timothy Bartik, an economist, estimated that welfare reform eventually would probably raise the total labor force by between one million and two million persons over the 1993–2005 period, with the obvious result that wages would fall (Bartik 1999). In many cases, the wage effect of welfare reform could be more dramatic than either Bartik or the Chamber suggested:

> New York Mayor Rudolph Giuliani cut 22,000 municipal jobs between 1995 and 2000, and most were replaced by workfare workers. Part-time welfare workers constituted 75 percent of the labor force of the Parks Department and one-third of Sanitation. The average city clerical salary was $12.32 per hour, while it was $1.80 per hour for Work Experience Program workers, who received no benefits. The city's Department of Homeless Services itself replaced unionized city workers with welfare recipients fulfilling workfare obligations. One Salt Lake City official told the *New York Times* that "Without the welfare people . . . we would have had to raise the wage . . . maybe 5 percent. (Pimpare 2004)

The Economics of High Wages

The initial rationale for the attack on labor was that much of what business saved on wages would add to profits and that profits would fuel the trickle down. At the time, the Golden Age was over. Profits were lagging. U.S. manufacturing was already being rocked by a wave of Asian imports. Business leaders applauded the slash-and-burn tactic of the right-wing revolution, including an assault on labor.

Each time major corporations announced massive layoffs, Wall Street bid up the price of their stocks. Given this perspective, the business press continues to expresses a deep fear that excessive wages will snuff out the opportunity to make profits.

In fact, high wages can actually benefit business. Although higher wages are a cost for any individual business, when the working class has higher wages, business finds a more ready market for its wares—an insight that was at the core of Keynesian theory. So, where wages are increasing throughout an economy—not soaring, but at a Goldilocks rate of moderately increasing wages—business will gain by having a ready market for its goods.

The extra demand arising from higher wages represents only one of the benefits of high wages. The most important effect of high wages comes in shaping methods of production. Where wages are low, business has little incentive to save on labor costs. High wages prod business to develop improved technology upon which economic growth and prosperity ultimately depend (see Naastepad and Kleinknecht 2004). As a result, high wages can actually improve profits.

Economists typically measure productivity in terms of output per worker. In 1970, at the dawn of the right-wing revolution, productivity in the United States was high. Since, much of the productivity growth has occurred because business has been shutting down less productive operations or moving them offshore.

Output per hour provides a more meaningful picture. In the United States, between 1970 and 2002, annual hours worked per capita rose 20 percent, while falling in most other advanced economies (Organisation for Economic Co-operation and Development 2004c, 6). The Organisation for Economic Co-operation and Development found a statistically significant negative correlation between productivity and workers' annual hours on the job for its 26 members, although the results for the most advanced countries were not quite strong enough to be statistically significant (Organisation for Economic Co-operation and Development 2004b, Box 1.1, p. 28).

For example, workers in the United States put in more than 34 percent as many hours as Norwegian workers. Norwegian workers produce 57 percent more output per hour than their counterparts in the United States. While the differences are not as extreme, Denmark, Switzerland, Ireland, France, Belgium, Germany, Netherlands, and Japan all enjoy productivity levels higher than the United States (Organisation for Economic Co-operation and Development 2004a, Table F, p. 312). Had labor been stronger in the United States, business would have faced pressure to increase productivity. In large part, the increasing hours of work in the United States was a response to falling real wages and benefits. Families had to put in more hours in an effort to maintain the same standard of living.

In the long run, even business will have to pay a hefty price for its greed in pursuing the short run goal of wage reduction. Common sense tells us that working smarter is better than working longer hours. Merely increasing hours of work will be insufficient to keep up with economies that are experiencing a much faster rate of productivity growth. Many families in the United States are already too strapped for time. Excessive hours of work are already taking a toll on people having difficulty juggling work demands with family responsibilities or education. Shortchanging either families or education will eventually cut into future productivity growth. Pressuring business to increase productivity rather than forcing people to work longer hours promises a better future.

A Thumbnail History of the Economy of High Wages

Despite the intense pressure to lower wages, historically the economy of the United States benefited from a scarcity of labor, which kept wages high relative to the rest of the world. Although most manufacturers in the United States responded to the incentive of relatively high wages by increasing productivity, in the South prior to the Civil War, employers chose another route, forcing slaves to do their bidding—although the slave masters were not wholly successful in this effort (see Chapter 8). In any case, business in the South had little need to turn to modern methods of mechanization. Given the primitive technology used, the leaders in the South did not have much interest in investing in the education of the common people, enslaved or free. Not surprisingly, the southern economy remained a backwater long after the demise of slavery because Jim Crow laws kept black labor cheap.

In the North, matters were different. Higher wages made labor-saving technologies economical, creating a relative prosperity that allowed workers to demand still higher wages, inducing further rounds of technical change. In fact, the historical record of the U.S. economy suggests that business often managed to create new technologies fast enough to make prices fall, even in the face of rising wages.

The rapidity of technical change struck most observers of the early United States. For example, the renowned French visitor, Alexis de Tocqueville, reported: "I accost an American sailor, and I inquire why the ships of his country are built so as to last for a short time; he answers without hesitation that the art of navigation is every day making such a rapid progress that the finest vessel would become almost useless if it lasted beyond a certain number of years" (de Tocqueville 1835, II, 420).

H. J. Habakkuk wrote an entire book about the positive effect of high wages on technical change in the United States during the nineteenth century. According to Habakkuk, "The Secretary of the Treasury reported in 1832, that the garrets and outhouses of most textile mills were crowded with discarded machinery. One Rhode Island mill built in 1813 had by 1827 scrapped and replaced every original machine" (Habakkuk 1962, 57; and the numerous references he cites).

The anticipation of early retirement of plant and equipment in the United States was so pervasive that manufacturers built their machinery from wood rather than more durable materials, such as iron (Strassman 1959, 88). Throughout the nineteenth century, commentators continued to echo de Tocqueville's observation that U.S. technology was designed to be short-lived (Schoenhof 1893). For example, in the late nineteenth century, the U.S. Secretary of State commissioned Joseph Schoenhof to inquire into the effects of high wages on the competitiveness of business in the United States. Schoenhof concluded that the employer of labor is . . . benefited by the inevitable results of a high rate of wages. . . . [T]he first object of the employer is to economize its employment.

Manufacturers introducing a change in manufactures have a machine built to accomplish what in other countries would be left to hand labor to bring about. Machinery, used to the limit of its life in Europe, is cast aside in America if only partially worn. (Schoenhof 1893, 33–34)

Cornell economist, Jeremiah Jenks asserted: "No sooner has the capitalist fairly adopted one improved machine, than it must be thrown away for a still later and better invention, which must be purchased at a dear cost, if the manufacturer would not see himself eclipsed by his rival" (Jenks 1890, 254; cited in Livingston 1986, 39).

David A. Wells was one of the most prominent advocates of high wages and the author of an influential book, *Recent Economic Changes*. Although not a trained economist, he was nonetheless the most influential economist in government during the nineteenth century. Besides serving in government himself, he was instrumental in placing other economists in government positions. Wells began his career as an ardent protectionist, but later converted to an equally strong free-trader faith. Wells grounded his belief in free-trade upon the conviction that U.S. technology was so advanced that the nation was thoroughly capable of meeting competition from imports produced by low-wage producers (D. Wells 1889, 105). For Wells, high wages and advanced technologies reinforced each other.

This pattern of rapid capital renewal made the manufacturing capacity of United States the envy of the world. By the turn of the nineteenth century, exports from the United States were inundating Europe, much the same as Japanese exports were displacing U.S. production around the 1970s. Just as people in the United States tried to discover the secret of Japanese ascendancy in popular books, English readers of those days pored over alarmist books with titles such as *The American Invaders* (1901), *The Americanization of the World* (1901), or *The American Invasion* (1902) (G. Wright 1990, 652).

By the late nineteenth century, rapid technical change brought productivity in the United States to such a high pitch that the rationale for high wages seemed self-evident to most observers. The belief in high wages continued well into the twentieth century. For example, Herbert Hoover, despite his undeserved reputation as a dogmatic advocate of *laissez-faire*, was another strong believer in high wages. As Secretary of Commerce and the most influential member of the Republican administration at the time, he told an audience on May 12, 1926, "The very essence of great production is high wages and low prices. . . . The acceptance of these ideas is obviously not universal. Not all employers . . . nor has every union abandoned the fallacy of restricted effort. . . . But . . . for both employer and employee to think in terms of the mutual interest of increased production has gained in strength. It is a long cry from the conception of the old economics" (Barber 1985, 30).

An anonymous employer echoed Hoover's sentiments during the following year: "In spite of the fact that wages in our factories have more than doubled in the past fifteen years our manufacturing costs are actually lower now than they were at the beginning of that period. High wages, forcibly thrust upon us by the war, and always opposed by those in charge of our business, have lowered our manufacturing costs, by making us apply machinery and power to tasks formerly done by hand" (Bernstein 1966, 51–52).

During the first part of the 1920s, Hoover began working closely with the National Bureau of Economic Research, an organization which figures prominently in Chapter 13. Perhaps the most important result of this collaboration was the report of the Commission on Recent Economic Changes, chaired by Secretary Hoover himself. The commission clearly connected its own work with Wells's earlier book. Hoover's introduction to the two-volume report of the commission underlined this connection in its second paragraph: "Forty years ago David A. Wells wrote his *Recent Economic Changes*, showing that the quarter century that ended in 1889 was a period of 'profound economic changes'" (Committee on Recent Economic Changes 1929, ix).

Of course, not all employers—especially those who ran small businesses—shared this appreciation of high wages, but many of the largest employers were willing to stand by their support for high wages even after the Great Depression began. For example on November 21, 1929, President Hoover summoned many of the nation's leading industrialists to head off the threat of a wave of wage cutting. According to a participant in the meeting, "[he] said that he would not have called them were it not that he viewed the crisis more seriously than a mere stock market crash; . . . that there were two or three million unemployed by the sudden suspension of so many activities; . . . that there must be much liquidation of inflated values, debts and prices" (Myers and Newton 1936, 26–27).

To prevent the stock market crash from turning into a catastrophe for society as a whole, Hoover asked that these employers refrain from cutting wages. The meeting seemed to have been a great success. Henry Ford even promised to raise wages (Vedder and Galloway 1993, 92). *Business Week* exulted with an article entitled "This Time They Did Not Cut Wages" (Anon. 1929). Business leaders and economists, in unison with popular opinion, supported the policy of maintaining wage rates (Vedder and Galloway 1993, 92–4).

Even with the onset of the Great Depression, a substantial portion of big business refrained from the expected wholesale cutting of wages. Later in life, Hoover recalled, "I felt that a most important part of our recovery in this period rested on the maintenance of wages and the avoidance of strikes" (Hoover 1952, 3, 43). He noted that during the depression in 1921, 92 percent of the firms reporting to the Bureau of Labor Statistics cut wages, in contrast only 7 percent cut wages in 1930. For the first 7 months of 1931, only 12 percent cut wages, compared to 54 percent in 1921 (Hoover 1952, 3, 46).

To maintain steady wages in the face of the Depression was an enormous accomplishment, especially since falling prices meant that a constant wage could buy more goods and services. Indeed, many large corporations seemed to go to great lengths to maintain the wage rate, although they did cut hours back significantly (Jensen 1989; O'Brien 1989). Economists recognized the uniqueness of this reticence to cut wages. In the words of Jacob Viner, "the Hoover Administration became apostles of the . . . doctrine that high wages are a guarantee and an essential [*sic*] of prosperity. At the beginning of the Depression, Hoover pledged industry not to cut wages, and for a long time large-scale industry adhered to this pledge" (Viner 1933, 12; cited in O'Brien 1989, 724–25).

A half-century after Hoover's report, neither the Republican Party nor the Bureau shared Wells's or Hoover's confidence in American competitiveness. Instead, employers preferred to rely on reducing wages and protectionism. Recall that about the time that Powell was circulating his manifesto, hourly wages in the United States (corrected for inflation) already peaked at a level that has not reached again after more than three decades.

Although the economy was already beginning to stumble by the time wages peaked, holding wages back was not a smart strategy. Not surprisingly, the subsequent rate of productivity growth suffered from the ongoing repression of wages.

Chapter 8

The Dangerous Consequences of Inequality

Inequality and Catastrophe

The trickle-down theory suggests keeping wages low in hopes of boosting profits, which is supposed to create investment, which will eventually allow prosperity to trickle down to the rest of society. The historical record is not kind to the trickle-down theory of economics. In 1980, when Jeffrey Williamson and Peter Lindert published what was the definitive study of inequality in U.S. economy at the time, they offered their brief overview of the history of inequality in the United States, which is worth quoting again:

> The period from 1860 to 1929 is thus best described as a high uneven plateau of wealth inequality. When did wealth inequality hit its historic peak? We do not yet know. We do know that there was a leveling across the 1860s. We also know that there was a leveling across the World War I decade (1912–1922), which was reversed largely or entirely by 1929. This leaves three likely candidates for the dubious distinction of being the era of greatest inequality in American personal wealth: c. 1860, c. 1914, and 1929. That each of these pinnacles was followed by a major upheaval—civil war and slave emancipation, world war, or unparalleled depression—suggests interesting hypotheses regarding the effects of these episodic events on wealth inequality (or perhaps even the impact of inequality on these episodic events). (Williamson and Lindert 1980, 51)

Like the negative association between the stock market and Republican administrations, the association between inequality and disaster might be just a coincidence. This chapter will explore some of the reasons for the disastrous consequences of inequality.

Back in 1936, Simon Kuznets, the same economist who later suggested that market forces could naturally eliminate inequality, remarked that inequality raises the intensity of both economic expansions and contractions (Kuznets 1936). History seems kinder to this observation than his later suggestion about inequality.

Consider the precedent of the 1920s. The situation during World War I led to a more egalitarian economy. Massive wars typically diminish inequality, partly for economic reasons and partly for social reasons. For example, the strains that all-out wars create typically require that the government place more controls on the economy, reining in the excesses of profit-making. Maintaining support for wars typically demands that sacrifices be shared across society.

Once World War I ended, business leaders succeeded in rapidly regaining their prewar advantages, amassing wealth and income at the expense of the rest of society. This pleasant interlude of inequality was not destined to last very long. Within a few years, the Great Depression brought down the booming economy of the 1920s and kept it down until wartime spending eventually revived the economy.

The Depression wiped out an enormous part of business wealth, so much so that I assume that in retrospect most business leaders would have gladly sacrificed the special advantages that they had gained during the 1920s if only they had been able to avoid the calamity of the Great Depression.

Like wars, depressions typically reduce inequality. Business wealth, especially of the speculative kind, disappears in a flash. Workers, of course, experience hardships during the depressions. In the case of the Great Depression, an estimated 25 percent of the labor force became unemployed, but the decline of their average income is small compared to the destruction of the wealth of the wealthy.

The Great Depression also destroyed much of business' credibility with the public at large, opening the door for New Deal reforms, which made a modest dent in inequality, although the Depression and the subsequent war were probably more important.

Although the present increase in inequality will lead to another calamity, its onset need not be as dramatic as the Civil War, World War I, or the Great Depression; it could resemble the proverbial frog swimming in a pot while the water comes to a boil, never noticing the danger because it would come gradually, after decades of slow economic growth. No matter whether this calamity comes as a sudden jolt or as a gradual decline, the right-wing revolution, unless it is quickly reversed, is setting in motion forces that are certain to undermine the economy and society as a whole.

The calamity scenario and the frog scenario are not mutually exclusive. An economy can grow slowly, stagnate, and decline for a while and then suddenly implode. Now, I will turn to a discussion of just how inequality can cause such stagnation.

Inequality and Growth

Two economists, Alberto Alesina and Roberto Perotti, investigated the association between inequality and economic growth by analyzing a sample of 71 countries for the period of 1960–85. Their data led to the conclusion that inequality had a substantial negative effect on economic growth. Indeed, a host of recent studies has borne out the proposition that a more unequal distribution of income causes the economy to grow more slowly (Alesina and Rodrik 1994, 485; Persson and Tabellini 1994; Easterly 2002, 265). One study estimated that a reduction in inequality from one standard deviation above the sample mean to one standard deviation below the mean would increase the long-term growth rate by approximately 1.3 percent per annum; however, this figure may well be an underestimate.

Using a slightly different technique, the increase from such a change in inequality would be 2.5 percent (Clarke 1995, 423). Even if a reduction in inequality were the only source of economic growth, meaning no growth of either population or productivity, a 2.5 percent increase would be sufficient to allow the economy to double in size in less than 30 years. To put this 2.5 percent growth rate into perspective, during the period under discussion, 1970 to 2005, U.S. economy grew at little more than 3 percent, due to factors such as population growth and improved technology. According to Clarke's estimate a reduction of inequality would almost double the rate of growth.

In analyzing 23 recent statistical studies of the links between inequality and growth, Roland Benabou concluded: "These regressions, run over a variety of data sets and periods with many different measures of income distribution, deliver a consistent message: initial inequality is detrimental to long-run growth. The magnitude of this effect is consistent across most studies" (Benabou 1996, 13).

Of course, just reducing inequality today does not instantly increase productivity. Some time will be required before a reduction in inequality can translate into more rapid growth. Even so, the conclusion that inequality creates a barrier to a healthy growth rate stands as a sharp rebuke to the basic justification of right-wing economic strategy.

According to the sacred tenets of trickle-down theory, the poor should accept policies that transfer wealth and income to those who are already rich, because in doing so future economic growth will be assured. But, in reality, the basic premise of the trickle-down is false. First, inequality actually hinders rather than promotes growth. Second, even if inequality were somehow consistent with growth, the less affluent sectors of society will not necessarily benefit from that growth. After all, the U.S. economy has grown since 1970 without the poor, or even the middle classes, sharing in that prosperity.

Finally, even if the basic premise of the trickle-down were true, empirical questions remain. In particular, how much inequality will society have to accept in order to produce a given rate of growth?

Proponents of the trickle-down theory expect society to take their theory as a matter of faith. In the long run, everybody, even the most poor, will share in the bountiful rewards from a growing economy. The long duration of the Great Depression suggests that the wait for the trickle-down payoff might be quite long—longer than the poor reasonably might be willing to accept.

How exactly does inequality hamper economic growth? To begin with, a healthy market economy requires balance. Shrinking the middle class and pushing more of the poor into destitution is almost certain to create imbalance. If too much wealth becomes concentrated in the hands of a relative few rich people, business will generally stagnate because the rich are less likely to spend their money than the poor. So without sufficient demand, business will suffer. This logic was central to the thinking of John Maynard Keynes.

The adverse negative impact of inequality on demand has a further negative consequence. To maintain an adequate level of demand, the monetary authorities must keep a relatively loose control of the money supply. Lowering the interest rate leads to the creation of asset bubbles, such as the stock market bubble of the 1920s and the dot-com bubble of the 1990s. Perhaps even more damaging, unequal societies create social problems that I will discuss later.

The negative relationship between inequality and growth makes an even stronger point—the policies that benefit the already rich are likely to hinder economic growth, suggesting the efficacy of a trickle-up theory.

Here is how the trickle up would work: by putting more resources in the hands of the less fortunate, the rate of economic growth will improve, allowing the rich to benefit in the long run once they can partake of the greater wealth made possible by a larger economy. In effect, the reduction of inequality would be like an investment that would pay off in the future.

Even people who ordinarily oppose redistribution from the rich to the poor and who do not accept the trickle up should recognize that something must be done to redress the imbalances that have built up over the past few decades.

Inequality and Economic Balance

The purely economic problem of income inequality goes farther than Keynes acknowledged. This logic is a bit technical but very important nonetheless. Modern business tends to have very high set-up costs, such as money spent on sophisticated equipment or on research and development. At the same time, in a modern economy, the cost of producing each individual unit of output, such as a computer program or a pill, is insignificant. Although writing the first copy of the program or producing the first few pills can be hugely expensive, producing a few more is not.

Elementary economics texts correctly teach that a competitive market tends to push prices down toward the cost of producing an extra unit of output—what economists call the marginal cost. When prices approach marginal costs too closely, business has no chance whatsoever of recouping its large outlays for set-up costs. As a result, a market economy has an inherent tendency toward deflation and depression.

Business's only hope seems to be to somehow find shelter from competition. When demand is strong enough, the competitive pressure to cut prices is weak, allowing prices to rise sufficiently above marginal costs to allow business to earn a profit after covering its set-up costs.

Advertising, which can create brand loyalty, offers one strategy to avoid competition. If Coke can make consumers regard its competitors' products as being an unacceptable substitute for its own soft drinks, the company has reduced the intensity of the competition that it faces. This strategy can be partially effective, but obviously not completely so. Other purveyors of soft drinks will eventually engage in counteradvertising, raising the cost and the effectiveness of this strategy.

Protection against imports can also help to blunt the effect of competition. Patents and other monopoly rights offer even more effective protection against competition. Finally, when a handful of companies control an entire industry, they can enter into implicit agreements not to compete on price. When demand slackens, they can cut production in order to maintain their price structure.

With the exception of natural boom-induced demand, all of these anticompetitive strategies violate the sacred dogma of the theologians of right-wing economics. The *laissez-faire* economists are correct, however, that although these anticompetitive strategies may help individual businesses or industries, they are counterproductive for the economy as a whole. These tactics raise prices and profits at the expense of consumers in general, in effect exacerbating the problem of inequality. They also reduce the need to improve productivity.

As increasing prices restrict demand, employment goes down, pulling demand down in other parts of the economy. This shrinkage in demand then accentuates the natural deflationary forces operating in the more competitive parts of the economy. Gardiner Means, an influential New Dealer, gave a telling example of how anticompetitive conditions in one part of the economy can intensify competition elsewhere. Between 1929 and 1932, while the Great Depression was sweeping across the economy, motor vehicle prices fell only 12 percent whereas production dropped by 74 percent. Other concentrated industries, such as agricultural implements, iron and steel, and cement demonstrated a pattern that was only slightly less extreme. At the other end of the spectrum, prices of agricultural commodities, which lacked protections against competition, fell 54 percent (Means 1975, 10, citing National Resources Committee 1939, 386).

In short, to the extent that inequality restrains demand, either business requires more extreme anticompetitive measures or the natural deflationary tendency gets worse in other parts of the economy. To the extent that the effect of these anticompetitive policies do not immediately set off a recession, they tend to exacerbate inequality and create economic rigidities that put off necessary adjustments. This delay is likely to make any future crisis even more dangerous.

Financialization

Nothing has contributed to imbalances in the economy so much as the outlandish expansion of financialization, which the right wing promoted through reckless deregulation. Talk of deregulation may evoke images of bulldozers free to tear up sensitive land or factories permitted to spew out toxic waste, but deregulation has other less obvious, but equally destructive, dimensions. Almost unnoticed in the background, business interests have convinced the government to mindlessly dismantle the supposedly arcane regulations meant to maintain order in the financial industry.

Many of these controls began after the Great Depression, which clearly demonstrated how an unfettered financial system, left to its own devices, can easily spin out of control. Business, having soon forgotten this lesson, bristled against regulations, arguing that meddlesome regulations do nothing to protect the economy; they merely prevent the efficient functioning of the financial system.

In reality, unregulated financialization works like a drug-induced euphoria. A get-rich-quick mentality spreads throughout the economy. Solid wealth-producing activities quickly lose their attraction. Recall the billion dollar incomes of hedge-fund managers.

In this environment, economic booms soon morph into bubbles that are certain to burst. Typical of the boom mentality, in 1986, a year before the stock market fell 508 points in a single day, 40 percent of the 1,300 members of Yale's graduating class applied to a single investment bank, First Boston (Lewis 1989, 24). The stock market recovered, but the frenzy began anew in the late 1990s.

Enron was emblematic of the mesmerizing lure of financialization and suggestive of its dangers. A once-sleepy, capital-intensive pipeline company, Enron became the darling of Wall Street after it converted itself into a major financial player during the frenetic 1990s boom. By December 31, 2000, Enron's stock reached $83.13. At this point, the stock market valued the company at more than $60 billion, 70 times what the company purportedly earned. *Fortune* magazine rated Enron as the most innovative large company in America in the magazine's survey of Most Admired Companies. Soon thereafter, the now-disgraced corporation declared bankruptcy, leaving its stock worthless (Healy and Palepu 2003, 3).

Not surprisingly, while the stock was soaring, Enron won friends in high places, including both Presidents Bush and Senator Phil Gramm, a former professor of economics who chaired the Senate Banking Committee at the time. Senator Gramm's wife, Wendy, another economist, won an appointment as chair of the Commodity Futures Trading Commission. In 1992, she exempted Enron's trading in electricity futures from oversight by the Commodity Futures Trading Commission. Doug Henwood, an outstanding observer of the financial world, writes of this incident:

> Enron happened to be a big funder of her husband, Texas Senator Phil Gramm (another friend of the free market who drew public paychecks almost all his working life). Six days after that ruling, Gramm left the CFTC, and five weeks later she joined Enron's board. In December 2000, Senator Gramm helped push a bill through Congress that deregulated trading in energy. Enron's electricity trading business swelled, and some of the firm's only real profits were made. Without owning a single California power plant, Enron came to control the state's market. Rolling blackouts became the norm, prices skyrocketed, and the same state racked up billions in debt. Phil Gramm blamed environmentalists for the crisis. Finally, price controls were imposed and the bubble burst. Deprived of its cash cow, Enron hit the rocks a few months later. (Henwood 2003, 200–1)

In short, much of the imaginary value represented by Enron literally disappeared. The inimitable John Kenneth Galbraith referred to such imaginary value as a "bezzle": "At any given time there exists an inventory of undiscovered embezzlement. This inventory—it should perhaps be called the bezzle—amounts at any moment to many millions of dollars. . . . In good times people are relaxed, trusting and money is plentiful. But even though money is plentiful, there are always people who need more. Under these circumstances the rate of embezzlement grows, the rate of discovery falls off, and bezzle increases rapidly. In depression all of this is reversed" (Galbraith 1961, 138).

A few high level employees who cashed out their stock in time and escaped prosecution can still laugh all the way to the bank. Some of the big banks also did quite well. Although they face continuing problems in the courts, their penalties will not be enough to deter them in the future.

We should not forget Wendy Gramm, the regulator, who also prospered: "from 1993 to 2001 her salary, attendance fees, stock option sales, and dividends totaled between $915,000 and $1.85 million. Her stock options swelled from $15,000 in 1995 to approximately $500,000 by 2000" (Prins 2004, 147). Ms. Gramm has continued her jihad against regulation. Later she ran the Mercatus Center, where she still serves as a senior scholar. Mercatus is the third largest recipient of conservative foundation funding, according to SourceWatch (http://www.sourcewatch.org/index.php?title=Mercatus_Center). According to the *Wall Street Journal*, this organization has been extraordinarily effective in eliminating all manner of regulations (see Davis 2004).

In effect, these winners pushed the cost of the bezzle onto others. The typical investors who saw their stock become worthless realized the consequences of the bezzle. So did the hapless Enron employees, especially those whose pensions consisted of Enron stock. Arthur Anderson, the accounting company that facilitated the fraud no longer exists, as its investors must bitterly know.

The California energy consumers did not escape unscathed. Many years from now they will still be paying off the inflated long-term contracts that the state signed in their name. Enron alone may not have controlled the California energy system, but it was among the handful of companies that did.

People around the country had bought houses, changed careers, and made life-altering decisions based on their mistaken belief that their stake in the Enron bubble represented true wealth. Others, who had no direct connection with the company at all, also got caught up with the Enron disaster. People set up businesses to service Enron employees or sold them goods on credit. Others, even further removed from Enron, paid a price when, unbeknownst to them, their pension plans had invested in the company. In the end, Enron caused irreparable harm to many thousands of people. By any calculation, losses that occur after a bubble bursts far outweigh the benefits that people enjoy during the boom.

Where does the blame lie? The criminal activity of some of the Enron executives and their abettors in the financial world is not surprising. A certain percentage of people will always cross the line when the opportunity presents itself. What is shocking is that the majority of the wrongs that Enron committed were actually legal, largely because of the regulatory laxity achieved by the right-wing revolution.

The need for stricter financial regulations is more urgent than ever. Since 1970, the ratio of total financial assets to the Gross Domestic Product (GDP) has more than doubled (Henwood 2003, 191). By the end of June 2004, the Bank for International Settlements estimated that the world financial market had $220 trillion worth of outstanding derivative contracts, or more than $35,000 for every single person on the face of the earth. The estimated daily turnover in foreign currency and interest rate transactions in April 2004 was $2.4 trillion, a 74 percent increase over a three year period (Bank for International Settlements 2005, 1, 21). In less than two weeks, these financial transactions would equal the total value of the annual production of all the economies of the world, which is estimated at about $30 trillion. In contrast, the New York Stock Exchange, with a typical daily turnover in early 2005 of a mere 1.5 billion shares worth about $50 billion, seems tame indeed.

While the relative size of the financial sector has ballooned, the manufacturing sector has shrunk. For example, the share of manufacturing represented 21.2 percent of the GDP in 1974; by 2004, that figure had fallen to 12.1 percent. In contrast, the Finance, Insurance, and Real Estate sector rose during the same period from 14.9 percent to 20.6 percent, effectively trading places with the manufacturing sector (President of the United States 2006, Table B-12, p. 296–97).

However, the data fail to reflect the full extent of the shift from manufacturing to finance because nonfinancial companies often earn substantial profits from financial operations, without reporting separate information for their financial operations. The magnitudes in question can be substantial. For example by 2005, General Motors and Ford earned almost all of their profits from their financial operations rather than from producing cars. For General Electric, financial operations produced almost half of the company's profit (Henry 2005).

While financialization is not as extreme for the entire corporate sector, by one estimate, financial profits as a share of total profits rose from around 15 percent during the 1960s to above 30 percent for most of the 1980s–1990s (G. Epstein and Power 2002). Using a different method, the Department of Commerce estimated that by early 2005 financial profits represented more than one-third of all corporate profits, up from little more than 20 percent a decade earlier, and continues to climb (U.S. Department of Commerce, Bureau of Economic Analysis 2005; Henry 2005). Both these breakdowns necessarily underestimate financial profits because many corporations do not separate their financial from their nonfinancial profits. As manufacturing continues to move abroad, the relative importance of financial profits will most likely continue its steady increase, at least until the coming depression.

The probable consequences will not be pleasant. New Enrons are growing at this very minute. They always do. Although the financial industry lobbies hard against regulation, effective regulation can limit the number and the size of future Enrons. In a healthy economy, the collapse of a few speculative ventures does relatively little harm. In a vulnerable economy, the size of the suddenly disappearing bezzle can set off a depression with a magnitude many thousands of times greater than Enron.

A healthy market economy requires that business invest for the future. Even in the unlikely situation in which every corporation "played by the rules," financialization represents a significant threat to the extent that the economy becomes "the prisoner of impatient capital" (Harrison 1994, 214). A financialized world without oversight where everything is arranged to improve the next quarterly financial report is a certain recipe for disaster.

Inequality and the Perverse Incentives for Efficiency

The financial revolution helped to create a level of inequality not seen since the eve of the Great Depression. The wide gap between the soaring executive salaries and the stagnant earnings of ordinary workers should be a source of embarrassment. As always, economics has a ready justification. Multimillion-dollar salaries are necessary to attract and motivate highly skilled executives. Executive salaries are necessary rewards and workers' wages burdensome costs.

How can anyone believe that compensation is a reward for the creation of value when executives who lead their corporations into disasters that destroy billions of dollars of value still continue to collect obscenely high salaries? In 2006, Barry Diller of IAC was the highest paid chief executive in America. Despite his company's poor performance, his take home pay was equivalent to 9.8 percent of company profits. IAC's proxy statement said that this money was necessary to "motivate Mr. Diller for the future," causing Nicholas Kristof to name him "the laziest man in America" (Kristof 2006).

Even if one grants that some inequality can create material incentives for more effort, increasing the extent of inequality beyond a certain point will not spur the less fortunate to work even harder. Certainly, the degree of inequality in the United States has long passed the point where a reduction in inequality would reduce effort. Common sense suggests that few people would work less energetically if the wealth of Bill Gates or Warren Buffett were to subside a bit.

In fact, Warren Buffett himself seems to agree with my assessment. Recall his earlier discussion of the right-wing victory as class war. Buffett was not celebrating the class war. Of course, Buffett is unusual among the super-rich in his willingness to recognize that society as a whole is the major source of his wealth. In a 1995 television interview, he openly admitted, "I personally think that society is responsible for a very significant percentage of what I've earned. If you stick me down in the middle of Bangladesh or Peru or someplace, you'll find out how much this talent is going to produce in the wrong kind of soil. I will be struggling 30 years later. I work in a market system that happens to reward what I do very well—disproportionately well" (Lowe 1997, 164; cited in C. Collins, Lapham; Klinger 2004).

Of course, Bangladesh and Peru have their own share of very rich people. What these societies lack is a sizeable middle class. Such unbalanced societies tend to stagnate. Unfortunately, the United States is moving in that direction.

Conservatives like to talk about entrepreneurship as the engine of progress. The meteoric rise of Enron and the dot-com companies seemed to vindicate the right-wing ideology that rampant individualism promises wealth and success for anyone with drive and ambition. Indeed, each success story seemed to be further evidence that egalitarianism is detrimental to prosperity, but in highly unequal societies, entrepreneurship necessarily takes a back seat. In the end, despite its supposedly libertarian values, Enron's growth depended more on influence than entrepreneurship.

Extreme inequality generally leads to a culture of corruption. Entrepreneurial energies are not likely to be rewarded nearly as well as influence. Jockeying for position not only consumes enormous quantities of time, energy, and resources; it contaminates all of society. The rich wisely use their money to invest in the acquisition of influence rather than in anything that even remotely promotes economic and technological progress (Glaeser and Saks 2004; Glaeser, Scheinkman, and Shleifer 2003).

Third world corruption may often be crude, but the supposedly more respectable corruption practiced in the United States is no less corrosive and just as effective a tool as the clumsy corruption endemic in poor countries. Those who want to purchase influence are permitted to contribute to politicians' political campaigns or provide gifts in-kind, such as the use of private or corporate jets. Influence peddlers can hire politicians' relatives for lavish salaries or pay the politicians exorbitant fees to give lectures or write books. In this shady world, highly paid specialists use their influence generally free from public scrutiny with the intent of getting public officials to do their bidding, allowing the wealthy to avoid taxes and to enjoy special privileges, such as protection from competition or regulation.

Even something akin to the outright purchasing of political candidates is considered to be legal in the United States; such practices are thoroughly undemocratic and frequently corrupt. Conservatives, however, even defend such actions as a form of free speech.

Those who want favors from politicians can also slip them secret information that can pay off handsomely. With respect to this form of influence, the evidence is indirect, but very strong. The average household, lacking inside information, earns about 1.5 percent less than the overall returns of the stock market. In contrast, corporate insiders as a whole profit about 5 percent more than the overall stock market average. Members of the U.S. Senate perform more than twice as well as corporate insiders, earning 12 percent more than the overall stock market (Ziobrowski, Cheng, Boyd, and Ziobrowski 2004).

The results of this thoroughgoing corruption—both legal and illegal—aggravate existing inequities. After all, only the rich and powerful have the resources to mount strong lobbying efforts, which bring them even more wealth and power, enabling them to lobby even more effectively (see Murphy, Shleifer, and Vishny 1993).

Consequently, the middle class pays more taxes and the typical citizen receives fewer services from the government. At the same time, corporate influence allows business to increase prices, reducing the buying power of ordinary people, thereby further increasing both inequality and unemployment. In addition, normal business activity becomes more sluggish because of the time and money wasted in the socially unproductive efforts to obtain influence.

Inequality and Hubris

Inequality also undermines economic growth by giving those on top an undeserved sense of privilege. Recall the earlier discussion of the executives' extravagant use of corporate jets. Do you believe that these corporate leaders felt the slightest bit guilty using company resources to fly their dogs or their children's beds around the world? These people certainly considered such expenditures reasonable, considering the "wonderful" work they believed they were performing.

Admittedly, in a perverse way, corporate jets can contribute to the profitability of individual corporations, which use their planes to curry favor with politicians. In return for letting politicians use their jets to ferry them around on campaign stops or for golfing junkets in luxurious locations, the politicians repay their benefactors through legislation or lucrative government contracts, which often can easily repay the cost of purchasing a fleet of jet planes. Such corruption, however, does nothing to make the economy or society any healthier. Instead, it merely fuels the fires of resentment.

Consider another element of CEO extravagance—the purchase of huge yachts, some longer than football fields. Some executives compete more vigorously in the acquisition of these yachts than they do in running their companies (Frank 2004). In fact, Daniel Gross, in a column for the online magazine, *Slate*, found that the performance the stocks of the companies run by the owners of the large yachts have performed very poorly. He suggests that while corporate jets could conceivably contribute to economic performance by speeding busy executives to their business, yachts would merely be a distraction from their corporate duties.

Of course, no one should begrudge anybody, even wealthy CEOs, their leisure activities any more so than workers on the assembly line. However, adding a few extra hundred feet to the size of a yacht would not seem to be a necessary component of relaxation. Instead, extending the size of a yacht is merely an exercise in conspicuous consumption intended to increase the gulf between the most successful CEOs and the rest of the world.

Within this corrupt culture of privilege, even the executives who run their companies into the ground "deserve" lavish rewards. As Warren Buffett told his shareholders, "Getting fired can produce a particularly bountiful payday for a CEO. Indeed, he can 'earn' more in that single day, while cleaning out his desk, than an American worker earns in a lifetime of cleaning toilets. Forget the old maxim about nothing succeeding like success: Today, in the executive suite, the all-too-prevalent rule is that nothing succeeds like failure" (Buffett 2005).

The great gap between the excesses of the corporate leaders, such as the abuse of corporate jets, and the salaries and treatment of ordinary workers must cause significant demoralization. Employees openly express their disapproval of such luxury, commonly referring to the jets as family taxis. As a result, the costs of executive extravagance go well beyond the direct costs of purchasing and maintaining the aircraft.

These extravagances also helped to fuel the hubris that ultimately brought down companies such as Enron. For example, a survey of 200 corporate executives found that those who supported a highly unequal salary structure also tended to rule out the role of ethics and values in their decision making, a perspective that justified their own narrow self-interest at the expense of broader community goals (Swanson and Orlitzky 2005).

Inequality, Resentment, and Growth

On a more subtle level, inequality alters the psychological make-up of a society. I have already mentioned the relationship between inequality and the channeling of resources into lobbying. Excessive inequality, together with the favoritism that the rich exploit to further their advancement, creates a general sense of unfairness. Common sense should tell us that once the overwhelming majority of a society comes to resent the undeserved privileges of the fortunate, society just will not work as well. Derek Bok, who should know about such matters from the vantage point of his two periods of tenure as president of one of the elite's more prominent institutions, Harvard University, observed, "The ultimate reason why we cannot ignore unjustified wealth is that it weakens the public's faith in the fairness of the economic system. Such faith is essential if we are to maintain support for the social order and inspire individuals to observe the laws, undertake the duties of citizenship, and extend the minimum of trust toward institutions necessary for communities to prosper" (Bok 1993, 231).

This sense of unfairness fosters conflict, which stifles growth. Samuel Bowles and Herbert Gintis, two prolific graduates of Harvard's own doctoral program in economics, offered a few examples of how such conflict makes society work less well, noting:

Inequality fosters conflicts ranging from lack of trust in exchange relationships and incentive problems in the workplace to class warfare and regional clashes. These conflicts are costly to police. Also, they often preclude the cooperation needed for low-cost solutions to coordination problems. Since states in highly unequal societies are often incapable of or have little incentive to solve coordination problems, the result is not only the proliferation of market failures in the private economy, but a reduced capacity to attenuate these failures through public policy. (Bowles and Gintis 1995, 409)

Bowles and Gintis expanded their analysis of the costs of inequality even further, writing:

Enforcement activities in the private sector may also be counted as costs of reproducing unequal institutions. Enforcement costs of inequality may thus take the form of high levels of expenditure on work supervision, security personnel, police, prison guards, and the like. Indeed, one might count unemployment itself as one of the enforcement costs of inequality, since the threat of job loss may be necessary to discipline labor in a low-wage economy. . . . In the United States in 1987, for example, the above categories of "guard labor" constituted over a quarter of the labor force, and the rate of growth of guard labor substantially outstripped the rate of growth of the labor force in the previous two decades. (Bowles and Gintis 1995, 410)

Unsurprisingly, the share of workers holding supervisory positions accelerated during the right-wing revolution, growing from 9.9 percent in 1966 to 15.7 percent in 2002. To put this data into perspective, Sweden devotes only 4.4 percent of its labor force to supervision (Bowles and Jayadev 2006). Yet since 1970,

Sweden's output per hour in manufacturing has grown 20 percent faster than in the United States (U.S. Bureau of Labor Statistics 2007, Table 1.1). The more modest role of supervisors throughout the more egalitarian Scandinavia is not accidental.

This toxic combination of dissatisfaction on the part of ordinary workers and arrogance on the part of upper management is not limited to a few well-publicized cases of corporate abuse in the United States. Instead, these reactions are endemic to highly unequal economies. To my knowledge, the existence of this weak spot in the theory of trickle-down economics has not entered into public debates. Instead, the bulk of the economics profession still echoes the virtues of trickle-down economics, although the message of professional economists is usually more nuanced than the rhetoric voiced by business leaders and politicians.

Inequality Undermines Efficiency at the Workplace

In fact, political demands for egalitarian policies tend to be more effective in societies that are already more equal (see Peltzman 1980, 209). As Peter Lindert noted, "History reveals a 'Robin Hood paradox,' in which redistribution from rich to poor is least present when and where it seems most needed" (Lindert 2004, 15).

So workers are more likely to express their resentment by taking measures that intentionally undermine the objectives of those that control their work. For example, before the Civil War in the United States, slave labor was quite inefficient. The sandy soils typical of the South were ideal for light equipment pulled by horses, yet the plantations typically used heavy tools drawn by mules. Frederick Law Olmstead, famous for having designed both Central Park in New York City and Golden Gate Park in San Francisco, brought this phenomenon to the attention of the world, just before the outbreak of the Civil War:

> I am shown tools that no man in his senses, with us, would allow a laborer, to whom he was paying wages, to be encumbered with; and the excessive weight and clumsiness of which, I would judge, would make work at least ten per cent. greater than those ordinarily used with us. And I am assured that, in the careless and clumsy way they must be used by the slaves, anything lighter or less rude could not be furnished them with good economy, and that such tools as we constantly give our laborers, and find our profit in giving them, would not last out a day in a Virginia corn-field—much lighter and more free from stones though it be than ours.
>
> So, too, when I ask why mules are so universally substituted for horses on the farm, the first reason given, and confessedly the most conclusive one, is, that horses cannot bear the treatment that they always must get from negroes; horses are always soon foundered or crippled by them, while mules will bear cudgeling, and lose a meal or two now and then, and not be materially injured, and they do not take cold or get sick if neglected or overworked. But I do not need to go further than to the window of the room in which I am writing, to see, at almost any time, treatment of cattle that would insure the immediate discharge of the driver, by almost any farmer owning them at the North. (Olmstead 1856, 46–47)

Were the slaves inherently clumsy or abusive people? Of course not. Their behavior was a rational response to an irrational situation. A society that consigned human beings to the status of property could not expect the same human beings to have much incentive to work very hard. On a hot, muggy day while the slave driver glanced away, a slave might be tempted to "stupidly" hurt a horse or damage a piece of equipment in order to take a brief break from unbearably hard labor.

Of course, slaves are not the only workers to feel resentment about their treatment. Economic literature is filled with examples of people in uninspired jobs who use their intelligence and creativity to make life better for themselves to the detriment of their employer. One of my favorite examples comes from Stanley Mathewson's classic description of an automobile worker's finding a loophole in a job description:

> A Mexican in a large automobile factory was given the final tightening to the nuts on automobile-engine cylinder heads. There are a dozen or more nuts around this part. The engines passed the Mexican rapidly on a conveyer. His instructions were to test all the nuts and if he found one or two loose to tighten them, but if three or more were loose he was not expected to have time to tighten them.
> [A supervisor who was puzzled that so many defective engines were passing along the line] discovered that the Mexican was unscrewing a third nut whenever he found two already loose. (Mathewson 1939, 125)

Sam Bowles and Rick Edwards reported on a 1983 study by the U.S. Department of Justice that found that more than two-thirds of workers in the United States engage in counterproductive behavior on the job, including excessively long lunches and breaks, slow, sloppy workmanship, and sick-leave abuse, as well as the use of alcohol and drugs on the job. One third of a sample of 9,175 randomly selected retail, manufacturing, and hospital workers admitted stealing from their employers. In-depth interviews with a smaller sample revealed that the workers were responding to a feeling of being exploited rather than to dire economic necessity (Bowles and Edwards 1985, 179).

These losses stemming from inequality are imperceptible in formal economic models. I doubt that many employers associate such inefficiencies with inequality. They would probably attribute such behavior to workers' personal defects. But then all problems in society seem to be attributable to the personal defects of subordinates.

The situation is even worse. Conflict in the workplace does not merely drag productivity down. People can suffer even more dire consequences from such conflicts.

The Hidden Cost of Workplace Strife

In an economy where workers perform their jobs for wages, conflict between labor and capital is more subtle than in the slave states before the Civil War. The conflict exists nonetheless. Take the case of Decatur, Illinois, a small industrial town that depended on three major employers: Firestone (tires), Caterpillar (heavy equipment), and a division of a giant British-based multinational, Tate & Lyle, A. E. Staley, which is a corn wet milling company, producing sweeteners, starches, ethanol, and animal feeds. During the early 1990s, all three corporations launched bitter antiunion offensives. The town as a whole became a major victim of the conflicts, so much so that Decatur became popularly known as the war zone (see Franklin 2001).

Alexandre Mas, a graduate student at Princeton, analyzed one dimension of the Caterpillar struggle, which spanned two strikes, dozens of brief walkouts, the use of replacement workers, threats to permanently replace the unionized workers, and 4,000 union members crossing the picket lines. Ultimately the conflict resulted in the National Labor Relations Board filing 443 complaints against Caterpillar, the most that had ever been issued against a single company (Mas 2003). Mas cited several sources to suggest that the labor turmoil caused quality to suffer in the factory:

> The UAW (United Automobile Workers) reported that the quality of Caterpillar machines produced during this period was substandard, citing a series of customer complaints that had been submitted to Caterpillar as evidence (Franklin 2001, 165). Additionally, the UAW cited an internal memo written by Aurora, Illinois plant manager Chuck Elwyn. The memo, a copy of which was provided to a reporter for the *Engineering News-Record* (1992), states that quality objectives for July 1992 had been missed by a wide margin ranking as "the poorest performance in the plant's history" and "the worst month by any plant in the entire corporation's history." Several months later, *The Economist* (1993) reported that Caterpillar "customers and dealers are beset with rumors of a slide in productivity and product quality." (Mas 2003)

Mas went beyond merely reporting anecdotes. His analyzed data from auctions of used Caterpillar equipment that occurred between 1994 and 2002 to estimate how antagonistic relationships caused the quality of production to deteriorate. Unsuspecting Caterpillar customers who purchased equipment produced during the strike apparently bought lemons, judging from these resale values.

Mas found that people who participated in the auctions must have recognized the diminished quality of the machines produced during the conflict. Auction prices for such machines were 4 percent lower on average than they would have been otherwise. The company also reduced the list price for new equipment produced amidst the turmoil by about 2 percent.

Mas conducted another study with Professor Alan Krueger of Princeton University. That work reveals a far more frightening dimension to the sort of defects that occur in the midst of a hostile workplace. Krueger and Mas traced the consequences of the Firestone strike, which the company initiated by making harsh demands on its workers, "Bridgestone/Firestone proposed deviating from the industrywide pattern bargain by moving from an eight- to a twelve-hour shift that would rotate between days and nights, as well as cutting pay for new hires by 30 percent. Almost immediately after 4,200 workers walked out on strike, the company hired replacement workers. A final contract, which included provisions to recall all strikers, was not settled until December 1996" (A. B. Krueger and Mas 2004, 254).

Following a rash of highway fatalities, the company recalled 15 million tires. These economists cleverly pieced together the effects of the strike with the subsequent deaths from defective Firestone tires. The economists were able to take advantage of a particular circumstance:

> Almost all the P235 tires were produced in three plants: Decatur, Illinois; Joliette, Quebec; and Wilson, North Carolina. For nearly three years—from April 1994 to December 1996—union workers at the Decatur plant either were on strike or were working without a contract; tires were produced by 1,048 replacement workers, union members who crossed the picket line, management, and recalled strikers in this period. The Wilson plant was nonunion, so it did not experience a strike. A Canadian union represents the Joliette plant, but labor relations there were much less contentious. Joliette had a six-month strike over fringe benefits at the end of 1995, but the plant did not hire replacement workers (which are illegal in Quebec). (A. B. Krueger and Mas 2004, 255–56)

Based on claims for compensation for property damage or personal injuries due to faulty tires, Krueger and Mas discovered that tires from Decatur produced during the labor strife were 15 times more likely to be defective than tires from the company's other plants. This large discrepancy in failure rates does not appear in other years, although the rate for 1993 was about double that of the other two plants (A. B. Krueger and Mas 1994, 265). They estimate that 40 people died in crashes as a result of a strike with which they had no direct connection.

Krueger and Mas observed that just about everybody came out a loser in this battle:

> The stock market valuation of Bridgestone/Firestone fell from $16.7 billion to $7.5 billion in the four months after the recall was announced, and the top management of Bridgestone/Firestone has been replaced. The company also closed the Decatur plant in December 2001 and considered abandoning the Firestone brand name. If antagonistic labor relations were responsible for many of the defects, even indirectly, this episode would serve as a useful reminder that a good relationship between labor and management can be in both the company's and the union's interests. (A. B. Krueger and Mas 2004, 287)

Because of the availability of the data on the defective tires, as well as the insight of Krueger and Mas in splicing together the strike and the highway fatalities, some of the costs of the Decatur incident became public. Surely, other negative consequences occurred as well, even if they were not as dramatic as the accidents in which defective tires killed or maimed victims.

This incident has a larger lesson. The Decatur tire factory represents a microcosm of the shortsighted, often vindictive efforts on the part of capital to win a victory at the expense of others.

Again, the logic of these strikes flowed directly out of the right-wing revolution. Not long after he assumed the presidency, Ronald Reagan broke the air-traffic controllers union, signaling that attacking labor was a respectable way of doing business. The courts, administrative agencies, and legislatures at both the state and federal levels all began to work overtime in an effort to undermine labor's bargaining power. After all, doing so was expected to increase the rate of profit. In many cases, this expectation was borne out—at least in the short run.

At the same time, this belligerent attitude toward labor must have taken a serious toll on productivity. Yes, of course, business can squeeze out greater productive efforts by pushing labor harder. But if business drives labor too hard by resorting to antagonistic policies, business will deny itself the potential collaborative creativity of its workers, a loss that will prove costly in the long run, even if the consequences are not as dramatic as the Bridgestone/Firestone case.

Hopefully, society will become aware of the larger costs of the right-wing capture of American society to prevent repetition of such disasters as were associated with Decatur.

Preserving Inequality

The resentment that excessive inequality breeds permeates through society. For example, property becomes insecure once the poor come to regard the social structure as unjust. Adam Smith, writing during an earlier time of great inequality, warned that the working classes were possessed by "passions which prompt [them] to invade property, passions much more steady in their operation, and much more universal in their influence" (A. Smith 1776, V.i.b.2, 709). Later in the text, he returned to his fear that "in the poor the hatred of labour and the love of present ease and enjoyment, are the passions which prompt [them] to invade property, passions much more steady in their operation, and more universal in their influence" (A. Smith 1776, V.i.f.50, 781–82). Consequently, Smith proposed that government is necessary to protect the property of the rich (A. Smith 1776, V.i.b., 670ff). He even went so far as to teach his students, "Laws and government may be considered in . . . every case as a combination of the rich to oppress the poor, and preserve to themselves the inequality of the goods which would otherwise be soon destroyed by the attacks of the poor, who if not hindered by the government would soon reduce the others to an equality with themselves by open violence" (Smith 1762–66, 208, 404).

Adam Smith understood that where inequality is rampant, the state must mobilize valuable resources in order to contain the anger and resentment of the poor. Despite his measure of realism regarding inequality, Smith was, deep down, very conservative. He attributed the problems of inequality to the irrationality of the poor—what members of Smith's class at the time referred to as their passions. Presumably, Smith would have us believe that a dispassionate analysis of the state of affairs in a highly unequal society would lead the poor to accept the wisdom of trickle-down economics—that inequality can contribute to a healthy rate of growth.

Today, many conservatives are disinclined to see passions as the driving force of criminal activity. They tend to understand that where people see few legal opportunities open to them, they are more likely to see crime as a rational choice

(Freeman 1996). For example, study after study has shown that unemployment is strongly associated with crime.

According to the U.S. Department of Justice, the average inmate was below the poverty level before entering jail. Almost 45 percent of jail inmates in 2002 reported incomes of less than $600 per month in the month before their most recent arrest (U.S. Department of Justice 2004, 4, 35). In 1997, little more than 20 percent of prisoners in state facilities have earned a high school diploma; in federal prisons, the figure is still only 27 percent (U.S. Department of Justice 2003, 511).

Similarly, low wages encourage criminal activity. Since the mid-1970s, real wages paid to all men 16–24 years old who work full time have fallen 20.3 percent. Real hourly wages paid to all male hourly workers between 16 and 24 years old fell by 23 percent (Grogger 1998, 784). They have almost certainly fallen faster for those who grew up in poverty. According to an earlier study, the decline in wages for unskilled men from 1980 to 1994 explains up to an estimated 60 percent of the increase in property crime and only 8 percent of the increase in violent crime during that period (Gould, Weinberg, and Mustard 1998).

Another study of arrests for a wider range of crimes reported even more dramatic results. The response to a 20 percent fall in wages for young people is an estimated increase in youth participation in crime of 20 percent (Grogger 1998, 785). Indeed, between the early 1970s and the late 1980s, arrest rates for 16- to 24-year-old males rose from 44.6 to 52.6 per 1,000 population, a gain of 18 percent.

In other words, inequality is responsible for a good deal of the crime that troubles the public. International comparisons offer further support for the association between crime and inequality: the more unequal the distribution of income, the higher the incarceration rate (Doyle 1999).

So, a reasonable person might conclude that a more egalitarian society would have less crime, fewer and less expensive measures to protect against crime, and a more modest criminal justice system.

The potential saving from a reduction in crime is substantial. As of year-end 2004, more than 2 million people were in federal or state prisons or in local jails, and an additional 4.9 million adults were under probation or parole jurisdiction (U.S. Department of Justice 2004).

Between 1982 and 2001, the cost of the criminal justice system in the United States soared from $37.8 billion to $167 billion dollars, representing about $600 per person. During the same period, employment in the system rose from 1.2 million to 2.3 million people (Bauer and Owens 2004, 1). No doubt, the figures have risen considerably since then. In California, prisons now claim a greater share of the state budget than higher education. Presently, uneducated prison guards make more than assistant professors in the state college system with a PhD.

Perhaps, not coincidentally, by 2003 the number of inmates reached more than six times the level in 1972, the year after Powell's memo. Incarceration rate in the United States is five to eight times as high as in Canada or Western Europe. Perhaps symbolic of the end of the cold war, the United States has now displaced Russia as the world's leading incarcerator (Mauer 2003).

Inequality and Drugs

Quite a large number of prisoners owe their present state to running afoul of increasingly stringent drug laws, which were part and parcel of the Richard Nixon's effort to change the political environment. Those sentenced under these drug laws tend to be the sort of people who troubled Lewis Powell. At the same time, those with whom people like Powell socialized could escape prison by going to posh drug rehabilitation centers for a few weeks.

Inequality seems to increase the consumption of drugs and the associated crimes. Studies of alcohol consumption lend support to this conjecture. International comparisons of drinking habits found that eleven-year-old children in countries with high degrees of inequality drank more alcohol than children elsewhere (Elgar, Roberts, Parry-Langdon, and Boyce 2005). At the present time, cocaine may be doing more damage to society than other drugs—since alcohol is not classified as a drug. This drug seems to be most attractive to people on either extreme of the economic spectrum.

While crack cocaine seems to have penetrated deeply into some of the poorest parts of our society, powdered cocaine seems to be especially popular among the richest strata. Both groups seem to be seeking an escape with this drug—the poor from the hopelessness of poverty and the rich from the boredom of an affluence that makes everything permissible. For example, affluent children are more inclined to substance abuse, anxiety, and depression (Luthar 2003). In this respect, Warren Buffett's incisive observation on inequality is worth pondering, "I hear friends talk about the debilitating effects of food stamps and the self-perpetuating nature of welfare and how terrible that is." Billionaire Warren Buffett said, "These same people are leaving tons of money to their kids, whose main achievement in life had been to emerge from the right womb. And when they emerge from that womb, instead of a welfare officer, they have a trust fund officer. Instead of food stamps, they get dividends and interest" (Harpaz 2000).

Neither the humiliation and degradation of poverty nor the excessive sense of privilege associated with extreme wealth provide for a healthy society. Although my hypothesis suggests that the drug epidemic disproportionately afflicts the very rich and the very poor, those in the middle are not unaffected by this epidemic.

Admittedly, we have very poor data about such matters, but if my suspicion is correct, then cocaine use might be a useful indicator of inequality.

Inequality and the Unnecessary Costs of Crime

Although spending on the criminal justice system represents a massive drain on public finance, for many conservatives the high cost of the criminal justice system represents more of an opportunity than a cost. Despite conservatives' expressed abhorrence of big government, they are more tolerant of this sort of spending for several reasons. First, they believe that an extremely punitive legal system will make people more accepting of harsh working conditions. Second, historically the penal system did not compete with the private sector. Finally, the rapid growth of the prison population has created a booming private prison industry.

Of course, some criminal activity creates real problems for society, most of which are never measured. For example, most economic estimates of the cost of crime do not take account of the burden that victims of crime impose on the medical system. Nonetheless, that cost is real. Also unmeasured are the physical, emotional, and economic costs to the victims of crime. We should also consider the contributions that these victims might have made had they not been caught up in criminal activity. Nor should we forget to consider the contributions that criminals themselves might have made if they had seen an opportunity for a different way of life. Finally, we might count the emotional costs to those who fear being the victims of crime, even if the extent of that fear might be irrational.

Other costs are even more subtle. As fear of crime increases, police become more militarized. They begin to take on a more antagonistic position against anybody whom they regard as suspicious. As a result, police often abuse their authority, creating still another class of indirect victims of the expansion of criminal activity. Such conflict no doubt creates a certain amount of disrespect for the law and may well contribute to further criminal activity.

Although the consequences of inequality-induced crime fall most heavily upon the poor, the rich cannot totally escape its consequences. Despite the enormous public expenditures intended to stem the threat of crime, the powerful law enforcement system seems incapable of providing sufficient security for the rich, who feel that they must go to great lengths to protect themselves. By 2002, more than a million people worked as security guards and gaming surveillance officers. Excluding the value of individuals' time, private expenditures on locks alone in 1985 was an estimated $4.6 billion (Laband and Sophocleus 1992, 961). That figure has certainly increased considerably since that time, as people turn to ever more sophisticated security gear. Toward the end of the twentieth century, the home security business had reached $14 billion a year, growing at a 10 percent annual rate (Parenti 1993, 192). Wealthy residents of Manhattan are spending $400,000 for accessorized bulletproof, steel-reinforced safe rooms (Pizzigati 2004, 230, citing Netburn 2002). Perhaps most visibly, many affluent people in the United States are seeking refuge in gated communities.

An Egalitarian Approach to Fighting Crime

Conservatives' acceptance of crime as the outcome of rational calculations leads them to the conclusion that harsher penalties will deter poor people from criminal activity (Becker 1968). Ironically, conservatives fail to apply the same logic to either the misdeeds of corporations or white-collar offenses. But, when the violator is a poor young person rather than a corporation or someone from the upper class, the only course of action is the strongest possible penalty.

In fact, the logic of punitive deterrence should be stronger for the corporate sector than for individual offenders. For a poor, desperate person with no good opportunities on the horizon, the threat of harsh punishment often does not act as much of a deterrent. With little to lose, such a person might rationally choose to engage in crime, fully cognizant of the possible consequences. In contrast, corporations, always sensitive to bottom-line considerations, would be likely to find strong penalties to be an effective deterrent.

In any case, if a small fraction of the funds used to fight crime were used to help lift those at the bottom of society, young people would see better opportunities for advancement than crime. Such policies would no doubt also help the economy prosper, enough perhaps to make this program pay for itself.

Consider the benefits that a more reasonable funding of poor schools would bring. Not surprisingly, employers usually offer very low wages to poor children coming from inferior schools. Lacking good opportunities, a few of these young people will drift from crime into thuggery, while others will develop sophisticated criminal networks requiring innate skills that would make a Harvard MBA proud. The great majority will just languish in poverty.

Unlike conservative economists, who largely interpret crime as a rational choice, many demagogic political leaders and the media casually label young children who fall into crime as incorrigible, or, even worse, as super-predators, never giving a thought to what these children could have been or how society could have benefited from their talents. Their parents, too, will come in for some criticism. But society as a whole will be held blameless for the millions of individual tragedies associated with these unfulfilled lives. Correcting the tragedies of excessive inequality would pay handsome economic dividends, but so far the public has been convinced that harsh measures are the appropriate corrective.

Ultimately, however, deterrence alone will be insufficient to reduce crime. Protection of property ultimately depends upon the willingness of the broad mass of people to condone its existing distribution. But the inequality that the right-wing victory has created was not won by informed consent, but through an abuse of power and misinformation.

If common people cannot receive what they consider to be a fair share of the fruits of their labor, preservation of the status quo through ever increasing coercion will ultimately fail. In the words of John Stuart Mill, probably the most important mid-nineteenth-century British economist, "Much of the security of person and property in modern nations is the effect of manners and opinion rather than of law" (Mill 1848, I.vii.6, 114).

Inequality and Education

Had society actually been trying to improve people's potential rather than allowing corporations to squeeze them both as workers and consumers, the economy, as well as society as a whole, would have been far healthier. After all, education is one of the keys to unlocking workers' potential. Indeed, the linkage between inequality and economic growth is especially clear in the case of education. Most studies indicate that the wealth of a society depends far more on a solid educational foundation than on the physical capital goods that many people associate with a successful economy.

We hear much about the importance of education for our economic future, yet unequal societies tend to have less widespread education (Fernandez and Rogerson 1996). Despite the reluctance to fund schools adequately, investment in education is still one of the best investments that any society can make, so long as the economy is flexible enough to absorb the educated people.

For example, after World War II both the Japanese and German economies recovered quickly, even though their factories and machines lay in ruins. What remained was the knowledge and skills of the people, who were able to use their abilities to resurrect their economies in short order. In contrast, the reconstruction of the Iraqi economy after the second Gulf War was a disaster because it neglected to take advantage of the expertise of the Iraqis themselves. One Iraqi engineer justifiably complained: "You need to have the people who spent twenty years running these irrigation canals or power plants to be there. They know the tricks; they know the quirks. . . . But the foreign contractors ignore Iraqis, and as a result they get nowhere!" (Parenti 2004, 17).

Nurturing all children should be one of society's highest priorities, but poor children lack virtually every conceivable advantage. They are more likely to grow up amidst greater family tensions, have poorer nutrition, and suffer from serious health problems, including lead poisoning, which degrades mental abilities (see Weiss, Del, and Fantuzzo 2001). Their connections and their role models all fall well short of those of the well-to-do. Worse yet, poor children are likely to internalize all the negativity that society associates with lower-class life. As a result, their behavior will often confirm the stereotypes that the rest of society holds. So, where children grow up with the disadvantages of poverty, go to impoverished schools, and get virtually no feedback, they are unlikely to develop the sort of skills that legal market forces will reward. Obviously, conventional roads to success are unlikely to be open to them.

A simple psychological experiment illustrates the deep inequities built into the educational system. A pair of psychologists gave teachers the results of a test that supposedly predicted which students would be "late bloomers." The test proved remarkably accurate, except that there was no test at all. Instead, the psychologists just chose the promising students at random. The teachers' acceptance of these imaginary test results strongly affected the way they treated their students. The selected students, in turn, responded positively, creating educational successes (Rosenthal 2002; 2003).

Class background creates something analogous to the fictitious test that purported to measure children's ability to improve in the near future. Teachers immediately recognize the stigmas of lower-class life in their students, especially if the children entrusted to their care are not white. Teachers have little reason to expect such children to succeed. After all, relatively few have succeeded in the past. The children, in turn, are likely to perform according to the teachers' low expectations, confirming what the teachers believed all along.

Even the successes, such as those resulting from the "late bloomer" experiment, may only be temporary. Herbert Kohl's heart-wrenching book, *36 Children*, tells the story of how a gifted teacher recognized students' potential and inspired them to excel. The rest of the educational system then worked to snuff out the children's earlier successes, possibly making them worse off than if they had been consigned to failure all along (Kohl 1967).

Recall how Finis Welch proposed that the existing structure of unequal rewards was an effective means of channeling people's efforts into the most productive activities. Welch, like most conservatives, ignored the role of society in shaping individuals. He never mentioned the many forces that channel the children of the rich and powerful in one direction and those of the poor in another.

If the playing field were more level, the right-wing myth might possibly have some merit. In reality, the cards are stacked in advance in favor of the rich and the powerful even before they are born.

Ideally, education works as a universal opening to success. Such a system could be a legitimate meritocracy in which the most talented people would find their way to the top. The prospect of unequal rewards in this hypothetical contest might inspire people to be more productive in the way Welch implied. Instead, unequal societies typically prevent the sort of selection process that might somehow justify some inequality.

The example of education illustrates how unequal economic systems reinforce inequality—just the opposite of what Kuznets suggested. Those with the most potential may languish within the underclass while the undeserving children of the rich and powerful get special treatment. For example, contributions or family connections get them into the finest universities; then they waltz into the most important posts in society. As a result, inequality leads to a relatively stratified society, in which an elite class monopolizes most of the desirable positions, consigning most of the rest to relatively demeaning work or unemployment regardless of their natural capabilities.

Although a few exceptional success stories make the class structure appear less rigid, the underlying system of inequality cripples the productive potential of an economy by allocating positions according to family origin rather than native talent. We are moving toward Thomas Piketty's earlier cited picture of an economy in which "a small group of wealthy but untalented children controls vast segments of the United States economy and penniless, talented children simply can't compete."

In late December 2004, the government compounded the problem of denying good education to deserving students by proposing to make Pell Grants, "the cornerstone of aid for low-income students" (S. Baum 2005), more difficult to obtain. By reducing grants for 1.3 million students and removing more than 89,000 from the program altogether, the government expected to save $300 million— a short-sighted move that is certain to cost society far more in the long run (Winter 2004; S. Baum 2005).

Eventually higher tuition costs will take a serious economic toll on society as well. For relatively privileged students, increased tuition does not present a serious problem. For others, the tuition costs make good education unaffordable, especially because their budgets are already stretched so thin. For example, in California the community college system raised its fees from $11 per credit in 2003–04 to $26 in 2004–05—a seemingly modest increase in a world in which tuition at elite schools exceeds $10,000. Because students' budgets were already tight, enrollment dropped by more than 300,000 students (California Community Colleges Chancellor's Office 2005).

Because community colleges tend to serve the least affluent students in higher education, such policies reinforce the already-discussed problems of inequality. All too many of those who do attend colleges and universities are hard-pressed to pay for their education. They must hold jobs during the school year as well as the summer. As tuition has grown, so too has the number of outside work hours. Forty-six percent of all full-time working students work 25 or more hours per week. Forty-two percent of these students reported that working hurt their grades (King and Bannon 2002).

The combined pressures of school and outside jobs are making college a grueling experience for many students. This stress takes a toll on students. For many students, the pressure is more than they can handle. One study of students' problems at the Kansas State University counseling center from 1988–89 through 2000–01 found that the number of suicidal students tripled (Benton, Robertson, Tseng, Newton, and Benton 2003).

My own experience confirms this survey. For decades, I have watched this growing workload increasingly distract students from their studies, depriving them of the opportunity to take advantage of their full potential. Instead, I see students who are too tired to benefit from the class or who become emotionally overwhelmed by the pressure. These pressures mean that higher education is unlikely to inspire students or even to give them a quality education.

Despite working part time to cover education costs, the average undergraduate debt was $18,900 in 2002, and is rapidly rising (S. Baum and O'Malley 2003). Those who drop out are also left with student debt, usually without the wherewithal to repay those debts (see Gladieux and Perna 2005).

All too often the burden of debt discourages promising students who beat the odds and earn a bachelor's degree from continuing with their graduate education. One can only guess how many potentially great scientists were unable to develop their talents because of college debts hanging over their heads. Nor can graduating students easily afford to take lower-paying public service jobs.

The prospects for educational reform will remain dim as long as our society maintains such a wide gulf between rich and poor. In unequal societies, the rich are blind to the social forces that impede social mobility. With a handful of exceptions, such as Warren Buffett, the rich are fully convinced that they owe their position to their own hard work and talent and that the poor remain poor only because of their own inadequacies.

With this mindset, we can expect that the electorate will continue to refuse to mobilize enough public funds to finance adequate education for the majority of students. After all, relatively few poor people vote. For the very wealthy, who exercise a disproportionate share in the electoral process, the price of sending a child to an expensive private school is trivial compared to the cost of paying their fair share in a tax system that supports quality education for all. Besides, the comforting rhetoric of school privatization conveniently puts the blame for inadequate education squarely at the foot of the teachers' unions.

Economists routinely produce studies that "prove" that merely increasing funding will not solve the "education problem." The lesson that they draw is that increasing funding is futile. Of course, financial support of the educational system alone will not be enough. The entire structure of inequality works against effective education.

Besides, if a society educates masses of people and then consigns them to unemployment or degrading jobs, the resulting disappointment may spell even more trouble for all concerned.

The Lesson of the GI Bill

Perhaps the greatest example of educational outreach came from the GI Bill. With the exception of a few schools, such as the City University of New York, the university environment was usually foreign to working-class children. Despite the expansion of both the state universities and the more widespread availability of technical training in higher education, prior to World War II, colleges and universities were still largely finishing schools for the children of the elite.

The end of World War II ignited fears that the economy was likely to sink back into a depression without the stimulus of military spending. Political leaders also wanted to prevent a repeat of a confrontation, such as the Bonus March, a Washington gathering of poor, World War I veterans only a little more than a decade before, in 1932, which General Douglas MacArthur violently routed.

To accommodate the returning soldiers, Congress passed the GI Bill, which funded university education for about one-half of the surviving veterans following World War II. This program dramatically broke with the elite academic traditions and triggered one of the most massive transformations of social capabilities in the history of the United States (Skocpol 1998, 96).

Not everybody applauded this policy at the time. Robert Maynard Hutchins, president of the University of Chicago, dreaded the prospect of swarms of veterans entering into the hallowed halls of academia. Hutchins was hardly a rabid conservative. In fact, he had a well-deserved reputation as a liberal and in many respects was one of the great visionaries of higher education. Hutchins warned that "colleges and universities will find themselves converted into educational hobo jungles" (Hutchins 1944; cited in Olson 1974, 33). In short, the GI Bill threatened the class structure of higher education.

More than a half century after the GI Bill began, Robert M. Berdahl, Chancellor of the University of California, Berkeley, lent some credence to Hutchins's instinctual reaction, "The GI Bill, I believe, came closer to being a social revolution than any event in American history in the twentieth century. It democratized universities by providing access to vast numbers of young men who would never otherwise have received an education. Equally important, it opened the doors of elite private universities to a much broader spectrum of the population. It produced an educated workforce that revitalized the American economy. Universities expanded in size and importance" (Berdahl 2000).

Although Hutchins seemed to be mostly concerned about maintaining the universities as elite institutions, some of his apprehensions seemed well-grounded at the time. Certainly, many of the returning veterans were not born into the aristocratic strata of the population that typically populated the elite colleges and universities, such as Hutchins's own University of Chicago. Besides, a good number of these veterans had just finished participating in a violent conflict. That experience would not seem to be appropriate training for aspiring college students. Hutchins may even have realized that many of the veterans would be suffering from what we now call posttraumatic stress disorder, perhaps threatening the tranquility of the cloistered environment of a major university. Most important, perhaps, Hutchins dreaded the prospect of colleges and universities turning into vocational schools (Olson 1974, 33–34).

In the end, all but the last of Hutchins's fears proved to be unfounded. By and large the veterans were far more serious about their studies than the typical well-bred, young college student. Judging from what I observed as a teacher during the Vietnam era, these enthusiastic veterans probably pushed many of the younger students to excel far more than they otherwise would have done, expanding the benefits of the GI Bill well beyond the ranks of the returning veterans. After graduation, many of these veterans rose to positions that would have seemed unimaginable before the war.

We get a feel for the profound importance of the GI Bill for lower-class citizens from an account of a reunion of the 1944 high school class from Turtle Creek, Pennsylvania, a poor, working-class community. The author, Edwin Kiester, Jr., himself a beneficiary of the GI Bill, wrote that his class had 103 male graduates in a high school class of 270. Kiester reported with some evident pride that

> thirty earned college degrees, nearly ten times as many as had in the past; 28 of the 30 attended college under the GI Bill of Rights. The class produced ten engineers, a psychologist, a microbiologist, an entomologist, two physicists, a teacher-principal, three professors, a social worker, a pharmacist, several entrepreneurs, a stockbroker, and a journalist [Kiester himself]. The next year's class matched the 30 percent college attendance almost exactly. The 110 male graduates of 1945 included a federal appellate judge and three lawyers, another stockbroker, a personnel counselor, and another wave of teachers and engineers. For almost all of them, their college diploma was a family first. Some of their parents had not completed elementary school—a few could not read or write English. (Kiester 1994, 132)

The experience of the Turtle Creek students was replicated throughout the country. As Kiester noted, "the first GI Bill turned out 450,000 engineers, 240,000 accountants, 238,000 teachers, 91,000 scientists, 67,000 doctors, 22,000 dentists, 17,000 writers and editors, and thousands of other professionals. Colleges that had languished during the Depression swiftly doubled and tripled in enrollment. More students signed up for engineering at the University of Pittsburgh in 1948 (70 percent of them veterans) than had in five years combined during the 1930s. By 1960 there were a thousand GI Bill-educated vets listed in Who's Who" (Kiester 1994, 130).

As the universities grew to absorb the returning soldiers, they created an infrastructure of buildings and faculty capable of handling a far larger population of students than ever before. To utilize these infrastructures after the wave of veterans graduated, colleges and universities maintained higher enrollments.

In this way, the GI Bill represented the great step forward in the democratization of higher education and society, paying huge dividends for many decades.

Nobody, to my knowledge, certainly no economist, has ever tried to take account of the full impact of the GI Bill, either for people such as Kiester's classmates or for the nation as a whole. Such a work would be daunting, to say the least, because the ramifications of this transformation are so extensive. Of course, the impact of the GI Bill goes far beyond the terrain that economists typically navigate.

Thomas Lemieux, a Canadian economist, and David Card, a fellow Canadian who teaches at the University of California, Berkeley and a recipient of the John Bates Clark award from the American Economic Association, studied the Canadian version of the GI Bill, although from a relatively narrow perspective. The Canadian law did not affect Quebec as much as the rest of Canada because the French-speaking universities made no provision for returning veterans. By comparing labor productivity in Quebec and Ontario, they were able to get an estimate of the effect of the Canadian version GI Bill on labor productivity. As would be expected, they found that productivity rose considerably faster in Ontario than Quebec.

This measure certainly understates the effect of the Canadian GI Bill, in part because their methodology assumes that the improvements in Ontario would not affect Quebec. Certainly, some of the productivity improvements in Ontario would have filtered into Quebec, either because workers moved from one province to another or because of the spread of technology developed in Ontario.

The GI Bill and the nature of the postwar economy reinforced each other. During the Golden Age, the economy was growing rapidly enough to offer opportunities to the new graduates. In addition, the Great Depression and the war loosened the grip of the old hierarchies making room for these new college graduates to apply their skills.

One other educational factor contributed to the success of the postwar U.S. economy: Nazi stupidity. Prior to 1939, the United States lagged far behind Germany in science. For example, Germany had earned five times as many Nobel prizes in chemistry than the United States. By driving many of its best scientists out of the country, Germany decimated its scientific heritage. The United States had the opportunity to welcome a good number of these scientists. Albert Einstein was the most famous of these émigrés, but he was one of many. The arrival of these scientists was an important factor both in winning World War II and in catapulting the United States into the front ranks of science (see N. Rosenberg 2000).

This infusion of science from the combination of the European refugees and the GI Bill came just in time. Although the effect of high wages and native ingenuity kept U.S. technology at a high level, postwar technology was much more dependent on scientific expertise than had been the case earlier.

The GI Bill was a magnificent achievement, perhaps the greatest economic policy success in U.S. history. It helped to keep inequality in check, while it stimulated economic growth. A new GI Bill or, better yet, universal access to education would allow many people to come closer to realizing their potential, even though educational reform would not directly aid in overcoming the stifling, hierarchical relationships that define most jobs.

A massive investment in public education could have an even greater impact, providing that social and cultural barriers to class mobility be dismantled. Every educator knows that education can be most effective when it touches students at a younger age. Shortchanging education, regardless of the reason, deprives society of the potential creativity of students numbed, humiliated, or even antagonized by the educational system. The full extent of these costs is immeasurable.

Ideally, the educational system would not have to contend with the complications that poverty creates for its students. But the reality is that one of every six children in the United States lives in poverty. For many of these children, violence and degradation is a common experience. Nobody can expect an educational system—especially one that is denied adequate resources—to undo all the damage that the rest of society does to its children. However, in the midst of oppressive poverty, the educational system should make special efforts to reach out to children in disadvantaged circumstances to help them tap their potential.

An equivalent of a GI Bill for poor children could inspire some young people, who might otherwise fall into criminal activity, to follow a different path. Ignoring the payoff that society would reap from nurturing their talents, the benefits from crime reduction alone would be substantial. For example, one recent study estimated the effect on the crime rate of an increase in overall male high school graduation rates in 1990—not just the rates for poor children, but for all children. This work seems especially credible since the authors used several different measures to confirm their findings. Each approach yielded similar estimates. They calculated that a small increase of just 1 percent in graduation rates would have resulted in "nearly 400 fewer murders and 8,000 fewer assaults. . . . In total, nearly 100,000 fewer crimes would take place" (Lochner and Moretti 2004, 182). The estimated economic savings from increased graduation was $1.4 billion.

Targeting the graduation rates for poor children would have an even more dramatic impact. Unfortunately, the No Child Left Behind Act actually gives educators an incentive to lower graduation rates. Administrators know that the tactic of removing difficult children from their schools leaves them with a larger share of high performers.

A Concluding Note on Inequality and Social Security

The growing divide between rich and poor also takes a toll on people who might feel unaffected by the afflictions of the poor. Consider Social Security.

In 1983, Alan Greenspan headed a commission that was supposed to put Social Security on a sound footing for the next 75 years. A couple of decades later, the updated deficit projection of the Social Security Trustees came in at $4 trillion over the next 75 years. Although this estimate is inflated (see Henwood 2005), a modest shortfall exists nonetheless.

L. Josh Bivens of the Economic Policy Institute estimated that shifts in two economic trends upset the earlier projections of the Greenspan commission: the slowdown in the growth of average U.S. wages and increasing income inequality.

Lower than expected wages meant that contributions would be lower. Although lower wages also mean a reduction in payouts, those payouts mostly take place after a delay. In the meantime, the unchanged obligatory payments will continue, even though less money than expected comes into the system, creating a shortfall.

Increased income inequality means that more of total wages goes to workers earning more than $90,000, which is the maximum taxable income for the program. As a result, more income will escape being taxed for Social Security. By 2005, the share of total earnings above the maximum taxable earnings base rose to 15 percent compared to 10 percent two decades earlier (Diamond and Orszag 2005, 15). None of those earnings contribute anything to Social Security. If it were not for these two changes—the slowdown in wage growth and the rise in inequality—the projected shortfall in Social Security would be only 60 percent as great (Bivens 2005).

Chapter 9

Obvious Contradictions

The Politicization of Funding Higher Education

Higher education has also fallen victim to the perverted political agenda of the right wing. The obsessive cutting of taxes both on the state and federal level has seriously diminished public financing of higher education. In the same speech in which University of California Chancellor Berdahl acknowledged the importance of the GI Bill, he associated the defunding of higher education with the phenomena of rising tuition, "State support for Berkeley's operating budget has fallen from over 60 percent in 1980 to 34 percent at the present time. In the process of privatization of public universities, the largest single group of private contributors is the students, who now contribute about 15 percent of the operating budget of the University" (Berdahl 2000).

Later, Berdahl observed that Berkeley had become a "state-assisted institution" rather than a public one. Berkeley is not alone in this respect. Nationally, the share of state budgets going to higher education has shrunk by more than one-third since 1980 (Washburn 2005, 8).

In the face of falling financial support for higher education, Congress compounded the problem. When the Republicans first won control over the Congress, they began to earmark funds for specific projects of their own choosing more than ever before. According to a *Chronicle of Higher Education* report, Congress earmarked more than $2 billion of funds for higher education (Brainard and Borrego 2003).

Earmarking undermines the educational mission in three ways. To begin with, grants for higher education typically came by way of peer reviewed competition. This approach was designed to make sure that money would go where it would be the most productive.

Admittedly, this system can give an unfair advantage to the most prestigious institutions. Instead, under the system of earmarking, funds are heavily weighted in favor of institutions represented by powerful congressional leaders. So, this particular method of allocation channels funds where they will be most effective—in furthering political rather than scientific objectives (de Figueiredo and Silverman). To bring this point home, Alan Krueger, who did the excellent work on the Bridgestone/Firestone scandal discussed earlier, published a valuable commentary on earmarking in the *New York Times*, which he aptly titled "The

Farm-Subsidy Model of Financing Academia," to emphasize the role of political clout (Kreuger 2005).

One of the more bizarre earmarks concerned Alaska Christian College, a five-year-old institution with only 37 students. The college is unaccredited and does not offer degrees, yet it has received more than $1 million in federal earmarks since 2003, although unfavorable publicity about the funding caused the government to order the college to cease using any unspent funds (see Faler 2005). A subsequent uproar caused Congress to abandon this particular earmark, but most earmarks go largely unnoticed, except by grateful constituents.

Dr. A. Abigail Payne, an economist at McMaster University in Canada, attempted to quantify the effect of earmarks. One commonly-used measure of the importance of an intellectual work is the frequency with which other researchers cite it. Dr. Payne found that articles supported by earmarks produce fewer than average numbers of citations (Payne 2002).

The second problem concerns the direct cost of winning earmarks. Academic institutions do not just sit back in hopes that Congress will favor them. Instead, they embark on expensive lobbying campaigns. Academic institutions reported spending a total of $61.7 million on lobbying in 2003, although not all expenses need be reported (Brainard 2004). Universities hire lobbyists for their ability to get the most out of existing political connections. In addition, lobbyists are free to take actions that are difficult for universities, such as donating money to politicians (Savage 1999, 107–10).

Such lobbying may be rational for an individual university. Successful institutions win more than a dollar in earmarks for each dollar spent on lobbying, but for the academic world as a whole the money spent on lobbying creates a serious drain on finances, unless that lobbying somehow increases total congressional outlays on education by more than the cost of the lobbying— a rather unlikely outcome.

Of course, to the extent that educational appropriations increase, other interest groups will then engage in counter-lobbying, which will require even more lobbying on behalf of education. Economists are virtually unanimous in condemning this sort of wasteful behavior as "rent seeking" (see A. O. Krueger 1974).

Finally, earmarking makes universities more vulnerable to the displeasure of powerful politicians. In the long run, this danger might be the most serious problem with earmarking. For example, I will discuss later how the right wing attempts to snuff out science when it runs afoul of its agenda.

In 2007, Congress began to address the abuses of earmarking. Hopefully, they will make some progress.

Health Care

Perhaps no sector of the economy illustrates how badly markets work than health care. The United States has the most advanced health care in the world. Unfortunately, such health care is beyond the means of the majority of society. Rising costs are making even barely adequate health care unaffordable for an increasing share of the population. Again, I will concentrate on the economic effects of health care rather than on questions of social justice.

By the 1980s, rising health care costs were already putting U.S. manufacturers at a serious competitive disadvantage with the rest of the world. Chrysler reported that its health care costs in its U.S. factories were already $700 per vehicle, compared to $233 in Canada, where the government provides health care (Wise 1989, 6). By 2005, General Motors saw its health care cost per vehicle in the United States more than double to $1,500 (Murray 2005).

By 1999, Ford's costs for pharmaceuticals alone reached nearly $2,800 annually for each active hourly worker (Bradsher 2004, 90). GM, Ford, and the DaimlerChrysler AG's Chrysler Group estimate that they spent $9.9 billion in 2003 to provide health care to nearly 2 million workers, retirees, and dependents (McCracken 2004). By 2005, the pressure of promised health care and pension costs helped to drive the credit ratings of Ford and General Motors below the threshold for junk bonds.

Already, by the late 1980s, corporate leaders in the United States began calling for the government to step in to contain health care costs (C. Gordon 1991). Conservative ideologues disagreed, insisting that market forces were better suited to solve the health care problem.

Newly elected president Bill Clinton promised to deliver an effective health care plan as the centerpiece of his administration, but strong industry pressure coupled with an aggressive public relations campaign derailed his initiative. To meet some of the objections that conservatives raised, Clinton compromised his proposal. In the end, he offered a clumsy bureaucratic mish-mash that pleased no one. Long after the inevitable defeat of the Clinton plan, it remained a powerful symbol of the supposed bureaucratic mess that any government health care plan would inevitably unleash.

Conservatives proposed that efficient corporate health providers could deliver substantial savings by monitoring health care to eliminate unnecessary expenditures. On its face, the idea made some sense. In fact, the Health Maintenance Organizations initially did manage to hold down medical costs, but not for long.

The conservatives' brand of health care had a fatal flaw: any company whose profits largely depended on keeping medical costs in check also had an incentive to deny as much care as possible—even when it was absolutely medically necessary. This emphasis on rationing had three dimensions: first, whenever possible providers would try to avoid responsibility for taking on people most likely to need care; second, they would try to deny care to those in need; finally, they would try to minimize the time spent with individual patients. Insofar as this last strategy is concerned, Health Maintenance Organizations turned to consultants who recommended that they apply techniques modeled on the Toyota assembly line (Head 2003, 125). Patients had little reason to rejoice that doctors were expected to work at a pace comparable to a harried assembly line worker.

Unfortunately, one expense dissipated much or all of these savings from stinting on health care. Once a corporation takes charge of a huge medical insurance fund, nothing can stop the managers from appropriating big chunks of money for themselves in the form of bloated salaries, benefits, and payouts for share-holders. Eventually, the excesses of management together with the monopoly profits from pharmaceutical corporations more than ate up the savings from the denial of medical services: health care costs soared once again, saddling the public with both higher costs and less care.

Today, huge Health Maintenance Organizations work to minimize available health care while siphoning off a shocking 31 percent of health care expenditures for administrative costs. In contrast, Canada's national health insurance program has an overhead of 1.3 percent. The U.S. health care industry continues to devote more and more of its energies to administrative tasks, despite the fact that computers have been reducing the need for tedious paper work. In fact, between 1969 and 1999, the share of administrative workers in the health care labor force grew from 18.2 percent to 27.3 percent (Woolhandler, Campbell, and Himmelstein 2003).

Excessive overhead and bloated corporate salaries do little to improve the delivery of health care. An editorial in the prestigious *New England Journal of Medicine* sums up the problem of the U.S. health care system: "The American health care system is at once the most expensive and the most inadequate system in the developed world, and it is uniquely complicated. In 1997 we spent about $4,000 per person on health care, as compared with the next most expensive country, Switzerland, which spent some $2,500. Yet 16 percent of our population has no health insurance at all, and many of the rest have only very limited coverage" (Angell 1999).

The corporations that led the movement for market-driven health care had little reason to cheer. After interviewing the head of General Motors, Alan Murray, a columnist for the *Wall Street Journal*, expressed their exasperation: "The U.S. spends a fortune on health care—15% of its total output, compared with 10% in Germany and 8% in Japan. But it gets a lousy return on that money. Forty-five million Americans lack health insurance. And errors are frequent: Recent studies show adults who visit a doctor or a hospital get what experts recommend as the best treatment only about half the time" (Murray 2005).

So in the end, commercial interests have trumped health concerns. The benighted corporate executives, such as those in the automobile industry, are the exception. In their case, ideology rather than commercial interests are trumping common sense.

Even within the U.S. healthcare system, nonprofit institutions are far more efficient than their commercial counterparts. For-profit hospitals spend 23 percent more on administration than do comparable private not-for-profit hospitals and 34 percent more than public institutions (Woolhandler and Himmelstein 1997).

Despite the fact that the United States lacks a government-run health care system, the government still pays for more than half of all medical expenditures. Per capita government spending on health care actually exceeds the total health spending (government plus private) of every other country except Switzerland. In effect then, the people of the United States pay the cost of a national health care system without the opportunity to take advantage of its benefits (Woolhandler and Himmelstein 2001).

So, despite the promise of market efficiencies, the inefficient health care system still leaves U.S. corporations at a serious competitive disadvantage when they have to pay for their workers' health care. The corporate response to the escalating costs of health care problems has been to shift more and more of the burden onto the underfunded government programs or onto the backs of workers through higher premium costs and copayments or, even worse, by the elimination of health care benefits altogether. By 2005, 45 million people in the United States lacked health care insurance. This problem is getting more serious by the day.

The proportion of Americans under age 65 covered by employer-sponsored insurance fell dramatically from 67 percent to 63 percent in the short period between 2001 and 2003. The cost of these policies for both employer and employee generally increased while the coverage narrowed (Strunk and Reschovsky 2004).

Those employers who continue to supply health care for their workers pass the costs onto the rest of the public through higher costs. In the end, the inefficiencies of market-based health care spill out into the rest of the economy.

Inequality and Health

While cutting health care costs may make sense for individual employers, on a national scale this practice is self-destructive. Health-care providers are obligated to give some care to the growing ranks of the uninsured. In 2005, the cost of this care, over and above what the uninsured themselves pay out of their own pockets, exceeded $43 billion nationally. The providers try to recoup some of these unreimbursed costs by passing them on to others, pushing up premiums. This problem partially explains why the average health insurance premium for those families who still have insurance through their private employers was $922 higher in 2005 (Families USA 2005). As a result, health care and inequality form a vicious circle. As premiums escalate, more employers refuse to offer health insurance, adding to the spiraling numbers of uninsured.

Many people, even with insurance, cannot afford health care emergencies. A survey of 1,771 personal bankruptcy filings in five federal courts, followed up with 931 in-depth interviews, found that half cited medical causes even though 75.7 percent of the people had insurance at the onset of illness (Himmelstein et al. 2005).

This combination of inequality and expensive health care costs reduces productivity. Obviously, a healthy workforce will be more productive. In addition, workers who are distracted by worries about how to pay for health care for themselves or their families will also be less productive. Finally, healthy families will be more likely to raise children who are more productive.

Even ignoring the question of access to health care, inequality by itself is detrimental to good health. In fact, emerging research indicates that inequality actually harms the health of the rich as well as the poor, although certainly not to the same extent (Wilkinson 1997). Even, the U.S. government's own Institute of Medicine reported: "more egalitarian societies (i.e., those with a less steep differential between the richest and the poorest) have better average health" (Committee on Assuring the Health of the Public in the 21st Century 2006, 59).

Just how does inequality harm the health of rich people? Unequal societies are more stressful because the privileged must exert control to protect their privileges from the poor. This control creates stresses for the controllers as well as the controlled. Recall how Adam Smith expressed the insecurity of the property owners who felt themselves to be under siege.

More ominously, when inequality is combined with millions of people without access to health care, the threats to health become multiplied many times over. People weakened by the stresses associated with poverty are less able to fight off diseases. The compromised immune systems of poor people without adequate health care provide an excellent environment for diseases to mutate, inevitably becoming more resistant to medical treatment or perhaps even lethal. Oftentimes, diseases that arise in such conditions have more social mobility than the people who carry them. As a result, the pathogens bred in poverty can strike the wealthy as well. So, the growth of the uninsured population presents a danger even for people with good health insurance.

To make matters worse, poverty tends to make people more susceptible to dangerous behavior patterns, such as the sharing of needles among drug addicts. Such activities leave them even more prone to disease, which ultimately puts the rest of society at risk.

With the increasing population of the uninsured, more and more people rely on emergency rooms for medical treatment. Faced with rapidly rising costs and modest government support, hospitals are responding by shutting down their emergency rooms, making the health care crisis even worse.

The elimination of emergency rooms represents a serious risk for society in the event of a disaster or epidemic in which large numbers of people require rapid treatment. This problem briefly came to public attention when people feared a widespread anthrax attack in October 2001, but this concern soon subsided. Since then, the disappearing emergency rooms attract only local attention in the communities left without adequate care.

The only answer to the dilemma of health care is an extensive national system that would relieve individual employers of the responsibility for health care of their workers and their families. Again, the automotive industry is giving signs that it may begin to weigh in on the side of national health care, and justifiably so. The Medicare Modernization Act provided the corporation with approximately $500 million in prescription-drug subsidies in 2004, equivalent to roughly half of North American auto profits. Even so, the cost of health care still adds more than $1,500 to every vehicle sold, and is rising at double-digit rates.

Although General Motors Chief Executive, Rick Wagoner, continues to express opposition to the idea of a national health care system (Murray 2005), GM Canada's Chief Executive Officer, Michael Grimaldi, along with his Canadian counterparts and Ford and DaimlerChrysler, have strongly endorsed the Canadian system (Lindorff 2005). In a joint statement with the Canadian Auto Workers, General Motors, Ford, DaimlerChrysler agreed that

Canada's health care system has been an important ingredient in the auto industry's performance. . . . The public health care system significantly reduces total labour costs for automobile manufacturing firms . . . ; these health insurance savings can amount to several dollars per hour of labour worked. Publicly funded health care thus accounts for a significant portion of Canada's overall labour cost advantage in auto assembly, versus the U.S., which in turn has been a significant factor in maintaining and attracting new auto investment to Canada. (General Motors, Ford, DaimlerChrysler, and the Canadian Auto Workers 2002)

John Devine, the finance chief at General Motors, and Jim Padilla, chief operating officer at Ford, along with a number of other high ranking executives associated with the industry spoke about the problem at a recent seminar. David Cole, chairman of the Center for Automotive Research in Ann Arbor and the seminar organizer said: "I think it's inevitable. I think we are on the road to some form of nationalized health care. . . . With so many more retirees and the Big 3 losing market share to the transplants that don't have all these retirees, there's more and more talk about it" (McCracken 2004).

Health Care in a Market Society

The health care system is not an isolated industry. The pharmaceutical industry has been a major contributor to escalating health care costs. Pharmaceutical companies claim that high drug costs are necessary because of the great expense of developing new drugs.

In fact, much of the pharmaceutical companies' research does not contribute to new medicines. Instead, these corporations devote enormous efforts to copying each others' drugs or suing other companies for copying their own drugs—resources that could have gone to developing new medicines.

Actually, the most important advances in the pharmaceutical industry did not come from the corporations' laboratories, but from those of the government and the universities. Corporations may patent these discoveries, giving themselves the privilege of charging monopolistic prices, but the heavy lifting came from the public sphere. The public, in effect, must pay twice for its medicines: first in the form of taxpayer support for public research institutions and once again in the purchase of medicines. As a result, the pharmaceutical industry remains one of the most profitable industrial sectors in the United States.

Sadly, the pharmaceutical industry spends more on marketing than on research. This marketing creates additional costs for the industry when advertising convinces ill-informed patients to demand high-priced drugs—sometimes for diseases that the industry invents, such as social anxiety disorder. Some doctors acquiesce rather than taking the time to explain the situation to their patients.

Many other commercial influences affect the public's health. For example, corporation interests have severely weakened regulations that protect people from harmful pollutants and questionable food industry practices. For example, the automobile industry, which is heavily burdened by health care costs, successfully lobbies to weaken regulations on vehicle emissions, which then create significant health care costs.

In fact, regulation of harmful pollutants represents one of the most economical health care measures that society could take. For example, the elimination of lead as a gasoline additive was not much of an economic burden, but that single regulation contributed greatly to national health.

A combination of competitive pressures, greed, and neglect has created a host of occupational accidents and diseases. Our analysis of the health care system can extend even further. Both the saturation of advertisements for junk food, together with the work demands that limit the time available for the preparation of wholesome meals, take a toll on the health of the population. In short, a whole complex of commercial pressures has undermined the health care system.

In fact, inequality, pollution, and education are all bound together with health care. For example, lead poisoning, asthma, and untreated toothaches undermine the education of poor children. Leaving the market to sort things out will further weaken the productive potential of the U.S. economy.

Environmental Protection

The crusade against environmental regulations has been a major part of the right-wing revolution. The distortion of science has been an integral part of this strategy to discredit regulation. This problem is not new. The distortion of science by both government and industry delayed the elimination of lead from gasoline by decades (Kitman 2000). Yet, as I mentioned earlier, the benefits of this regulation proved to be immense and the costs relatively small.

The right-wing revolution has intensified scientific distortion to an unparalleled level, yet the need for scientific analysis is greater than ever. Each year, a combination of growing population, increasing consumption, and the introduction of new toxins makes the environment increasingly susceptible to serious damage. A bare-bones list of industry's wasteful and destructive environmental practices would fill an entire volume. Enough books have been written about the specifics of the manifold environmental atrocities to fill an entire library.

The right-wing push for the elimination of environmental protections as quickly as possible may have increased profits in the short run, but like so much of the right-wing agenda, this strategy has detrimental long-term effects. The first consequence of lifting environmental protections is obvious. The economy, and even life itself, ultimately depends upon the environment. Some people feel the immediate effect of deregulation when environmental hazards attack their health. From a purely business perspective, the wanton use of resources hastens the day when rising resource costs bite into economic growth.

For example, the world has a finite supply of petroleum. Obviously, the more petroleum we use, the less that remains. The danger is not in using up the last drop of petroleum. That event will never happen. Instead, the problem is the exhaustion of easily accessible, low-cost petroleum, forcing suppliers to turn to increasingly expensive and more environmentally damaging sources.

Less obviously, the lack of environmental protection can put the United States economy at a long-run disadvantage because environmental regulations can actually stimulate productivity. The reasoning here follows the same logic as the earlier discussion of the advantages of high wages. Again, petroleum offers an excellent example, although I suspect that future shortages of water pose a far more serious threat to society. Expensive petroleum prices force business to develop better technologies. In Europe and Japan, because of stricter regulation and higher taxes people pay something closer to the full cost of energy. Because of this higher cost, industry is hard at work developing more efficient and even alternative energy sources.

Once the world has to face the stark prospect of much more expensive petroleum, these alternative technologies will become economically viable worldwide. By that time, the center of these technologies may well be firmly located in Europe or Japan, leaving the United States far behind. For example, when oil prices began to spike in the early years of the twenty-first century, raising interest in hybrid cars, U.S. automobile producers had to license the technology from Japanese companies.

By making petroleum more expensive today, either through taxes or environmental regulation, U.S. industry would begin to adjust to the inevitable situation when energy prices will be much higher. Having to make the transition too abruptly can wreak havoc with the economy. Although giving the energy industry a relatively free hand allows it to enjoy higher profits today, the long-run consequences for the economy may be disastrous. In short, over and above any environmental benefits, more careful regulation of energy production and consumption will pay handsome dividends, even for energy companies, once the need to make widespread adjustments becomes urgent.

Finally, because the environment is a seamless web, economic activities have repercussions well beyond the confines of any particular industry. Pollution that one industry creates imposes costs on others. In some cases, these costs may not be recognized for some time because of the complexity of the environment. Progress in environmental science is not keeping pace with the rapid growth and intensity of unexpected environmental problems that human activity is creating. To make matters worse, environmental regulation today largely depends upon bureaucratic rules, which are necessarily broad in scope. No such rule could possibly adequately address the full complexity of environmental issues, making careful monitoring more urgent.

Nonetheless, efforts to comply with relatively crude rules can still force industry to treat the environment more gently. For example, endangered species law has probably been the most effective environmental tool available in the United States. This law is far from perfect. In some cases, even the definition of a species is open to question. Nonetheless, the intense debates regarding the application of the endangered species law have done a great deal to protect the environment, while furthering both public and scientific knowledge, despite industry and governmental efforts to obfuscate.

One may debate whether the preservation of one particular species—usually the critics single out some unattractive insect or rodent—is worth the economic inconvenience. However, the preferred solution of the right wing—the absence of regulation altogether—represents a serious threat to all concerned. Hopefully, strong environmental regulation would push industry to develop more productive and less destructive methods, just as higher wages have historically pressured business in the United States to invent more productive technologies.

The stakes of the debates regarding environmental protection are monumental. The wrong choice can mean that the lives of many millions of people are put at risk or that hundreds of billion of dollars could be wasted on unnecessary expenses. Although certainty is unobtainable, rational people should be able to rely on the best available science.

Chapter 10

Attempting to Hold the Line

The Growing Crisis in Science

World War II ushered in what might be called America's Golden Age of science. Today, people have good reason to fear that the Golden Age of science might go the way of the economic Golden Age.

The current craze for improving results on standardized tests is not likely to inspire young people to follow a scientific career. First of all, the tests typically emphasize English and math rather than science. More importantly, "teaching to the test" will certainly dull students' interest in any subject. This ridiculous emphasis on testing will snuff out the creativity of many budding scientists, although it might boost the prospects for privatized education.

Already, relatively few students are pursuing careers in science and technology. In a talk on the occasion of his winning the Harold Berger Award presented biannually by the Penn School of Engineering and Applied Science, Dean Kamen, inventor of everything from medical devices to the Segway transporter, complained: "Last year the U.S. graduated 62,000 engineers. We graduated more students last year with degrees in sports management" (Rogers 2004).

The current emphasis on money and power is also making scientific and technical careers less attractive. Recall how 40 percent of Yale's graduating class applied for financial jobs at First Boston. Instead of making science as attractive a career as finance or sports management, the United States is denigrating science in a number of ways.

To begin with, science is becoming needlessly politicized. Rather than encouraging independent scientific investigations, the government is manipulating science to promote its narrow political agenda. The massive corporate effort to undermine scientific evidence—a crass effort to prevent unwelcome regulation—does little to encourage young people to follow a scientific career.

The perverse incentives that discourage science will cause incalculable damage in the future. A cross-country analysis indicates that economies with a high share of engineering college majors grow faster than those who train their youth as lawyers and financial experts (Murphy, Shleifer and Vishny 1991). The American Electronics Association expressed a sense of urgency in this regard, "China graduates almost four times as many engineers as the United States. Japan with less than half of the population of the United States, graduates almost twice as many engineers. South Korea—with 1/6th the population and 1/20th the GDP—graduates nearly the same number of engineers as the United States" (American Electronics Association 2005).

This neglect of scientific education points to a serious danger. After all, the demand for basic science has never been greater because of the growing complexity of a world populated with six billion people demanding an ever increasing standard of living built upon a shrinking resource base.

The Right-Wing Assault on Science

Everyone agrees that scientific advances are essential for economic improvement. Although much modern science is expensive and many avenues of research prove to be dead ends, the benefits of the rare scientific breakthroughs are so great that funding research still pays enormous dividends for society.

The United States arguably had good reason to see itself as the world leader in science. The GI Bill contributed to success of the United States in science, if for no other reason than the expansion of the size of higher education. The immigration of refugee scientists fleeing the Nazis significantly improved the quality of scientific research. In later years, generous public funding for the universities along with a relatively supportive atmosphere helped to advance science in the United States even further.

In recent years, science has come under intense attack. Powerful corporations are wealthy enough to always be able to find a handful of people—sometimes even people with decent credentials—to further corporate interests rather than scientific progress. Just think of the scientists who clouded the issue of the health impacts of tobacco successfully enough to protect the industry from lawsuits or regulation for many decades. These people did not have to prove that tobacco did not have harmful effects; they just had to raise enough doubts to confuse the issue.

The counterparts of these scientists are hard at work sowing confusion about the harmful effects of heavy metals, toxic chemicals, and global warming. The network of foundations that fueled the right-wing revolution heavily funds those who are willing to support corporate-friendly science, while attacking unwelcome results.

Major corporations and their allies are raising their opposition to science to a new level, even funding sophisticated smear campaigns against researchers who dare to point to environmental dangers that corporate behavior creates. The corporate-friendly anti-regulators use harsh rhetorical terms, such as Peter Huber's phrase "junk science," to denounce studies that support the case for regulatory or compensatory actions. Unlike the "junk science," practiced by those whose work supports the need for regulation of corporate behavior, researchers funded by corporations purport to use only "sound science"—at least according to the prevailing corporate rhetoric. Peter Huber himself, whose book, *Galileo's Revenge: Junk Science in the Courtroom*, set off the gallant movement to counter "junk science," once he explained what he meant by that term. He included under the rubric of junk science "anything that associated with victim harm, with toxic exposure, or medical negligence" (Alliance for Justice 1993, 54).

The government has enthusiastically jumped in with its own antiscientific jihad. For example, in early 2004, the Union of Concerned Scientists issued a report, signed by 48 Nobel Laureates detailing a number of instances in which the Bush administration seriously violated scientific principles. The report charged that the administration ignored or even distorted scientific information when findings disturbed its political agenda and that the administration stacked scientific panels with people with strong industry connections rather than scientific credentials.

One particular incident concerned White House interference with an Environmental Protection Agency report on the dangers of global warming (Union of Concerned Scientists 2004). This stance was consistent with the administration's vigorous dismissal of the scientific concerns about the dangers of global warming: the administration preferred instead to rely upon the reassuring insistence from the petroleum industry that global warming does not represent any threat at all.

The denigration of serious scientists by those who try to blunt criticisms of corporate behavior does not create a conducive atmosphere for science. Instead, such antiscientific actions create a negative climate in which science appears as an arena in which petty people work in an atmosphere of confusion—hardly an image to win public support or inspire a new generation of scientists.

The attack on science is spilling into the classroom. Education, especially early education, is crucial for promoting science. Childhood experiences that awaken scientific interests generally spark the careers of most great scientists.

The right wing has crippled scientific education in other ways. For example, the right wing has to accommodate its fundamentalist constituency. Because of religious antipathy to the theory of evolution, some schools now require teachers to avoid straightforward discussions of the subject of evolution. Some go further, expecting teachers to instruct their students about creationism. Discussion of human reproduction and safe sex has also come under censorship. Eventually these restrictions are likely to have serious consequences. As teachers become timid about what they can teach, they lose the ability to inspire potential scientists, let alone educate students.

The negative consequences of restrictions of federal spending on stem cell researchers could be coming much more quickly. Several distinguished scientists in this field have already relocated to other countries, where they can work in a more hospitable climate, although some state governments are attempting to fill this gap. Many people are justifiably leery about the abuses associated with human cloning, yet the long-run medical benefits from this technology seem virtually unlimited.

The attack on science also includes a foreign-policy dimension. The Office of Foreign Assets Control of the United States' Department of the Treasury issued a measure prohibiting U.S. scientific magazines and publications from reviewing, publishing, or modifying works of authors from countries which are the object of a "commercial embargo," including Cuba, Iran, Sudan, and Libya. Violators would be subject to severe fines and prison terms. The irrationality of this policy even extended to a book by Shirin Ebadi, who won the Nobel Peace Prize for her work in pursuing democracy in Iran, although the government eventually had to relent in this particular case.

Censoring Science

The destructive corporate influence on academic research reaches into higher education. For example, in 1998, Berkeley negotiated a comprehensive agreement between its Department of Plant and Microbial Biology and the Novartis Agricultural Discovery Institute. Novartis was to provide long-term monetary support worth $25 million for basic research and, in exchange, receive first rights to license the discoveries made within the department. The agreement actually allowed corporate personnel to sit in on academic committees, including those that make hiring decisions. Presumably, the company also would be able to directly influence what will and will not be researched. Considering the stakes, $25 million is not a trivial sum, but in an age when a single patent can be worth one hundred times that amount, $25 million spread over a few years is not a particularly generous contribution.

Ignacio Chapela was an up-and-coming young scientist in the department. Earlier, he had worked for the Swiss biotech pioneer Sandoz, which, in turn, had merged with Ciba Geigy to form Novartis, the company in question. He also had been a member of a National Academy of Science's committee reviewing the impacts of genetic manipulation of crops. Nonetheless, Chapela was skeptical about genetic engineering of food crops and was opposed to the Novartis deal. Neither position was likely to advance his academic career.

To make matters worse for him, Chapela, along with a graduate student, published an article in the prestigious journal *Nature* showing that transgenic corn was intermixing with native Mexican corn (Quist and Chapela 2001). This finding was alarming because Mexico has the most diverse reservoir of indigenous corn in the world.

I once served on a U.S. Department of Agriculture task force dealing with the importance of maintaining such diversity. For millennia, breeders have drawn upon naturally occurring traits, such as those found in Mexican corn, to develop strains that can increase yields or protect against insects or plant diseases. Destroying this diversity would be an irreparable loss for the world.

The director of a Mexican corporation approached Chapela, first offering a "glittering research post if he withheld his paper, then told him that he knew where to find his children." When this approach did not work, corporate interests applied a different type of pressure. In the words of British journalist, George Mombiot:

> In the U.S., Chapela's opponents have chosen a different form of assassination . . .
> On the day the paper was published, messages started to appear on a biotechnology listserver used by more than 3,000 scientists, called *AgBioWorld*. The first came from a correspondent named "Mary Murphy." Chapela is on the board of directors of the Pesticide Action Network, and therefore, she claimed, "not exactly what you'd call an unbiased writer." Her posting was followed by a message from an

"Andura Smetacek", claiming, falsely, that Chapela's paper had not been peer-reviewed, that he was "first and foremost an activist" and that the research had been published in collusion with environmentalists. The next day, another email from "Smetacek" asked "how much money does Chapela take in speaking fees, travel reimbursements and other donations . . . for his help in misleading fear-based marketing campaigns?" The messages from Murphy and Smetacek stimulated hundreds of others, some of which repeated or embellished the accusations they had made. Senior biotechnologists called for Chapela to be sacked from Berkeley. *AgBioWorld* launched a petition pointing to the paper's "fundamental flaws." (Monbiot 2002)

The two leaders of this attack on the article were actually fictitious creations of a British public relations organization, the Bivings Group. Real or not, they stirred up enough of a firestorm to pressure the journal to take unprecedented actions. The editor called upon three outside reviewers, then overruled the majority of the reviewers and finally made the first retraction in the history of the journal (Monbiot 2002).

Chapela's problems did not stop there. He was up for tenure at the university. At first, his chances looked good. Those with the most knowledge of Chapela's skills as a researcher and teacher—his peers in the department—supported him. A departmental committee voted in favor of tenure (32 to 1, with three abstentions). At the college level the vote was unanimous. The next stage should have ensured tenure. An *ad hoc* committee composed of five faculty members chosen for their ability to evaluate Chapela's research then voted unanimously in his favor. His dean also signed off on the tenure decision.

At this point, the powers-that-be gathered strength. The vice-provost intervened, asking the *ad hoc* committee to reconvene in order to review Mr. Chapela's research once again. The chairman resigned and disavowed the committee's report, saying he did not have the expertise to judge Mr. Chapela's research. The chairman did not tell any of the members of the committee about his decision at the time.

This special committee then compiled a dossier and forwarded it to the Academic Senate Committee on Budget and Interdepartmental Relations, a faculty committee that routinely reviews tenure decisions. This committee then advised the chancellor to reject Mr. Chapela's tenure bid—which the chancellor did. Apparently, the senate committee that had appointed the *ad hoc* committee asked it to reconvene to review Mr. Chapela's research again.

This bureaucratic maneuver was highly unusual. One member of the *ad hoc* committee, Wayne M. Getz, a professor of environmental science, stated, "I've been here 24 years, and my understanding is that if the department and the ad hoc committee recommend for tenure, you get tenure" (S. Walsh 2004). Later, after a storm of adverse publicity and an impending lawsuit, the university relented and granted Chapela tenure.

What about Novartis? One outside committee later asked by the University to review the entire Novartis contract concluded, "Regardless of whether Chapela's denial of tenure was justified, there is little doubt that the UCB-N agreement played a role in it" (Busch et al. 2004, 42).

Corporations influence the tenor of science even when they have no direct contact with researchers. Promotion and tenure in universities often depends, at least in part, on a person's ability to win research grants. The pressure to get grants is especially strong in science and technology.

Once grants are awarded, corporations censor science in a heavy-handed fashion. For example, pharmaceutical companies routinely require academic researchers to sign contracts that give the company control of the scientists' data and prevent them from publishing without the company's consent (see Perelman 2002).

Short-Circuiting Science

The United States benefited mightily from a brain drain in which some of the most talented people in the world have left their homeland to make their future in the United States. Between 1901 and 1991, 44 of the 100 Nobel Prizes awarded to researchers in the United States were won by the foreign-born or their children (Paral and Johnson 2004). The immigration of brilliant scientists escaping from Nazism was a case in point.

Colleges and universities are often the gateways for skilled immigrants. A U.S. Department of Energy study based on information from 2001 found that 71 percent of foreign citizens who received science/engineering doctorates from U.S. universities in 1999 were still in the United States in 2001. Students in computer/electrical and electronic engineering, computer science, and the physical sciences were more likely to stay than those from other fields (Finn 2003).

Today, rather than welcoming potential Einsteins into the United States, the government is presently treating would-be immigrants with suspicion. The belligerent foreign policy of the United States, together with the tightening of immigration policies, is making the United States a less attractive destination for graduate students.

Foreign graduate students in science and engineering are now less likely to study in the United States. In 1998—a relatively low point—the number of first-time graduate students fell in every field except biological sciences (Thurgood 2004).

More than 30 prestigious organizations, including the National Academy of Sciences, the American Association for the Enhancement of Science, the Association of American Universities, the American Council on Education, and the National Academy of Engineering endorsed an unprecedented joint statement warning about this trend:

> [T]here is increasing evidence that visa-related problems are discouraging and preventing the best and brightest international students, scholars, and scientists from studying and working in the United States, as well as attending academic and scientific conferences here and abroad. If action is not taken soon to improve the visa system, the misperception that the United States does not welcome international students, scholars, and scientists will grow, and they may not make our nation their destination of choice now and in the future. The damage to our nation's higher education and scientific enterprises, economy, and national security would

be irreparable. The United States cannot hope to maintain its present scientific and economic leadership position if it becomes isolated from the rest of the world (Association of American Universities 2004).

In light of the nationalistic political climate, other countries are trying to make their higher education more attractive to foreign students at the same time that the United States is defunding higher education.

The Central Intelligence Agency's National Intelligence Council sounded the alarm that Japan and China are becoming "educational magnets" for Asian students (National Intelligence Council 2005, 38), perhaps echoing an earlier statement by Microsoft chairman Bill Gates, who lamented to the luminaries before a gathering of world leaders that tough U.S. visa policies threaten the status of the United States as "the IQ magnet of the world. . . . There has been a 35 per cent drop in Asians coming to our computer science departments" (Gapper and Larsen 2005).

In response to these warnings, the government promised to speed up the visa process, but visa delays are only part of the problem. Even before the September 11 attack, visa applications required incoming students to express their intent to return to their country of origin.

These graduate students benefit the United States in several ways. First, these students bring an estimated $13 billion to the United States (Adam 2001; see also Vincent-Lancrin). Second, foreign students account for a large portion of graduate education, especially in the sciences. In 2000, nonresident aliens received 36.5 percent of the doctoral degrees awarded in the physical sciences, 50.7 percent in engineering, and 25.7 percent in the life sciences (Borjas 2005; U.S. Department of Education. Digest of Education Statistics, 2002, Tables 270, 272).

By increasing the demand for scientific education, these students also help to build up the scientific infrastructure within the university, just as the GI Bill did after World War II. As a result, foreign students make economies of scale possible. The cost per student of a laboratory built to serve twenty students will be far less than one designed to serve only four students. By helping to increase the scale, these students can benefit current and future American students.

For those students who return to their countries, the science and technology that they create will benefit the entire world—not just their own country. Those students who never return home bring even more benefits to the United States.

After the 1989 protests at Tiananmen Square, Senator Lamar Alexander, then president of the University of Tennessee and who would later become Secretary of Education under President George H. W. Bush and finally U.S. Senator again, recognized an excellent opportunity. Alexander suggested to Bush that the 30,000 Chinese students in the United States be given the chance for immediate citizenship. Alexander later speculated that welcoming these students as citizens could have had an impact comparable to the influx of German scientists fleeing the Nazis (Alexander 2005).

Patent data suggests the benefit of retaining foreign graduate students in the United States. Economists often use patent data as a rough indicator of the state of science and technology. One study estimated that a 10 percent increase in the number of foreign graduate students would raise U.S. patent applications by 3.3

percent, successful university patent grants by 6 percent and successful non-university patent grants by 4 percent (Chellaraj, Maskus, and A. Mattoo 2004).

The response of Bill Gates to the drop-off in foreign graduate students suggests that the major corporations have little interest in short-circuiting science. Even so, the corporate sector has done much to fund the right wing, which has used nationalistic fervor to distract the electorate from real issues. In this sense, the corporate sector, along with the right wing as a whole, bears responsibility for this problem.

The Neglect of Basic Science

Science comes in two flavors. One is applied, addressing questions of the form—how can you accomplish a particular goal, such as making computer chips run faster or improve yields in a particular crop? The other flavor is basic science, which often has no particular application in mind. Instead, basic science merely investigates questions about the natural world for their own sake.

Basic science generally produces the revolutionary breakthroughs that make possible great leaps in knowledge. Applied science generally depends on previous work in basic science. Of course, science is a two-way street. Work in applied science also contributes to basic science but not nearly as much as basic science contributes to applied work.

Without continual research in basic science, applied science will eventually lose its vigor. Typically basic scientific discoveries require several decades before they turn up in practical applications.

The bulk of basic science comes from the universities and public agencies. For example, Francis Narin and his colleagues attempted to track down the funding source of the scientific research that patent applicants cited on the first page of their applications. They found that 73 percent of the main science papers cited by American industrial patents in two recent years were based on domestic and foreign research financed by government or nonprofit agencies. Even IBM—famous for its research prowess and numerous patents—was found to cite its own work only 21 percent of the time (Narin et al. 1997).

Now, recall Louis Powell's recommendation that universities be reined in. The right wing largely accomplished this objective by severely restricting government funding of education, even though the cost of doing cutting-edge science has been rapidly escalating in most fields.

Cut off from adequate funding, academic administrators were forced to turn to the corporate sector for support. Corporations were more than willing to get involved with those parts of the university with the most potential to develop commercially viable technologies. The universities, in turn, proved equally willing to embrace corporate funding.

This corporate support comes at a steep price, as the Chapela case suggests. Corporations have little interest in pursuing basic science—the kind of science that can transform future technologies. The reasons are not hard to understand.

Corporate donors typically expect something tangible in return from the university—something more tangible than a potential scientific breakthrough

30 years from now. For example, Novartis did not renew its contract because it had not yet reaped enough benefits. Instead, corporations prefer greater emphasis on applied science that will produce profits quickly. You might recall Harrison's comment about "impatient capital."

Benefits from breakthroughs in basic science are also too uncertain for corporations. No one can predict which lines of research will be important or the sort of applications that important discoveries will eventually make possible.

Corporate influence harms research in other ways. Ideally, science flourishes in an open environment in which researchers freely share ideas. As the academic environment becomes ever more entrepreneurial, disinterested scientific research must surely suffer. Grants become, in effect, a property right, giving researchers control over money and people. Secrecy becomes a high priority in the quest for profit.

The stakes can be quite high. A recent editorial in *Nature*, entitled "Is the University-Industrial Complex Out of Control?" suggests the scope of this problem. According to the editorial, "One-third of all the world's biotechnology companies were founded by faculty members of the University of California" (Anon. 2001).

The resulting neglect of basic science will not cause immediate damage to the economy because, as I already noted, basic discoveries take a while before they are ready to emerge as a new technology. This delay no more justifies short-changing basic science than would the elimination of education for preteenagers on the grounds that such a policy would not have an immediate impact on the economy.

In the process of wooing corporate donors, universities have begun to emulate corporations, even adopting current management fads. In the process, university presidents have become more like CEOs than academic leaders. Their salaries are steadily inching up to CEO levels, with more than 100 earning one half million dollars or more in 2005 (Anon. 2006).

University administrations have also begun to emulate corporate behavior in their ungenerous treatment of less skilled workers. Like corporate CEOs, these academic CEOs adopt perspectives that are foreign to the academic values that have contributed to the traditional strengths of colleges and universities.

Most directly, the effect of this corporatization of the university has been to marginalize those parts of the university with less commercial potential, such as literary criticism or history, and to focus on fostering those parts of the university that could lure more corporate support. Universities naturally became more cautious about hiring people who might be critical of the corporate world.

In the process of corporatization, universities are bidding up the salaries of star research professors who have the potential to attract wealthy corporations. At the same time, they save money on teaching costs by drastically reducing the number of full-time tenured professors, replacing them with contingent instructors, just like the corporate sector. For example, between 1998 and 2001, the number of full-time tenured faculty declined by 6.2 percent, while full-time, nontenure track faculty increased by 35.5 percent and part-time faculty by 19.1 percent (J. Curtis 2004). Part-time faculty members bear a disproportionate share of the teaching load. Those teachers, who often have to shuttle between teaching assignments at different institutions to make ends meet—sometimes called "roads scholars"—do not have much time to devote to their students, further undermining the quality of education.

Many universities have also embarked on ambitious building programs, in part designed to attract corporate interest. The combination of these extra costs together with the curtailing of government funding put universities in a bind. The universities responded by saddling students with ballooning tuition and fees.

Finally, the quest for corporate funds has deflected universities from its mission of producing basic research. None of these trends promise much good.

So in the end, Lewis Powell and his followers won by neutering the universities, but at a serious cost to the long-term economic prospects of the United States. At the same time that other nations are building up their educational prowess, the United States is witnessing a slew of dangerous trends: universities with more attention to the bottom line than education, students without the kind of training they deserve, an unfriendly atmosphere for foreign students, and science bottled up in secrecy and litigation. Eventually, the corporate sector will have to pay a steep price for pursuing such short-sighted policies, especially as the scientific leadership of the United States fades.

Intellectual Property Rights vs. Science

Finally, intellectual property rights—supposedly the ultimate trump card in the American economic arsenal—are severely compromising modern science. In recent decades, intellectual property rights have become so excessive that they seriously threaten the flow of technological and scientific progress. Theoretically, the right to obtain a monopoly on the fruits of scientific research should create a strong incentive to delve deeper into the secrets of nature. This idea might make sense if we think of science as a product of a single individual.

However, technological and scientific advances build upon a complex stream of ideas and information. Each breakthrough depends on the work of many others. For example, nobody invented the computer. Instead, the computer depended upon a massive array of work from people in physics, mathematics, electrical engineering, material sciences, and other disciplines. Theoretically, within the context of a market economy each contributor deserves a reward commensurate with his or her particular input. But how can anybody measure their relative contributions?

Instead, the current system of intellectual property rights assigns credit for an invention or discovery to a single owner, although the owner might have to pay royalties to others holding rights to particular objects or processes used in the invention. Within this arrangement, disputes are inevitable. Disgruntled participants have no recourse but to turn to the courts, creating a flood of litigation, leading to horrendous multimillion dollar patent fights.

To make matters worse, a whole new industry has emerged. Patent trolls buy up obscure patents that have never been used and then look for profitable businesses that they can sue for infringement. Often times, even if the suit has little merit, paying off the claimant is cheaper than mounting a defense in the court-room. As these trials multiply they create what people in the industry refer to as a patent thicket. This explosion of business litigation is ironic given the furious corporate campaign to limit individual's right to sue the corporate sector.

Strengthening intellectual property rights was supposed to provide business with security over its scientific and technological investments, which could provide an incentive to put more resources into furthering technology. Legal dis-putes undermine security, drain away potential profits from intellectual prop-erty rights, and force business to devote energy to accumulating more patents as a defensive measure. This defensive strategy also imposes its own costs, because as patent coverage becomes denser, the likelihood of legal disputes increases even further.

In this litigious environment, only the largest corporations have the where-withal to withstand the challenge of expensive trials. Here again, the result is not favorable to economic vitality since large corporations, which the system favors, tend to be laggards in pushing the boundaries of science and technology. Small innovative companies are not likely to prosper in this environment. Even if a small company has the capacity to make an important contribution, investors might be leery because of the potential legal barriers such a firm might face. Favoring the large corporations also reinforces the growing trend of economic inequality.

Ironically, the same large corporations that have been the strongest advocates of strong intellectual property rights have become proficient in circumventing the intellectual property rights of others. They become especially expert in reverse engineering—that is, finding a way of effectively duplicating an exist-ing device, pill, or a program by creating an equivalent without violating existing patents. The pharmaceutical industry's efforts on developing what the industry calls me-too drugs, which merely duplicate protected products, are an obvious example.

The single-minded quest for intellectual property rights also deforms the sci-entific process by emphasizing work that will have relatively quick payoffs.

Perhaps most damningly, the quest for more intellectual property rights inhibits scientific communication. What makes modern science work most effectively, over and above providing sufficient funds to the best available people, is open communication. When scientists become more intent on producing intellectual property rights than on discovering the secrets of nature, open com-munication threatens to erode the probability of economic success.

Robert K. Merton once wrote about the importance of open communication in science:

> "Communism", in the nontechnical and extended sense of common ownership of goods, is . . . [an] integral element of the scientific ethos. The substantive findings of science are a product of social collaboration and are assigned to the community. They constitute a common heritage in which the equity of the individual producer is severely limited. "Property" rights in science are whittled down to a bare mini-mum the rationale of the scientific ethic. The scientist's claim to "his" intellectual "property" is limited to that of recognition and esteem which, if the institution

functions with a modicum of efficiency, is roughly commensurate with the signif-icance of the increments brought to the common fund of knowledge. (Merton 1942, 121)

More than a half century after Merton's observation, the emphasis on intellec-tual property rights is inflicting considerable damage on scientific research.

Globalization and Intellectual Property Rights

High wages and environmental regulations are not the only pressures that can push industry to modernize. Low-cost competitors from abroad can also force business to modernize. As countries, such as Korea, Taiwan, Singapore—not to mention Japan—began to develop modern manufacturing sectors, they began to export relatively simple, low-cost, labor-intensive products, such as textiles. Gradually, countries steadily expanded their production into ever more sophis-ticated commodities.

Competitors in the United States had several options. They could lower wages to match their competition's costs, but given the extreme difference in wages, this tactic is usually not practical. Alternatively, business could move its manufacturing abroad to take advantage of cheap wages elsewhere; it could go out of business altogether; or it could respond to the competition by radically improving its productivity. As mentioned earlier, the stance of the U.S. govern-ment in Vietnam made the first alternative of moving offshore more attractive.

Relatively few companies have chosen to increase productivity. As a result, manufacturing employment in United States is shrinking at an alarming rate. Outsourcing is also spreading into services. Although still relatively small, it is growing rapidly.

The response of government to competitive pressures should be to invest massively in education, retraining, and scientific research. The purpose of this investment should be to make sure that the economy has the capacity to respond to low-wage competition with a modern, high-tech capacity. Instead, the gov-ernment of the United States is pinning its hopes on an entirely different strat-egy based largely on the enforcement of often-questionable intellectual property rights. The idea is that the United States will become an exporter of movies, music, software, pharmaceuticals, and business services—all of which will be protected by intellectual property rights.

In the movie business today, skilled professionals from all over the world are working in the American film business, but production of films is increasingly moving to lower-wage parts of the world. The present dominant position of Hollywood is no longer its geography, but rather its distribution system. Over time, this dominance is likely to erode, especially as markets in Asia become more affluent.

Similarly, the center of gravity in other highly favored industries, such as pharmaceuticals and software, is shifting as corporations begin to rely more heavily on skilled professionals from other countries. Adam Segal of the Council on Foreign Relations warned, "Craig Barrett [former CEO] of Intel has said that the Chinese are now 'capable of doing any engineering, any software job, any managerial job that people in the United States are capable of.' And Microsoft has reportedly contracted with the Indian companies Infosys and Satyam not only to do simple software coding, but also to provide highly skilled software architects" (Segal 2004).

Elsewhere, without batting an eyelid, Barrett said: "If the world's best engineers are produced in India or Singapore, that is where our companies will go" (Rajghatta 2005). Similarly, the pharmaceutical companies are also reaching out to tap the rapidly increasing pool of Chinese expertise (Santini 2004). So, business is even beginning to outsource what *Business Week* called "the vanguard of the next step in outsourcing—of innovation itself" (Engardio and Einhorn 2005).

The blasé attitude of much of the business community reminds me of the ironic response of Adam Smith's contemporary, Samuel Johnson after his friend, James Boswell, remarked about the lack of industry in Litchfield, Johnson's birthplace: "Sir [said Johnson] 'We are a City of Philosophers: we work with our Heads, and make the Boobies of Birmingham work for us with their hands'" (Boswell 1934–64, ii, 64).

The current philosophers of intellectual property believe patents and copyrights alone will be able to protect and even expand the existing powers of business in the United States. Their hopes do not seem to be well-founded, given the scrimping on the basic science, which will be required for creating the next generation of products. As a recent report prepared for the Central Intelligence Agency's National Intelligence Council concluded: "China and India are well positioned to become technology leaders, and even the poorest countries will be able to leverage prolific, cheap technologies to fuel—although at a slower rate—their own development" (National Intelligence Council 2005, 11).

Ultimately, the enforcement of the intellectual property rights of U.S. corporations depends on the military power of the United States. The full might of the United States can be brought to bear upon any country that stands by idly while evildoers within its borders dare to create knock-offs of a Disney cartoon or a Nike swoosh. In the clever formulation of Thomas Friedman, perhaps the most enthusiastic proponent of corporate globalization at the *New York Times*, "The hidden hand of the market will never work without a hidden fist—McDonald's cannot flourish without McDonnell Douglas, the designer of the F-15. And the hidden fist that keeps the world safe for Silicon Valley's technologies is called the United States Army, Air Force, Navy and Marine Corps. . . . Without America on duty, there will be no America Online" (T. Friedman 1999, 373).

Friedman's ironical linking of McDonald's and McDonnell Douglas brings to mind two further ironies about the role of the military in protecting the market. First, despite loud claims of absolute faith in markets, neither business nor the political leaders of the United States have ever made much of an effort to apply market principles to the military. Yes, much of the military has been privatized in recent decades, but, as I shall discuss in the case of Lockheed Martin, the private companies that win the contracts owe far more to political connections than to market competition. One might fairly conclude that the Pentagon represents one of the largest, and insofar as economic efficiency is concerned, least efficient socialist economies that mankind has ever devised—a socialist economy sworn to uphold the market.

Second, the mind-boggling cost of protecting corporate assets abroad is itself a threat to the U.S. economy. Although no other country in the world poses a conventional military threat to the United States, the official military budget for the fiscal year 2006 is close to $500 billion. This amount seriously understates the military budget because funding for the wars in Afghanistan and Iraq comes from supplemental expenditures. In addition, a good deal of military spending occurs outside of the official defense budget. For example, the nuclear weapons program is part of the Energy Department and the some of the biological weapons labs are within the Agriculture Department. Some estimates put the actual military budget at more than twice the official figure by including the ongoing cost of past wars—such as veterans benefits—and interest on the national debt resulting from earlier military spending.

Ironically, the obscene binge in military spending is likely to undermine U.S. military strength in the long run. In the days of the Vikings and Genghis Khan, impoverished countries could just send their hordes abroad to loot other societies. Today, a powerful military rests first and foremost on a strong domestic economy. The U.S. victory in World War II largely depended on the ability of its factories to pour out airplanes, tanks, ships, and other materiel. Today, the manufacturing base is shrinking and the domestic high-tech sectors are rapidly losing their lead. In addition, the neglect of basic science will eventually take a toll.

A One-Man Military-Industrial Complex

Thomas Friedman, in lumping together McDonalds and McDonnell Douglas, put his finger on the close association of intellectual property rights and military Keynesianism. Except as a local issue when a new weapons factory opens or a military base closes, military Keynesianism rarely appears in public dialogue. Instead, a relatively tight network of well-placed politicians and weapons manufacturers, along with the inhabitants of conservative think tanks construct the basic framework of military Keynesianism and present it to the public as a *fait accompli.*

Bruce Jackson, whose career, deserves an entire book, seems to personify this brand of insider military Keynesianism. Jackson was born into the stratosphere of the military-industrial complex. His father, William Harding Jackson, was deputy director of the Central Intelligence Agency from 1951 to 1956.

Perhaps then nobody should be surprised that the Army assigned a young intelligence officer of such noble pedigree to work in the Pentagon as a military intelligence officer in the 1980s. During the Reagan and Bush Senior administrations, he labored under leading Pentagon hawks, such as Richard Perle, Paul Wolfowitz, and Dick Cheney.

Jackson left the military to begin a brief career in investment banking with Lehman Brothers between 1990 and 1993—no doubt with the expectation that his Pentagon contacts would prove valuable. Jackson also joined in with the Project for a New American Century (Project for a New American Century

2001). Indeed, Jackson's wide network must have paid off. In 1993, he catapulted himself into a high position with a leading military contractor, Martin Marietta, as Director for Corporate Development Projects and Director for Strategic Planning. In 1995, Martin Marietta merged with Lockheed.

At the newly formed Lockheed Martin, Jackson assumed the position of Director of Defense Planning and Analysis. In 1997 the company promoted him first to Director of Global Development and finally to Vice President for Strategy and Planning.

The newly formed Lockheed Martin was the ideal employer for Bruce Jackson. Although the company may be most famous for selling the government $640 toilet seats, such trivial transactions are nothing for the most powerful weapons contractor in the world. Tim Weiner, the *New York Times*'s crack reporter on the defense beat, sketched out the breadth of Lockheed's ties with the government:

> Lockheed Martin doesn't run the United States. But it does help run a breathtakingly big part of it. Over the last decade, Lockheed, the nation's largest military contractor, has built a formidable information-technology empire that now stretches from the Pentagon to the post office. It sorts your mail and totals your taxes. It cuts Social Security checks and counts the United States census. It runs space flights and monitors air traffic. To make all that happen, Lockheed writes more computer code than Microsoft. . . . It creates rockets for nuclear missiles, sensors for spy satellites and scores of other military and intelligence systems. The Pentagon and the Central Intelligence Agency might have difficulty functioning without the contractor's expertise. But in the post-9/11 world, Lockheed has become more than just the biggest corporate cog in what Dwight D. Eisenhower called the military-industrial complex. It is increasingly putting its stamp on the nation's military policies, too. . . . "It's impossible to tell where the government ends and Lockheed begins," said Danielle Brian of the Project on Government Oversight, a nonprofit group in Washington that monitors government contracts. "The fox isn't guarding the henhouse. He lives there." (Weiner 2004)

In 2005, Lockheed Martin earned $37.2 billion. A mere 2 percent of its revenue came from sales to the private sector. Another 13 percent of its sales came from foreign governments, mostly close military allies to the United States, such as Israel, Saudi Arabia, South Korea, and Chile. Here again, influence with the U.S. government pays healthy dividends. As Bob Elrod, a senior executive in Lockheed's fighter plane division, explained, all of these foreign sales are guaranteed by the U.S. government (St. Clair 2005, 150).

The U.S. government awarded many of its contracts to Lockheed without even requiring that company to make a competitive bid on them. In fact, Lockheed won 74 percent of its $94 billion in Pentagon contracts for the fiscal years 1998 to 2003 without competition (Makinson 2004).

Although money flows freely from the government to Lockheed, little returns back to the government. The company paid an effective 2002 tax rate of a mere 7.7 percent in 2002. Although Lockheed Martin may be stingy about the taxes it pays, the company is quite magnanimous with its political donations, giving more than $2.2 million in that same year.

The massive privatization of the military, along with the extensive revolving door in which personnel move back and forth between private industry and the Pentagon, is rapidly changing the nature of the military-industrial complex. One author counted 16 current and past Lockheed executives and directors in the George W. Bush administration (Juhasz 2006, 102).

The Pentagon seems to be morphing into a branch office for Lockheed and the other leading defense contractors, while these companies seem to function as a virtual retirement home for people who leave powerful positions in the Defense Department. Symbolic of this symbiosis of government and the defense contractors, Lockheed moved its headquarters to a suburb of Washington.

Bruce Jackson was an ideal representative for Lockheed Martin, a company that has applied political influence so handsomely. For example, Jackson played a leading role in many organizations that lobbied for increased military spending. He served on the board of the Center for Security Policy, run by Frank Gaffney, another former Reagan Pentagon official, once described as "the heart and soul of the missile defense lobby" (Hartung and Ciarrocca 2000). Jackson was a founder, along with William Kristol, Irving's son, and Robert Kagan, of the Project for a New American Century, often credited with designing the foreign policy of the George W. Bush administration, including the war on Iraq (Hartung and Ciarrocca 2000).

A *New York Times* article described Jackson's exploits as director of the U.S. Committee to Expand NATO during the run-up to the 1998 U.S. Senate vote to ratify the inclusion of Poland, Hungary, and the Czech Republic into the North Atlantic Treaty Organization (NATO), "At night, Bruce L. Jackson is president of the U.S. Committee to Expand NATO, giving intimate dinners for Senators and foreign officials. By day, he is director of strategic planning for Lockheed Martin Corporation, the world's biggest weapons maker. Mr. Jackson says he keeps his two identities separate, but his company and his lobbying group are fighting the same battle. Defense contractors are acting like globe-hopping diplomats to encourage the expansion of NATO, which will create a huge market for their wares" (Gerth and Weiner 1997).

Jackson put so much energy into this project because the expansion of NATO meant building a much larger client base for Lockheed Martin weapons. According to the *New York Times*, "Billions of dollars are at stake in the next global arms bazaar: weapons sales to Central European nations invited to join the North Atlantic Treaty Organization. Admission to the Western fraternity will bring political prestige, but at a price: playing by NATO rules, which require Western weapons and equipment" (Gerth and Weiner 1997).

Lockheed's reach extends far beyond NATO, "Lockheed now sells aircraft and weapons to more than 40 countries. The American taxpayer is financing many of those sales. For example, Israel spends much of the $1.8 billion in annual military aid from the United States to buy F-16 warplanes from Lockheed. Twenty-four nations are flying the F-16, or will be soon. Lockheed's factory in Fort Worth is building ten for Chile. Oman will receive a dozen next year. Poland will get 48 in 2006; the United States Treasury will cover the cost through a $3.8 billion loan" (Weiner 2001).

The more weapons Lockheed sells abroad, the more convincing the demands for greater domestic military weapons sound, especially after former allies appear more threatening. In short, Lockheed helps the Pentagon engage in an arms race with itself.

Jackson also operated on a more direct political level. He was co-chairman of the national finance committee for Senator Dole's presidential campaign in 1995–96. In 1996 and again in 2000, he was a delegate to the Republican National Convention, where he served on the Platform Committee and the Platform's subcommittee for National Security and Foreign Policy. In 2000, Jackson served as Chairman for the subcommittee. He bragged at an industry conference in 1999 that he would be in a position to "write the Republican platform" on defense if Bush gets the nomination (Hartung and Ciarrocca 2000). Jeffery St. Clair commented, "Naturally, the platform statement ended up reading like a catalogue of Lockheed weapons systems. At the top of the list, the RNC platform pledged to revive and make operational the $80 billion Missile Defense program supervised by Lockheed" (St. Clair 2005, 154–55).

In 2002, the Bush administration called on Jackson to set up the Committee for the Liberation of Iraq. "People in the White House said, 'We need you to do for Iraq what you did for NATO,'" Jackson said in a phone interview (Judis 2003). Jackson succeeded in rounding up ten East European governments to support a tough line on Saddam Hussein. According to some reports, he even drafted their statement.

Jackson is certainly not the only influence peddler for the military-industrial complex. His career does serve to symbolize the process of creating public policy behind the scenes in a way that starves needed parts of society while heaping riches on military contractors and those who serve them.

Of course, Lockheed's influence did not suddenly blossom with the appearance of Bruce Jackson. One of its early patrons was Richard Russell of Georgia, who was so respected by his peers that the Senate named its office building after him. Russell was legendary in his ability to use his lengthy chairmanship of the Senate Armed Services Committee to bring government spending into his district.

In August 1965 while the Vietnam War was raging, Russell began making sounds like an antiwar protester. He told a national television audience during a Meet the Press interview that if an election were held, Vietnam would certainly elect Ho Chi Minh as its president. He lectured the Senate: "Whenever the people go to calling their leader 'Uncle,' you better watch out. . . . They have a man in whom they have explicit confidence, you are dealing with a very dangerous enemy." By November, Lockheed's plant in Marietta, Georgia won a huge contract for the monstrous C5–A transport planes (Fite 1991, 443–45; Goldsmith 1993, 138).

After the award of the contract, Russell's public doubts about the war suddenly evaporated. The Russell episode is a reminder that not everything changed with the right-wing takeover—that in many respects the change was a matter of degree, although the degree is extreme enough to be alarming.

Enter the Neoconservatives

The agenda of the neoconservative movement, which originally grew out of the hawkish military-Keynesian wing of the Democratic Party, meshes comfortably with that of the defense contractors. The momentum of the right-wing revolution provided space for the neoconservatives to flourish. They proved to be adept in bureaucratic maneuvering, gaining traction within the halls of government, usually away from the public eye. Their relative obscurity was an advantage because their policies would not have been particularly popular with the public.

Prior to the election of George W. Bush in 2000, the views of those few neoconservatives who served in more prominent positions did not seem to be too far out of line with the times. With the end of the Soviet Union the neoconservatives became more vocal about pushing their agenda of total U.S. military dominance, especially in the Middle East. Only with the Bush administration did the public begin to realize what the neoconservative agenda meant. Certainly, their push for a second war against Iraq had little public enthusiasm, despite a full throttle propaganda campaign for the war largely based on falsehoods and deception.

The casualties of this war will go beyond the many young soldiers and the countless Iraqis whose lives this war has destroyed. Business will also pay a price in the end, over and above the obscene direct economic costs of the war. Coming on top of the nonstop series of tax cuts, the Iraq war is creating a fiscal imbalance that is certain to create substantial economic damage.

The neoconservatives, however, could not have amassed the power that they wielded without the momentum created by the business offensive. For example, a more aggressive media might have prevented the disaster in Iraq.

After business-funded think tanks stifled critical voices, the corporate press rarely dared to question authority, including the government's blatant misinformation about Iraq. Journalists knew where to find alternative analysis, but they did not dare publish such information.

Although the defense industry certainly has reason to appreciate the influence of the neoconservatives, intelligent business leaders must have understood that the aggressive neoconservative unilateralism poses serious risks for the corporate sector as well as the country. In light of a cornucopia of generous government largesse, business dared not protest.

De-Globalization

Most corporate leaders understand that the U.S. economy is closely bound up with the rest of the world. American corporations depend upon the global economy for markets, raw materials, and even the production of many of the products that they sell or use as inputs.

Parts of the world that had previously worked closely with the United States for decades now increasingly see the United States as a threat to world stability. Will they be as receptive to U.S. business in the future? What about the companies, such as the entertainment industry, whose exports depend upon an admiration of U.S. culture? At the time of this writing, sales of once popular U.S.

brands seem to be declining in reaction to aggressive U.S. policies, even though a declining dollar should be making these goods more affordable (Benoit, Roberts, Silverman, and Thornhill 2004).

Even scientists themselves may be caught up in nationalist fervor following the September 11 attack. For example, an analysis in the *British Medical Journal* of five of the leading scientific journals in the United States—*Journal of the American Medical Association, New England Journal of Medicine, Lancet, The British Medical Journal, Nature,* and *Science*—found that these journals published far fewer French authors following the decision by the French government not to endorse the invasion of Iraq (Bégaud and Verdoux 2004).

In Seattle in February 1999, massive protests against globalization made headlines around the world. Although the protests were fully justified, the word "globalization" was not. What angered the protesters was not globalization, but rather the dogmatic imposition around the world of the same sort of right-wing policies that already threaten prosperity in the United States.

Although the United States is not the only wealthy country insisting that other countries adhere to the narrow, destructive form of globalization that infuriated the protesters in Seattle, the version of globalization that the United States prefers is the most extreme. A proper understanding of globalization would welcome a free international exchange of ideas and information rather than a flood of advertisements for American commodities. A proper globalization would not preclude the social provision of education, health care, or water.

The present tendency toward what de-globalization—cutting the country off from so much of the creativity of the rest of the world—is a dangerous move that will benefit few, but will hurt the United States most of all. The corporate sector recognized the danger of de-globalization insofar as government policies were making the United States a less attractive venue for students. But, for the most part, the corporate sector has been relatively silent about the dangers of de-globalization.

Chapter 11

How Things Fall Apart

Earlier Right-Wing Revolutions

No country in the world has ever developed on the basis of *laissez-faire*. The United States is no exception. Government has always played a central role in the development of the U.S. economy. In the few times that the government has lurched in the direction of *laissez-faire*, serious economic depressions have soon followed.

The first brush with a more thoroughgoing reliance on market control came during the presidency of Andrew Jackson. As was the case in the late twentieth century, the Jacksonian movement rebelled against the presumed elitist character of John Quincy Adam's administration.

The rising entrepreneurial class, which lacked the political connections to profit from lucrative corporation charters, represented one of the largest constituencies behind the Jacksonian movement. One writer astutely characterized the Jacksonian period as "the democracy of expectant capitalists" (Simons 1925, 210). Another long-time employee of the Federal Reserve who was an expert on this period offered a description of the leaders of the Jacksonian movement that sounds quite modern, "People were led as they had not been before by visions of money-making. Liberty became transformed into *laissez faire*. A violent, aggressive, economic individualism became established. . . . It opened economic advantages to those who had not previously had them; yet it allowed wealth to be concentrated in new hands only somewhat more numerous than before, less responsible, and less disciplined" (Hammond 1957, 327).

The leaders of the Jacksonian era abolished the Bank of the United States to allow for an unregulated banking system. They severely limited the federal provision of public works, although the states continued to be actively involved. Nonetheless, the Jacksonians were not dogmatic advocates of *laissez-faire*. Many of them just wanted to get rich. In this spirit, they attacked whatever inconvenienced them in this endeavor. As a result, the erection of higher tariff barriers to protect the emerging industrial structure did not necessarily offend their principles. Nor did the brutal relocation of Native Americans or the extension of slavery seem to trouble them unduly. Fate rewarded the efforts of the Jacksonians with the most severe depression that the country had ever known.

The late nineteenth century witnessed an even stronger depression. This time, the economic conditions rather than the politics bore an even closer resemblance to the contemporary United States. Not long after the boom of the Civil War and the greatest revolution in technology that the country had ever seen, a select few people, known as robber barons, had accumulated enormous wealth at the expense of the public at large. Mark Twain appropriately dubbed the period the Gilded Age on account of the great inequities of the time— grandiose fortunes alongside a broad swath of poverty. Unlike the Golden Age, the prosperity of the Gilded Age was superficial.

The economy was severely out of balance. The purchasing power of the poor was insufficient to keep the factories of the rich busy. Cutthroat competition ravaged business, ending in a brutal depression. To recover, *laissez-faire* was cast aside as business formed cartels, trusts, and monopolies. World War I temporarily brought both a system of national planning, soaring demand, and greater equality (Perelman 2006).

By the 1920s, business had quickly regained control. As the earlier discussion of the utility industry suggested, the methods foreshadowed the current right-wing revolution, with Bolsheviks playing the role now assigned to Muslim terrorists. The result was the devastation of the Great Depression of the 1930s.

The current right-wing revolution, however, is by no means enthusiastic about free markets and *laissez-faire*. After all, providing pork to its contributors is a central part of its strategy. Instead, the right wing is intent upon changing government to make it almost entirely responsive to the needs of its base.

The government is hell-bent on enacting policies that put enormous pressures on the economic system in order to pump as much immediate profit as possible to the giant corporations and the superrich. In doing so, the right-wing revolution is setting off speculative impulses comparable to that of a pure *laissez-faire* regime, except that the government will try to bail out the giant corporations that fall by the wayside.

In short, the current policy mix is even more risky than either a strict *laissez-faire* approach or a more regulated system. It lacks the controls that might help steer the economy away from more serious dangers, as well as the efficiencies that might come from a system that depended less on government largesse. In such a climate business will be less able to respond to challenges.

Taking Stock of the Revolution

The traditions of the old South were central to the right-wing revolution. Recall how Lewis Powell harkened back to the genteel customs of the South. Richard Nixon's Southern Strategy was a key political tactic in the revolution. In this sense, the revolution was a stunning success because the economy of the United States is coming to resemble the old South.

Ironically, the Southern economy remained backward until New Deal regulations began to integrate it into the larger economy. Southerners, like Richard Russell, developed an expertise in winning defense contracts. Northern factories fleeing to the South promoted a belated modernization. Even so, almost a century and a half after the abolition of slavery, the South as a whole still has not caught up with the more advanced parts of the nation.

In saying that the United States is coming to have some of the earmarks of the old South, I don't mean to suggest that slavery has returned, even though the heavy reliance on undocumented labor occasionally bears a resemblance to slavery. Rather, the sharp divisions of the new economy have a distinctly Southern flavor. Just as the resentment of the slaves sabotaged productivity, the ill treatment of workers restricts productivity. In addition, the current emphasis on holding down wages discourages the introduction of more productive technology, just as it did in the old South. Finally, the recent emulation of the old South, with continual recourse to antagonism toward various elements of society, whether ethnic, racial, or cultural, does little to further economic progress.

A united society produces a stronger economy. Fear, of course, can unite society when it is directed toward a common enemy as happens during wars. Indeed, World War II united virtually all of the United States. For example, wartime necessity gave blacks more opportunity both in the military and in industry. The same Robert Lucas who praised inequality estimated the average level of wartime economic efficiency for the U.S. economy by calculating the trend of the ratio of output per unit of capital between 1890 and 1954. Lucas discovered that during the war years, 1944 through 1946, the output per unit of capital surpassed the trend line by more than 20 percent. At no time, before or after, did the U.S. economy ever match this remarkable performance (Lucas 1970, 154). The British wartime economy also exceeded expectations (Kaldor and Barna 1941, 263).

This spurt of productivity occurred even though the government was ill-prepared to convert to a wartime economy in which the military absorbed half the output. To make matters more difficult, business faced a confusing system of controls and the government was fitfully shifting its organizational structure throughout the war (Kostinen 2004).

Incidentally, this spurt of labor productivity occurred even though the monetary incentives for hard work, which conservatives consider to be the prime motivator of humanity, were not particularly strong. After all, real after-tax wages were lower than either before or after the war (Mulligan 1998).

Admittedly, overtime was a factor in boosting productivity, but I suspect a sense of shared purpose that came during the war was even more important. The dangers of wartime ignite a sense of urgency that allows a mobilization of resources that neither market forces nor the ordinary rhythms of traditional society can harness. Some of the largely destructive energy that war unleashes moves into positive channels. For example, wartime emergencies often encourage technological innovations, some of which turn out later to be useful for the civilian sector, although this phenomenon is far weaker today.

Finally, war often creates progressive social improvements. In effect, the need to mobilize public support for battle frequently makes rulers declare a truce in their class war. Finally, by destroying old and obsolete equipment, war encourages the erection of more productive plant and equipment.

Almost a century ago, the philosopher, William James, gave a famous lecture entitled "The Moral Equivalent of War," in which he suggested:

So far, war has been the only force that can discipline a whole community, and until an equivalent discipline is organized, I believe that war must have its way. But I have no serious doubt that the ordinary prides and shames of social man, once developed to a certain intensity, are capable of organizing such a moral equivalent as I have sketched, or some other just as effective for preserving manliness of type. It is but a question of time, of skillful propagandism, and of opinion-making men seizing historic opportunities. . . .

The martial type of character can be bred without war. Strenuous honor and disinterestedness abound everywhere. Priests and medical men are in a fashion educated to it, and we should all feel some degree of its imperative if we were conscious of our work as an obligatory service to the state. (James 1911, 292–93)

In 1977, in the midst of the oil shock, President Jimmy Carter, who had been quite popular up until that time, picked up James's theme in a televised speech on April 18: "Tonight I want to have an unpleasant talk with you about a problem unprecedented in our history. With the exception of preventing war, this is the greatest challenge our country will face during our lifetimes. The energy crisis has not yet overwhelmed us, but it will if we do not act quickly. It is a problem we will not solve in the next few years, and it is likely to get progressively worse through the rest of this century. . . . This difficult effort will be the 'moral equivalent of war'—except that we will be uniting our efforts to build and not destroy."

Following this speech, Carter's popularity plummeted, leaving him irrevocably branded as weak and indecisive. This reaction sealed his fate and opened the floodgates to the right-wing revolution. Yet, Carter and James were on the right track. They certainly posed the correct question: Why in the world do advanced societies require the spur of war in order to mobilize people and resources to accomplish their goals?

I don't pretend to have all the answers, but I can say with confidence that the right-wing tactic of emphasizing wedge issues to divide society makes social progress more difficult. The absence of regulation and the crippling of social programs compound the problems.

Now I want to turn to the reasons for the silence of economics on such matters.

Part 4

The Impotence of Economics

Chapter 12

Taming Economists

Madmen in Authority

John Maynard Keynes once recalled an encounter with Max Planck, an originator of quantum theory. Planck told Keynes that he had considered studying economics when he was young, but he found the subject too difficult (Keynes 1924, fn 186). How in the world could Professor Planck, whose work rivaled that of Albert Einstein, be intimidated by the study of economics? Keynes himself suggested an answer to that question in a letter to a fellow economist: "Economics is a science of thinking in terms of models joined to the art of choosing models which are relevant to the contemporary world. It is compelled to be this, because, unlike the typical natural science, the material to which it is applied is, in too many respects, not homogeneous through time" (Keynes 1938, 296).

Keynes's explanation is very sophisticated considering its brevity. On the simplest level, he is saying that economies, like life itself, are in a constant state of flux. In contrast, physical processes operate the same way from year-to-year. Dropped apples invariably fall toward the earth. Nobody expects them to somehow float toward the sky like a helium balloon.

Keynes could have added that economies, like people, are far too complex to reduce to laboratory experiments, despite recent technological advances in monitoring brain activity. As a result, we economists lack the ability to come to a scientific consensus. What consensus does appear owes far more to conformity than to any objective standard.

Although economists largely agree about basic issues, they have strong disputes about secondary matters. For example, I can think of more than a dozen explanations for the Great Depression, all of which have the support of some well-respected economists.

Most of these explanations have a grain of truth, but again economic processes are far too complex to reduce to simple, one-dimensional explanations. But the simplified models to which Keynes referred are of little use in sorting out the relative importance of the various causes.

Finally, many economists do not behave like dispassionate scientists; instead, they tend to have strongly held social, political, and economic beliefs that permeate their analysis. Economists rarely acknowledge their pervasive biases in their ways of looking at the world; instead, they pride themselves in following a scientific discipline that allows them to remain above crass self-interest.

This stance is particularly ironic because economic theory is the study of self-interested behavior. So here are the economists adopting an Olympian pose in which the rest of the world behaves according to its own self-interest, while the economists alone remain aloof from personal considerations in their unvarnished quest for the truth. George Stigler, a very conservative, Nobel Prize–winning economist was one of the very few to take note of this pretension, observing that "economists do not relish an explanation of their own scientific behavior in ordinary economic terms. To tell an economist that he chooses that type of work and viewpoint which will maximize his income is, he will hotly say, is [sic] a studied insult" (Stigler 1982, 60).

Economists may claim that their work is objective, but all too often objectivity consists in merely repeating the mantra that market forces are the solution. This attitude leaves no place for a Keynes-like appreciation of the complexity of economic processes.

According to the prevailing economic pseudoscience, free markets are expected to be the exclusive answer to any conceivable problem. Imagine a health care system in which every doctor was rigidly trained to diagnose every ailment as a cold. No matter that the patient has a broken leg, cancer, or even a knife stuck in his back—the diagnosis is still a cold. More and more, economists are behaving as if they were no better than these imaginary doctors.

The prescription for every problem is the removal of excessive interference with market forces, which prevents the system from working properly. Market forces, left to themselves, are supposedly capable of treating poverty, pollution, and every other problem in society.

OK, I overstate the problem, but not entirely. Economists may vehemently disagree about some small points. For example, what passes as leftist analysis within the world of academic economics is typically the idea that some minor tweak in the market is required for optimal performance. Insofar as larger issues are concerned, the economics profession is almost unanimous. Open dialogue is the exception rather than the rule among economists. Today, after decades of systematically removing critical voices, right-wing censorship is no longer necessary.

Despite the narrow ideological perspective, economists' dogma has significant influence on the course of political events. In a famous passage Keynes wrote, "Practical men, who believe themselves to be quite exempt from any intellectual influences, are usually the slaves of some defunct economist. Madmen in authority, who hear voices in the air, are distilling their frenzy from some academic scribbler of a few years back. I am sure that the power of vested interests is vastly exaggerated compared with the gradual encroachment of ideas. Not, indeed, immediately, but after a certain interval" (Keynes 1936, 383).

Keynes, having been born into the highest reaches of English academic life, never gave any indication that "madmen in authority" could exert significant influence on an "academic scribbler," let alone an eminent economist with a pedigree as distinguished as his own. In the United States, economic and political pressure has long been a determining factor in the way economics is taught.

In fact, for most of the history of the country, little effort has been required to ensure that academic economists behave according to the wishes of the "madmen in authority."

Economists and *Laissez-Faire*

From the dawn of higher education in the United States, conservative interests have exercised enormous power over academic economics. Before the Civil War, academic economics religiously followed the orthodoxy of *laissez-faire* and free trade. This perspective might have seemed ironic since the country did not actually practice *laissez-faire*. For example, the government largely financed the canals and railroads and protected industry with high tariffs.

At the time, however, colleges in the United States had a strong financial motive for teaching *laissez-faire*. Prior to 1860, colleges were largely religious institutions that depended heavily on merchants for their funding. Unlike the manufacturers, who favored protection for their industries, the merchants were firm believers in free trade.

Typically, economics was taught as part of the course on moral philosophy. The president of the college, usually a member of the clergy, would teach these courses to ensure that the content would satisfy the local merchants. The merchants, in turn, were expected to express their gratitude in the form of generous donations (see O'Connor 1944).

The late 1870s marked a radical transition in the U.S. economy with numerous, widespread, and violent strikes, destructive competition, growth of cartels and large enterprises, economic depression, and a growing awareness of poverty and destitution, especially in rapidly growing cities.

Students from the United States flocked to Germany, which then had the finest university system in the world. Germany had been slowly and painfully built up out of a hodge-podge of independent and semi-independent German states. The path to unification was slow. As late as 1792, about 1,000 states existed with 300–400 fully independent units. Twenty-five years later a little over thirty still remained. Germany only reached full unification by 1871.

Because of the great diversity among these once-independent states, German economists paid close attention to the way different institutions and customs affected the economy. Despite the obvious difficulties in piecing together the numerous mini-states, the German state successfully used education to jumpstart the country, which had historically been a European backwater, into one of the leading economies of the world.

German economics reflected the German economic experience. There, students learned a very different type of economics, which made them skeptical about the sort of abstract theorizing, which was the core of academic economics in the Anglo-Saxon world.

When these young, German-trained economists returned to the United States, they chafed under the dogma of *laissez-faire*. Instead, they embraced the emerging Germanic historical approach, which tried to understand economies in terms of their unique conditions, rather than attempt to develop an abstract theory that was supposed to fit every situation.

Their German experience also taught these young economists how the state could actively promote economic growth. The revolutionary role of the railroads in the United States emphatically confirmed the effectiveness of state action. Many of these economists were also attracted to the Social Gospel, which taught that the market economy should try to uplift people and relieve their poverty. Some were even sympathetic to a mild form of socialism.

Led by Richard T. Ely, whom Schumpeter once called "that excellent German professor in American skin" (Schumpeter 1954, note 874), a small core of 50 economists in 1885 founded the American Economic Association.

In the spirit of his German training, Ely called for the abandonment of "the dry bones of orthodox English political economy for the live methods of the German school" (Ely 1883, 235; Ely 1884, 64). When Ely drafted his first statement of principles for the new organization, it read: "We regard the state as an agency whose positive assistance is one of the indispensable conditions of human progress" (Ely 1936, 144).

The American Economic Association eventually grew to become the dominant professional association for economists in the United States. As many as 15,000 economists now attend their annual conventions. Although the highlight of the annual meetings of the American Economic Association is the Richard T. Ely address, in recent decades the subject and substance runs directly against the ideals that Ely had advocated. Just recall Welch's advocacy of inequality.

Despite their superior training, the academic world was unreceptive to these young, German-trained economists with their skepticism of *laissez-faire*. Many of the founders of the American Economic Association learned that the administrators of colleges and universities would not tolerate any deviations from orthodoxy, especially at a time when labor had embarked on a militant challenge of the status quo. As Francis A. Walker, one of the very few established economists who sympathized with the younger generation, wrote that *laissez-faire* "was not made the test of economic orthodoxy merely. It was used to decide if a man were an economist at all" (Walker 1889, 26).

Ely should have been relatively safe, since he landed in Johns Hopkins, a university uniquely modeled on the German system. Even there, conservatives launched a violent attack on him. After failing to win a promotion, Ely moved on to the University of Wisconsin. Again, he experienced repeated attacks by conservatives, although a trial before the Board of Regents eventually vindicated him. Even so, he soon retreated to Northwestern (Ely 1938, 174–78, 218–33).

Some less fortunate economists were hounded out of academic life altogether. After more than a century of repeated purges and careful selection of safe candidates, on almost any campus around the country the economics department is among the most conservative. Professor Fred Lee of the University of Missouri, Kansas City has compiled an extensive dossier of the numerous cases in which professors lost their job, but much of the effect of this repression necessarily falls from view. How can anybody account for the many professors, who seeing the fate of those economists who voiced progressive views, quickly fell into line. Nor can anybody calculate the number of young academics whose job applications were rejected out of hand because of their progressive leanings.

New Business Influence

Gradually, as manufacturing became a greater force than merchant activities, the dogma of *laissez-faire* receded in importance. At the same time, the American Economic Association gradually became relatively disinterested in social reform. For example, the organization even offered a platform to F. C. S. Schwedtman, vice president of National City Bank of New York and secretary of the National Association of Manufacturers, to deliver "a carefully prepared address before the joint session of the American Association for Labor Legislation and the American Economic Association at the St. Louis meeting in 1910, and after the address endeavored to indoctrinate a number of college professors with his views" (P. Wright 1915, 243).

The rise of manufacturing also changed the justification of higher education, which to a large extent had previously been a place to provide some polish and refinement to the children of the affluent. Business began to see universities as an engine of economic progress. For example, the historian, David Noble, detailed how the early growth and development of the Massachusetts Institute of Technology harnessed the faculty to serve the needs of science and industry (Noble 1979). These corporate ties generally persisted, while some of the more applied programs, such as engineering, became more academic.

Not everybody applauded this transformation of education. Based on his discouraging experience at the University of Chicago, Thorstein Veblen, probably the most important U.S. economist of the time, published *The Higher Learning in America: Memorandum on the Conduct of Universities by Business Men* to protest the degree to which business interests dominated the academic world (Veblen 1918). Veblen, however, was swimming against the tide, but then he made a career of swimming against the tide. He even claimed that his original subtitle was *A Study in Total Depravity.*

By the 1920s, business won unprecedented powers over society. In 1925, Calvin Coolidge summed up the temper of the times while addressing the American Society of Newspaper Editors with a speech that he entitled "The Press Under a Free Government." According to the president, "After all, the chief business of the American people is business." According to an influential history book, "So profoundly pro-business was the national temper and so successful were business efforts in keeping the favor of the public, that other groups might combine, publish, speak, and vote, and still industrial business could assert itself above all competitors for public favor . . . business associations were so powerful in the twenties that none of these groups could withstand them. Business had, [Roger Babson, a famous investment advisor and founder of Babson College] said, 'the press, the pulpit and the schools'" (Cochran and Miller 1942, 343–44).

By 1930 businessmen, bankers, and lawyers, who were often engaged in corporate law or who sat on corporate boards, controlled from two-thirds to three-quarters of all positions on university governing boards (Barrow 1990, 33–34).

Despite the conservative, probusiness temper of the times, on some issues the public still opposed commercial interests. The corporate takeover of the generation of electricity offers an instructive example. During the early part of the twentieth century, the demand for electricity was increasing by leaps and bounds.

Business recognized the huge profit potential of the electricity market, but in 1912 a third of the power companies in the United States were publicly owned, and most generated their own electricity. These public operations provided reliable and inexpensive power because they focused on service rather than profits. The private power companies used unscrupulous methods both to swallow one another and even more to replace public power providers. Insofar as the latter goal was concerned, the private power companies went to great lengths to change public opinion. When they failed to sway the public, as was generally the case, they resorted to less savory techniques, such as bribery, to make sure that public officials and regulators behaved obediently (Beder 2003, 23–24).

At the time, the private power industry spoke nonchalantly about the ease of buying the services of college professors, knowing full well that business pressure had already led to the purging of many of those who opposed the industry's practices. For example, M. H. Aylesworth, the managing director of the industry trade association, the National Electric Light Association (NELA), "issued an exuberant advisory directive to member utilities in a 1923 speech that became part of Federal Trade Commission investigation records. What it lacked in subtlety, it possessed in explicit counsel on how to buy an educator":

> I would advise any manager who lives in a community where there is a college to get the professor of economics—the engineering professor will be interested anyway—interested in our problems. Have him lecture on your subject to his classes. Once in a while it will pay you to take such men and give them a retainer of one or two hundred dollars per year for the privilege of letting you study and consult with them. For how in heaven's name can we do anything in the schools of this country with the young people growing up, if we have not first sold the idea of education to the college professor? (Rogers 1972, 71–72)

The multifaceted Reverend Dr. Charles Aubrey Eaton, a New Jersey congressman, who also happened to be a manager of the industrial relations department of the General Electric Company, recognized that teaching in college was one of the "starveling professions" (Rogers 1972, 72). The reverend counseled the industry:

> Here is a professor in a college, who gets $2,500 a year and has to spend $3,000 to keep from starving to death, who walks up to his classroom in an old pair of shoes and some idiot of a boy drives up and parks a $5,000 automobile outside and comes in and gets plucked. Then because that professor teaches that boy that there is something wrong with the social system, we call him a Bolshevik and throw him out.
>
> What I would like to suggest to you intelligent gentlemen is that while you are dealing with the pupils, give a thought to the teachers and when their vacation comes, pay them a salary to come into your plants and into your factories and learn the public utility business at first hand, and then they will go back, and you needn't fuss—they can teach better than you can. (Rogers 1972, 72–73)

Had professors at the time been more committed to intellectual integrity, I doubt that the industrial leaders would have spoken so casually about purchasing their services. Indeed, much of the academic community behaved compliantly to express its gratitude for the funds that the private power industry was generously spreading around. The industry also managed to purge public school textbooks that were not to its liking (Rogers 1972, 72–80; Beder 2003, chap. 2).

Some scholars even went so far to please their benefactors as to publish false data to lend support to the industry's claims (Rogers 1972, 77–78). This disregard for the truth might not be surprising. After all, Samuel Insull, the leading utility executive and head of the industry trade organization, modeled his propaganda campaign on the work of Phineas T. Barnum, whom Insull once personally consulted (Beder 2003, 38).

Barnum, you might recall was the showman famous for the quotation, "There's a sucker born every minute." Although the words were from one of Barnum's rivals, that statement certainly caught the spirit of Barnum's career. Through indoctrination by way of extensive public relations campaigns and influence over education, the industry eventually managed to successfully equate public ownership of utilities with Bolshevism in the public mind.

Insull took the lead in pursuing another tactic to make the public more accepting of private power companies: he promoted the idea of government utility regulation. Why would business take such a stand? Throughout this book, I have noted modern business's almost fanatical opposition to regulation.

Historically, however, business's attitude toward regulation was much friendlier. Business had commonly promoted regulation both as a way of protecting itself from market forces and to deflect the public's anger about business practices. Recall how a few decades earlier, business had welcomed the Interstate Commerce Commission because regulation could defuse popular antagonism toward the power companies. In the case of the utilities, Insull hoped that the public again might expect that regulators would prevent the utilities from engaging in abusive behaviors (Beder 2003, 27).

Of course, the industry knew that nothing of the kind would occur. The regulators would not earn high salaries, making them every bit as vulnerable as the "starveling" college professors. In addition, the business leaders realized that regulation could prevent competitors from entering into the industry, protecting their monopolistic positions.

Decades later, after the popular support for public power had receded into the distant past, the country embarked on a process of deregulation of the public utilities—with disastrous consequences. Relatively few economists raised their voice in protest.

The New and Improved Richard T. Ely

Despite the intensive efforts to snuff out all matter of dissent, "Disquieting reports of articles in economics journals that 'stirred up some of the members of the association,' suggested that not all the university research was laundered to the satisfaction of the subsidizers" (Rogers 1972, 77).

At this point, Richard T. Ely enters into the picture once again, illustrating how thoroughly business influence had corrupted the ivory towers. Martin G. Glaeser, economics professor at Wisconsin State University, had written a book called *The Outlines of Public Utility Economics*, only to find that the Institute for Land Research and Public Utility Economics at Northwestern University, which paid part of his salary, was receiving generous contributions from many utility corporations.

The founder of this institute was none other than Richard T. Ely, who still served as director. Glaeser thought, as he later testified before the Federal Trade Commission, that only the National Electric Light Association and a single Milwaukee light company had put up money for his research. Professor Glaeser, with some indignation, rejected Ely's suggestion that Glaeser share authorship with a public utility official. Glaeser also turned down a guaranteed purchase order from the NELA of as many as 40,000 copies, with proceeds to go to the Institute (Rogers 1972, 80). The intervention of the utility companies was extraordinary:

> With the book in galleys at the Macmillan Company in New York, Professor Glaeser was distressed to receive, in advance of publication, criticism of his work from the NELA Educational Committee. In fact, the association's publicity director, of all people, asked that parts of the introduction be eliminated. . . . Although piqued that proofs had somehow reached alien hands, Professor Glaeser agreed to drop one paragraph, written by Dr. Ely, because he said he never liked that section of the introduction anyway. He said he made other amendments, too, as requested by utility officials, but only those he thought valid. The utilities liked the revised book very much and launched a movement to get it distributed to all the high school principals in Missouri, for a start. (Rogers 1972, 80)

Although Glaeser was a mild critic of the power companies, he knew from the start that the private power industry was partially subsidizing his work. Once published, the utilities distributed it widely to prepare themselves for meeting its criticism.

Ely's role is of interest as well. Here was an economist who once appeared to represent the cutting edge of academic economic radicalism, who even earlier expressed strong fears about the ability of the giant corporations to dominate the economy (Hawkins 1960, 179). Also, Ely had long been a proponent of public power.

Despite these progressive sentiments, Ely was far from radical even in his early years. He denounced Marxist socialism as "a pseudo-scientific presentation . . . full of revolting crudities." Instead, he favored what he called "all-classes socialism," which, not surprisingly, resembled the German society of the time (Ely 1894, 14, 179).

Although Ely repeatedly expressed justifiable fears about the likelihood of being run out of his job (Hawkins 1960, 181), by this time Ely had little to fear, so considerations of job security cannot account for his transformation.

Ely used personal prejudice to explain his change of heart. According to his own account of his conversion, public ownership had been economical in Germany and in the upstate New York where he grew up because of the character of the people, implying that the majority of people in the United States had become less capable because of the waves of immigration (Ely 1938, 260). Writing during a time when the eugenic movement was strong, Ely proposed that the "most general statement possible is that the causes of poverty are hereditary and environmental, producing weak physical, mental and moral constitutions" (Ely 1891, 402; cited in Cherry 1976). Not surprisingly, Ely lumped together the cases of the "Jukes" and the "Tribe of Ishmael" (Ely 1891, 402–3; cited in Cherry 1976).

Ely vehemently denied that financial motives had anything to do with his change of heart, even though the utilities provided substantial funding for his Institute for Land Research and Public Utility Economics at Northwestern University (Ely 1938, 264). Instead, much like the business leaders of the 1970s, he expressed sympathy for the poor, downtrodden businessmen: "At the present time, however, big business has been cowed, and is in many cases an under dog [*sic*]. Big men in the business world are now often afraid to come forward boldly and assert their rights, even though they are undoubtedly at the same time in the social interest. The world has changed, and they are the true progressives who have changed their mind in this changing world" (Ely 1938, 263).

Still, in his autobiography, Ely also revealed how he relished working with the rich and powerful by this time. The allure of rubbing shoulders with the elites provides still another incentive for identifying with business.

Ely's trajectory is not that unusual. A young economist may begin with some progressive sympathies. Conditioned by the desire for job security and the temptation of corporate money, the economist soon falls into a conservative mode of thought and does his best to see that the next generation of economists follows his compromised example.

Chapter 13

Economists' Sins of Omission and Collaboration

Making Economics Safe and Irrelevant

The Great Depression temporarily disrupted the longstanding lovefest between business and academic economics. This catastrophe shook many economists' confidence in the market, just as it did for most of the population. Quite a few economists began to wonder how such a breakdown could have happened. Was the problem part and parcel of a market economy? Even so, the firing of economics professors for their ideas and pressure from legislatures continued. For example, in the late 1930s the Texas legislature attempted to make the University of Texas dismiss Robert Montgomery for advocating public ownership of power companies. Businessmen pressured the university to fire some other economists along with Montgomery. Finally, in 1942, the university dismissed or refused to rehire three junior faculty members for their political views.

The relative openness to new ideas during the Depression was temporary. By the time World War II ended and the cold war commenced, right-wing activism began in earnest once again, this time in the name of anticommunism. Recall the Keynesians retreat to military Keynesianism. Some universities began to require faculty to sign loyalty oaths. A few principled, liberal professors and even a handful of conservatives, refused, but most of the faculty went along with the requirement. Recall how these pressures even intimidated an economist of Paul Samuelson's stature.

In this environment of intimidation, economics departments became careful about whom they hired and how they taught the next generation of economists. By 1960, the attacks on radical academics finally ended, with a handful of exceptions, because nobody was left to attack (see Lee 2004).

During the 1960s, when protests briefly flourished, the Vietnam War was widely discrediting the government. With enrollments booming, universities hired a number of radicals. Their influence, however, was short-lived, except in fields such as literary criticism. With the growing success of the right-wing revolution, corporate pressure blanketed the universities, destroying any hope of critical influence emanating from the ivory tower.

In the academic world of today, the dean of the school of business at the University of California is now officially known as the BankAmerica Dean of the Haas School of Business. Professors occupy positions, such as "Bell South Professor of Education through Telecommunication at the University of South Carolina; McLamore/Burger King Chair at the University of Miami, McCoy-BancOne Corp Professor of Creativity and Innovation at Stanford University, John M. Olin Professor of Humanities at New York University, Olin Professor of Law and Economics at Yale Law School, Sears Roebuck Professor of Economics and Financial Services at the University of Chicago, Ronald Reagan Professor of Public Policy at Pepperdine University, James Baker III Institute for Public Policy at Rice University, Center for the Study of American Business at Washington University, Center for Corporate Community Relations at Boston College" (Draffan 2003, 11; Press and Washburn 2000, 41).

Something else, something less obvious, was at work within the economics profession. During World War II, many of the leading economists, both liberal and conservative, worked hand-in-hand with scientists and mathematicians on military projects. Some developed new techniques to help military planners, such as strategies for conducting nuclear war; others worked directly on military hardware, such as automated firing mechanisms to aid aircraft gunners.

Virtually all of these economists became enamored with the new techniques that they encountered during the war. When these economists returned to academia, they began to use these same techniques in building abstract models that purported to demonstrate how well a peacetime, market economy worked or could work with a few minor modifications. Many of the most influential articles during the early postwar period were merely sanitized versions of work that these economists had done earlier for the military. The military and the established foundations, such as Ford and Rockefeller, generously funded these abstract model-builders, much to the detriment of the relevance of economics (Amadae 2003; Mirowski 2001).

Soon, economists who could produce such sophisticated but unrealistic models of the economy began to displace those who studied difficult problems that real people faced. The models that were most likely to find favor among professional economists were those with elegant mathematical solutions.

Such elegance tends to require models that depict a world in which everything works smoothly and predictably; in other words, perfectly functioning markets have desirable mathematical properties. As this ridiculous quest for elegance at the expense of relevance proceeded, professional pressures pushed economists to neglect more than ever the sort of close observation of the actual functioning of the economy that might provide valuable insights.

Decades ago, when the right-wing revolution was first beginning to gain traction among economists and the premium on modeling became extreme, some leaders in the field protested this false scientism. For example, Wassily Leontief, an earlier Nobel Prize–winning economist, used his presidential address to the American Economic Association to warn: "Uncritical enthusiasm for mathematical formulation tends often to conceal the ephemeral substantive content of the argument behind the formidable front of algebraic signs" (Leontief 1971, 1–2).

Similarly, Frank Hahn, himself a highly respected modeler, observed in his presidential address to the Econometric Society:

> [T]he achievements of economic theory in the last two decades are both impressive and in many ways beautiful. But it cannot be denied that there is something scandalous in the spectacle of so many people refining the analysis of economic states which they give no reason to suppose will ever, or have ever, come about. . . .
>   It is an unsatisfactory and slightly dishonest state of affairs. (Hahn 1970, 1–2)

The habit of thinking in models even permeates economists' conversations. Robert Solow, a Nobel Prize–winning economist lamented: "Today, if you ask a mainstream economist a question about almost any aspect of economic life, the response will be: suppose we model that situation and see what happens" (Solow 1997, 43).

Young economists soon learn that success as an economist depends on publishing arcane articles. Engaging serious problems, especially if that exercise involves questioning market efficiency, will not further one's career. Mark Blaug, one of most articulate skeptics about model building reported on the dismay of John Hey, then managing editor of the prestigious *Economic Journal*, the leading economics journal in the United Kingdom, who was evaluating his over ten years of editorship. Hey described the type of papers that economists submitted to the journal:

> Many of the submissions do not appear to be written in order to further economic knowledge. Whilst I fully understand the pressure on authors, particularly young academics, it is still disheartening that so many economists seem to be playing the "journal game," i.e. producing variations on a theme that are uninteresting and which do not enlighten. A large number of purely theoretical contributions come into this category: On the other hand, the key theoretical pieces shed light in areas where it is needed. I fear, however, that few economists ask themselves what are the crucial economic problems facing society. If they did so, they might well produce more relevant material. . . . It often appears that the model has been constructed for no other purpose than to produce a result which is a stylised fact observed by the author. That may be an interesting exercise but it needs to be supplemented with a discussion of whether this particular explanation for the stylised fact is useful and better than the alternative explanations. Simply producing a model that comes up with a desired result is a test of the cleverness of the author not a test of the relevance of the theory. (Blaug 1998, 12, citing Hey 1997)

The tiny population of enlightened academic economists was not alone in their dismissal of modern economics. Dissatisfaction even existed in business. Citicorp is the most powerful financial corporation in the world today, but in the 1980s, its predecessor, Citibank, was tottering on the edge of bankruptcy. In 1984, the company replaced its chief executive, Walter Wriston, who frequently published books and articles popularizing the economic philosophy of his friend, Milton Friedman. The new chief executive, John Reed, was appalled that conventional economics offered so little guidance for the real world. Reed gave heavily to a group of physicists and economists who were attempting to build a new form of economics based on the mathematics of chaos theory. Addressing these researchers in 1986, Reed complained bitterly. According to Mitchell Waldrop, who wrote an influential book about this attempt to build an alternative analysis, "Reed had decided that professional economists were off with the fairies. Under Reed's predecessor, Walter Wriston, Citicorp had just taken a bath in the Third World debt crisis. The bank had lost $1 billion in profits in one year, and was still sitting on $13 billion of loans that might never be paid back. And not only had the in-house economists not predicted it, their advice had made matters worse. So Reed thought that a whole new approach to economics might be necessary" (Waldrop 1992, 91).

Waldrop described a 1996 meeting, where Reed addressed the researchers:

> Reed, armed with a fistful of overhead transparencies, went first. Basically, he said, his problem was that he was up to his eyeballs in a world economic system that defied economic analysis. The existing neoclassical theory and the computer models based on it simply did not give him the kind of information he needed to make real-time decisions in the face of risk and uncertainty. Some of these computer models were incredibly elaborate. . . . And yet none of the models really dealt with social and political factors, which were often the most important variables of all. Most of them assumed that the modelers would put in interest rates, currency exchange rates, and other such variables by hand—even though these are precisely the quantities that a banker wants to predict. And virtually all of them tended to assume that the world was never very far from static economic equilibrium, when in fact the world was constantly being shaken by economic shocks and upheavals. In short, the big econometric models often left Reed and his colleagues with little more to go on than gut instinct—with results that might be imagined.
>
> Following the advice of their in-house economists, said Reed, Citicorp and many other international banks had happily lent billions of dollars to these developing countries. (Waldrop 1991, 93–94)

While the technical direction of academic economics diminished the potential of economists to make positive contributions, conservatives were delighted about the economists' political message. Peter Warren told readers of a Heritage Foundation magazine:

> The creeping rot of multiculturalism, feminism, deconstructionism, and other fashionably radical intellectual trends has spread to nearly every branch of study in American universities. But economics appears to have developed an immunity to such diseases. It is one of the few disciplines in which radical Left ideology has failed to take root. Market capitalism—anathema to the bulk of the professorate—flourishes in economics departments, where Keynesians have been unable to prevent the growth of various offshoots of classical free-market thought. This lack of political correctness is one of the reasons why U.S. economics programs are considered to be among the best in the world. (Warren 1994, 72)

The Evolution of Trained Incapacity

Despite the growth of abstract model building, in the early 1960s, many older economists, with their memories of the Great Depression, still adhered to Keynesianism. Relatively few of the younger economists did.

Several factors contributed to the decline of Keynesianism. Obviously, right-wing activism took a serious toll. In addition, the disintegration of the Golden Age disoriented many economists, just as it did to the businessmen who later devoured Lewis Powell's manifesto.

In addition, economics displays a herd-like behavior. Economists cannot win recognition if they work too far from the mainstream. Besides, as the political tides moved to the right, so too did the economics profession. These two factors reinforced each other.

Finally, Keynesian theory suffered a fatal flaw: it was not particularly amenable to elegant models. So, as suddenly as Keynesian theory swept across the economics profession, it began to disappear. Conservative economics, which blamed the slowdown on the government rather than on the natural workings of a market economy, began to fill the vacuum void by Keynesianism.

Robert Lucas, a conservative, Nobel Prize-winning economist whom we encountered earlier in discussing his theories regarding inequality, is one of the most influential modern practitioners of the craft of turning sophisticated mathematics into models of the economy, reveled in this changing of the guard. Writing in 1980, he chortled, "One cannot find good under-forty economists who identify themselves or their work as 'keynesian'. Indeed, people even take offence if referred to as Keynesians. At research seminars, people don't take Keynesian theorizing seriously any more; the audience starts to whisper and giggle at one another" (Lucas 1980b).

What did Lucas's own models offer to replace the supposedly giggle-inducing work that had preceded his own? Although the Keynesian approach might not have had the trappings of scientific rigor that modern, mathematically oriented economists value so highly, the models now in vogue are decidedly unrealistic. Lucas repeatedly reminded his readers that his models are indeed artificial (Lucas 1980a, 271; Lucas 1981, 563). He considers the artificiality of his fantastic models as a badge of honor, insisting that looking at the world as it appears to us can be a source of error. Lucas cited the poet, Wallace Stevens, with approval: "It helps to see the actual world/ to visualize a fantastic world" (Lucas 1992, 233).

Unfortunately, Lucas never acknowledged that artificiality by itself is no guarantee of scientific rigor, if by science we mean something that furthers our knowledge of the world. For example, since 1969, Lucas has produced a spate of supposedly pathbreaking models intended to prove that unemployment is voluntary, rather than a symptom of economic weakness (Lucas and Rapping 1969). Lucas set out to explain "why they [the unemployed] prefer it [unemployment] to all other activities" (Lucas 1987, 54). In Lucas's abstract world, unemployed workers simply have a higher preference for leisure than for wages.

Of course, any economist is free to claim that all unemployment is voluntary. Such an economist could possibly even find some data that might be consistent with that explanation, even though this theory seems to defy common sense. In the end, though, empirical proof of involuntary unemployment is impossible.

These models, however, serve an important political purpose. As one commentator noted: "To say that someone is involuntarily unemployed is to relieve him of the responsibility for his condition; it is to suggest that he is unemployed 'through no fault of his own'" (Coddington 1983, 27). So, Lucas shifts the blame for massive unemployment away from a defective economic system to the personal preferences of the unemployed.

In one of the last Richard T. Ely lectures leaning toward Keynesianism, Alan Blinder, a distinguished Keynesian economist and later vice-chair of the Federal Reserve under Greenspan, despaired about the failure of economists to address high unemployment. Not surprisingly, he alluded to Lucas's appraisal of the profession, recalling: "By 1980, the adage 'there are no Keynesians under the age of 40' was part of the folklore of the (American) economics profession" (Blinder 1988, 278). But far more had disappeared than Keynesianism. A decade later, Welch would use the occasion of his Ely lecture to praise inequality.

Lucas's performance, along with that of the majority of the economics profession, confirms the accuracy of Thorstein Veblen's accusation from almost a century ago regarding what he called a state of "trained incapacity"—meaning a proliferation of skills together with a narrowing of vision that creates an inability to come to grips with the real world (Veblen 1914, 347).

The Dangerous Turn of Modern Economics

In 1992, a group of economists, including four Nobel Laureates and a future one, placed an advertisement in the May issue of the *American Economic Review*, entitled "A Plea for Pluralistic and Rigorous Economics," in which they complained about "the threat to economic science posed by intellectual monopoly. Economists today enforce a monopoly of method or core assumptions. Economists will advocate free competition, but will not practice it in the marketplace of ideas."

The core assumptions, of course, are those that are fundamental to those models in which markets work perfectly. Such complaints have become almost nonexistent in the United States, especially from the leading economists of the day. The phalanx of conventional economics is stronger than ever.

George Stigler once observed "that learned bodies are each run by a self-perpetuating clique" (Stigler 1982, 118). Today, the clique marginalizes those economists who study the real problems of workers or the poor, while those who approach the same subject abstractly by applying some new statistical technique to a large database are likely to win professional acclaim. Those who blame people for their own situation can hope to win a Nobel Prize.

Because of the emphasis on abstract modeling, the training of young economists today is comparable to a dysfunctional medical school in which young surgeons learn detailed information about sophisticated medical devices without needing to study anything regarding anatomy. Indeed, a survey of graduate students of economics at elite universities found that "[s]ixty-eight percent believed that a thorough knowledge of the economy was unimportant; only 3.4 percent believed that it was very important" (Colander and Klamer 1987, 99).

In this environment, economists win prestige for their technical accomplishments rather than their ability to engage in real life problems. In other words, economists' training and promotional ladders coerce them to work in ways that prevent them from confronting real world problems in a fashion that help people understand how to improve their lives. Instead, they keep producing abstract models that show that people should put their faith in market-based solutions. In the evocative phrase of Steven Shapin, "elegance trumps pertinence" (Steven 2002), but, I should add, ideology trumps elegance.

Even after finding an academic job, economists still face disincentives to delve into studies that challenge the status quo. For example, for many professors winning grants is often an important consideration in being retained or promoted (Colander 1989). And those who supply the grants rarely favor progressive policies.

The emphasis on technical virtuosity has profound effects. For example, prior to the Powell memo, most economists were willing to accept a role for environmental regulation, which was needed to correct failures of the market. Today, most economists reject the idea that markets need much correction. Only about half of economists accept that the government should increase fuel efficiency standards or that greenhouse gasses will pose a problem in the future. In terms of greenhouse gasses, more than 7 percent believe that they can actually increase the GDP and only 12 percent believe that they pose much of a threat by lowering the GDP by more than 10 percent by 2100 (Whaples 2006).

In conclusion, a combination of a narrow educational process together with compelling job pressures has led to a deadening conservatism in the field of economics, much to the delight of conservatives. As I have been arguing, this aspect of the right-wing victory should be a concern for all since economists should have a duty to alert society to dangers rather than lulling people to sleep.

A Brief Interlude of Supply-Side Economics

Outside the corridors of elite universities, some economists were turning to a cruder sort of economic thinking than that of the abstract modelers. In November of 1974, a young economist named Arthur Laffer drew a diagram on a napkin for President Ford's young deputy chief-of-staff, Richard Bruce Cheney. Laffer suggested that simply lowering taxes could stimulate the economy so much that tax cuts could actually increase tax revenues (Cannon 1982, 236n; Wanniski 2003). This demonstration deeply impressed Jude Wanniski, then an associate editor of the *Wall Street Journal*. He used the influence of his paper to popularize the idea, which Wanniski labeled supply-side economics.

Wanniski, the self-styled "primary political theoretician in the supply-side camp," maintained that Republican campaigns could never be successful by promising to accompany tax cuts with austerity (Wanniski 1999). Instead, he recommended a "Two-Santa" approach in which the party would promise generous government programs along with tax cuts (Wanniski 1976). Within a short time, supply-side economics broadened its claims, insisting that eliminating taxes and regulations would promise universal prosperity, while still cutting the federal budget deficit, a claim so preposterous that George H. W. Bush dismissed it as "voodoo economics" in his 1980 debate with Ronald Reagan during their competing presidential campaigns.

The disenchantment with Keynesian economics together with the extravagant promises of supply-side economics, all backed up by the prestige of the *Wall Street Journal*, briefly made this new brand of conservative economics attractive during the early Reagan era, although it failed to win any lasting acceptance within academia.

Irving Kristol in particular was extremely effective in promoting supply-side economics. He also helped Wanniski get generous financial support for his book on supply-side economics (Wanniski 1979; Goodman 1981). In later years, Kristol said that he understood the weakness of supply-side economics all along, but actively worked to propagandize it nonetheless. He justified his actions in terms of political strategy rather than the overblown claims of supply-side economics: "I was not certain of its [supply side economics'] economic merits but quickly saw its political possibilities. . . . The task, as I saw it, was to create a new majority, which evidently would mean a conservative majority, which came to mean, in turn, a Republican majority—so political effectiveness was the priority, not the accounting deficiencies of government" (Kristol 1995, 35).

Lowering the tax burden of the rich and powerful was a major objective of many of the proponents of supply-side economics. Ronald Reagan's head of the Office of Management and Budget, David Stockman, gave a famous interview to William Greider in which he described how supply-side economics actually operated:

> The hard part of the supply-side tax cut is dropping the top rate from 70 to 50%—the rest of it is a secondary matter," Stockman explained. "The original argument was that the top bracket was too high, and that's having the most devastating effect on the economy. Then, the general argument was that, in order to make this palatable as a political matter, you had to bring down all the brackets. But, I mean, Kemp-Roth (tax cut) was always a Trojan horse to bring down the top rate" (Greider 1981, 46). Stockman conceded: "when one stripped away the new rhetoric emphasizing across-the-board cuts, the supply-side theory was really new clothes for the unpopular doctrine of the old Republican orthodoxy. "It's kind of hard to sell 'trickle down,' so the supply-side formula was the only way to get a tax policy that was really 'trickle down.' Supply-side is 'trickle-down' theory." (Greider 1981, 46)

Although supply-side economics never achieved dominance, a good number of reputable economists took up the supply-side program. By advocating supply-side economics, these economists became more likely to gain entry into the seats of power, winning grants or appointments to high positions in Washington. In effect, Keynes's "madman in authority" was able to influence these economists. Once harsh reality refuted some of the more outlandish claims of supply-side economics, the fad quickly receded. Even so, the fact that supply-side economics won a substantial toehold in academic economics reveals the mercenary side of the discipline.

A more respectable form of conservative economics, known as monetarism, moved into the breach. The monetarist conservatives agreed with the supply-siders that market forces were the only route to efficiency and prosperity. Both approaches called for the elimination of government influence, especially with respect to taxes and regulation. Despite their similar objectives, the monetarists were just more circumspect in their presentation.

The National Bureau of Economic Research

Supply-side economics was unique because the basic theory largely emerged from outside of the economics discipline. For the most part, economists do not wait for right-wing activists to package a theory for them. They are perfectly capable of defending business interests on their own. These homegrown theories have a more long-lasting effect than the brief burst of supply-side economics.

In recent decades, no organization, not even Ely's American Economic Association, has been more influential in shaping the economics profession than the National Bureau of Economic Research. Thomas Edsall, a distinguished journalist who was surveying the changing political scene in 1984, concurred: "Perhaps the most prestigious of the institutions that have helped to push the economic debate to the right is the National Bureau of Economic Research" (Edsall 1984, 118).

The original purpose of the National Bureau of Economic Research was entirely different. In 1920, the founders' objective was not to narrow economics down to a business-friendly dogma. Instead, they intended "to conduct economic research effectively on a factual basis." They reasoned: "In these days of conflicting economic opinions and skillful propaganda, the interests of economic knowledge can best be served by the presentation and analysis of data, objectively collected and interpreted. Unless some guarantee of impartiality can be given, results will be viewed with distrust by many" (W. Mitchell 1936, 7).

Toward this end, the Bureau aimed at discovering the truth by including as wide a range of people as possible, "from extreme conservative to extreme radical who should associate with them representatives of all the important organized interests in the country" (cited in Fabricant 1984). Within a few decades, however, the Bureau fell considerably short of its goal of inclusiveness.

Although the noble idea behind the National Bureau of Economic Research—to examine every aspect of economic knowledge—would seem to exclude political involvement, only a few years after its creation, the Bureau began its collaboration with Herbert Hoover. The Bureau maintained a rather progressive perspective at the time, but as its political engagement became more institutionalized, its political leanings turned more conservative.

Since 1945, two highly placed economists almost continually dominated the Bureau. The first of these economists, Arthur F. Burns, a close friend and teacher of Milton Friedman, became Director of Research in 1945, where he remained until 1953, when President Eisenhower appointed him as head the Council of Economic Advisers. After three years, he returned to academia and then served as president of the Bureau for ten years. In 1969, President Nixon first appointed Burns as an economic counselor, and then one year later named him chairman of the Federal Reserve Board, where he served from 1970 to 1978. Incidentally, Burns was also the mentor of Alan Greenspan, a more famous leader of the Fed.

Burns played a highly political role at the Fed. He used his powers to stimulate the economy to ensure Nixon's reelection, even though this action was certain to create both inflation and dangerous imbalances in the economy after the election.

Later, Burns tried to explain why he had not managed to stem the inflationary tide in a famous lecture, melodramatically entitled, "The Anguish of Central Banking." In this central banker's retrospective equivalent of the Powell memo, Burns held the unruly behavior of the masses to be ultimately responsible:

> [T]he rapid rise in national affluence did not create a mood of contentment. On the contrary, the 1960s were years of social turmoil in the United States, as they were in other industrial democracies. In part, the unrest reflected discontent by blacks and other minorities with prevailing conditions of social discrimination and economic deprivation—a discontent that erupted during the "hot summers" of the middle 1960s in burning and looting. In part, the social unrest reflected growing feelings of injustice by or on behalf of other groups—the poor, the aged, the physically handicapped, ethnics, farmers, blue collar workers, women, and so forth. In part, the unrest reflected a growing rejection by middle-class youth of prevailing institutions and cultural values. In part, it reflected the more or less sudden recognition by broad segments of the population that the economic reforms of the New Deal and the more recent rise in national affluence had left untouched problems in various areas of American life—social, political, economic, and environmental. And interacting with all these sources of social disturbance were the heightening tensions associated with the Viet Nam War. (Burns 1979, 690)

Burns endorsed Reagan's inconsistent promises during the 1980 campaign that the Republicans could raise defense spending, cut taxes, and still balance the budget. Later, he explained to Herbert Stein that he did so because "if you dissented from it, your whole usefulness in the organization was lost" (Judis 2000, 150).

In 1977, the National Bureau of Economic Research turned to Martin Feldstein as its next president. To his credit, Feldstein was not one to construct abstract models with no connection to reality. However, his work is more openly ideological than that of the abstract model builders. Throughout his career, Feldstein has carefully constructed his models to make the case that government activities, such as the collection of taxes and especially the maintenance of Social Security, create destructive disincentives that weaken the economy.

Feldstein carefully used the Bureau to further his own political agenda. Even Arthur Burns was moved to criticize the new turn of the Bureau. Burns maintained that the institution once confined itself to objective research, ignoring policy issues, and acting as a check on Federal statistics, but he lamented that "work of that kind does not come across my desk from them anymore" (S. Golden 1980).

A recent article in the monthly magazine of the International Monetary Fund referred to Feldstein's approach as "supply-side lite" (Loungani 2004). Feldstein himself offers a different account, explaining: "I'm a true supply-sider. . . . At the time, some of the extreme statements people were making were giving it a bad name" (Bernasek 2004). In short, Feldstein offered supply-side policy rec-ommendations, but with a patina of academic respectability.

Feldstein first came to national attention in 1974, the same year that Arthur Laffer produced his famous napkin. Feldstein published a model that "proved" that Social Security caused enormous losses for the U.S. economy. According to Feldstein, Social Security was reducing personal savings by 30–50 percent. He estimated that if Social Security had not existed, the stock of plant and equip-ment in the United States would have been as much as 50 percent larger and total personal income 20 percent greater than the level in 1971 (Feldstein 1974). Since Social Security had only been functioning 24 years at the end of the time period that his data covered, Feldstein's article implies that the present effect of Social Security on total personal income today would be far higher—perhaps almost 50 percent since the program has had another 35 years at the time of this writing.

The same Jude Wanniski, who popularized supply-side economics, later recalled, "I came across a paper that a fellow at Harvard had written on Social Security, saying it was causing the national saving rate to decrease. And I thought, 'Great . . . I've got to publish it'" (Bernasek 2004). In other words, because Feld-stein's results were welcome, people of influence rushed to embrace him.

The only problem was that Feldstein's work was seriously flawed. A few weeks before the election of Ronald Reagan at the 1980 annual meeting of the Ameri-can Economic Association in Denver and after Feldstein had already ascended to the head of the National Bureau of Economic Research, two less famous econ-omists, Selig D. Lesnoy and Dean R. Leimer, reported that they were unable to replicate Feldstein's results (Leimer and Lesnoy 1982). Upon analyzing Feld-stein's work, they discovered that his results critically depended upon an ele-mentary programming error. With that error corrected, Feldstein's data no longer had the disastrous effects Feldstein claimed. Instead, his model showed that Social Security could have actually had a positive impact on savings.

In all fairness, errors in economic model building are extremely common. In 1982, the *Journal of Money, Credit, and Banking* began a project to replicate pre-viously published articles. The results were unsettling to say the least. Sixty-six percent of the authors were unable or unwilling to supply the materials neces-sary to rerun the model. The authors who responded did so after an average delay of 217 days. All but one of these articles had problems, including pro-gramming errors, such as Feldstein committed (Dewald, Thursby, and Anderson 1986). This project was hardly likely to inspire confidence in the scientific rigor of economics.

Feldstein admitted his programming error. Undeterred, he soon rejiggled his model. By adding a few new assumptions, he was able to "prove" once again that Social Security was still destructive. Some years later, in 1996, Feldstein gave his own Richard T. Ely lecture. There, Feldstein regaled his audience with new data demonstrating one more time the harmful effects of Social Security. According to Feldstein, the present value of privatizing Social Security would be an astounding $20 trillion dollars—about twice the GDP of the United States (Feld-stein 1996, 12).

In a 2005 *Wall Street Journal* opinion piece, disingenuously entitled "Saving Social Security," Feldstein returned once more to his *bête noire*. This time he was arguing in support of an unpopular piece of Republican legislation to mix Social Security and private accounts. Feldstein promised great benefits from this "reform": "A higher national saving rate would finance investment in plant and equipment that raises productivity and produces the extra national income to finance future retiree benefits" (Feldstein 2005b). So, Feldstein would rescue Social Security by gutting it.

Earlier in the year, the American Economic Association had given Feldstein a platform to renew his attack on Social Security in his presidential address. Here Feldstein adopted a new pitch. He protested that the program did too little to redistribute income from the rich to the poor. His argument was that, because the rich live longer than the poor, they will have more opportunity to benefit from Social Security (Feldstein 2005a).

Without bothering to contest Feldstein's questionable calculations about the redistributional impact of Social Security, this last attack is especially notable for its unusual rhetorical turn. Not too long ago, the same Professor Feldstein discussed the question of inequality with the *New York Times*. Feldstein began as if he took the subject seriously, observing, "Why there has been increasing inequality in this country has been one of the big puzzles in our field and has absorbed a lot of intellectual effort." Feldstein's own intellectual effort in this debate left something to be desired. Rather than address the question of inequality seriously, he trivialized the question, responding to the reporter: "But if you ask me whether we should worry about the fact that some people on Wall Street and basketball players are making a lot of money, I say no" (Stille 2001).

This dismissal of the question of inequality was not some uncharacteristic, offhand remark. In an earlier article, entitled "Reducing Poverty Not Inequality," Feldstein described the proper approach to an imagined increase in inequality occurring because a small number of affluent people received $1,000 each at no cost to the rest of society. For Feldstein, only a "spiteful egalitarian" would not welcome such an improvement in society (Feldstein 1999, 34).

Of course, Feldstein and his fellow "spiteful inegalitarians" have been adamant in their hostility to any redistribution of income toward the less fortunate. Such policies threaten to hinder the magical trickle down upon which all progress supposedly depends. Suddenly, however, when it gave credence to his attack on Social Security, Professor Feldstein refurbished himself as a populist advocate of redistribution of income from the rich to the poor by arguing that Social Security benefited the rich. Professor Feldstein never bothered to explain why the rich are so hostile to this program that benefits them so lavishly.

One might expect such a flurry of conflicting arguments from an unscrupulous salesman who wants to earn his commission from a confused customer, but not from one of the most prominent academic economists in the country. One might suspect that what is at work is ideology rather than an objective search for the truth.

Feldstein did not limit his political activism to Social Security. For example, he used the *Wall Street Journal* to publicize his work predicting that Clinton's economic taxes would harm the economy while raising little revenue (Feldstein 1993). Unlike his Social Security work, this article made a specific prediction. Unfortunately for Feldstein, his estimates turned out to be demonstrably false. The economy experienced a sudden burst of prosperity during the rest of the Clinton administration.

Alicia H. Munnell, a former student of Feldstein whom he thanked in the acknowledgements to his original Social Security paper and who later rose to become a member of the President's Council of Economic Advisers and Assistant Secretary of the Treasury for Economic Policy, offered this damning verdict in a *Business Week* article following the Denver meeting: "I get the feeling that the NBER does adopt a position on an issue—explicit or implicit—and then they go about generating research to support the position" (Anon. 1980). In light of Feldstein's later work, I see no reason to revise her evaluation.

Even if an economist avoids rudimentary programming errors and questionable procedures in handling the data, problems with economic models still remain. The economy is far too complex to reduce it to a mathematical equation or a computer model, even a very large and sophisticated one. As a result, such models necessarily rely on simplifying assumptions.

Although Feldstein proved nothing with his unrelenting attacks on government programs, he demonstrated how clever economists, armed with sophisticated mathematical and statistical techniques, along with the help of well-trained graduate assistants, are capable of manipulating models to get whatever results they desire. As economists like to joke: "If you torture the data long enough they will confess." So, although economists such as Feldstein can give their work the appearance of scientific precision, their work must necessarily remain suspect.

For example, Social Security's presumably negative effect on savings was at the core of Feldstein's model, but saving has a contradictory effect on the economy. Some models assume that saving encourages investment, while others assume that saving depresses demand, which, in turn, holds back investment. No matter which assumption about the effect of saving economists choose, they can point to reputable theories and models that support them. Admittedly, as economists marginalized Keynesian theory, the models that show the positive influence of savings have become more common. That shift does not reflect an advance in knowledge, but rather a consequence of the right-wing offensive.

Also, economists can pick and choose among various time periods and data sets, avoiding combinations that do not confirm what they want to find. While such models—including many of the models to which I have referred in this book—might suggest new lines of research or raise questions about previously accepted truths, they cannot constitute proof by any means.

So, economists may build their models and pundits or politicians can foist the results of these models on the unsuspecting public as if they were scientific evidence, but they are not grounded in science. For example, almost two decades after the errors in Feldstein's original model were revealed, conservative ideologists, such as those at the Heritage Foundation, continue to trumpet his long-discredited calculation as serious evidence of the damage done by Social Security (see D. Mitchell 1998).

I believe that Social Security is one of the most effective government programs ever devised in the United States, but I can neither prove nor disprove that assertion with a computer model. In fact, Feldstein's results might possibly turn out to be correct after all, but nobody can know for certain. Different economists have come up with a wide range of estimates (see Lesnoy and Leimer 1985).

Unfortunately, the public rarely has the opportunity to hear about the full range of economic information. Ideological filters determine who gets hired or tenured in economics departments. Those economists who manage to defy the conventional wisdom face the added barrier of getting their work published in "reputable" journals. Even if such papers manage to find their way into journals, they lack the "megaphone" of powerful agencies, such as the Heritage Foundation, which give wide distribution to long-discredited material without much fear of being exposed. So, ultimately what the public learns about how the economy works are those results that conform to the desires of the rich and powerful.

How to Succeed in Economics

Feldstein's career illustrates how bountiful rewards flow to clever economists who can effectively cater to the rich and powerful. Shortly before the Denver meetings, the *New York Times Magazine* published a glowing report of Feldstein's career, entitled, "Superstar of the New Economists" (S. Golden 1980). After the debunking of his paper at Denver, the press briefly reported on the controversy. Then Feldstein's career continued its rapid ascent.

Two years after Feldstein's error came to public attention, to the surprise of few, Ronald Reagan recruited Feldstein to be his chief economic advisor. Within another couple of years, Thomas Edsall credited Feldstein as perhaps "the most influential . . . force pushing economic policy to the right" (Edsall 1984, 219). Edsall is not alone in his verdict. When the Center for Economic Studies chose Anthony Atkinson to deliver its Munich lectures, he also singled out Feldstein as the major force moving economics to reject the welfare state (Atkinson 1999, 4). The historian Robert Collins's summary of Feldstein's career, shows how attractive Feldstein must have appeared to an administration enamored with supply-side economics, "Harvard's Martin Feldstein made the National Bureau of Economic Research (NBER) an outpost of supply-side emphasis, if not doctrine, when he became the organization's president in the mid-1970s . . . unifying most of his scholarship was a deep interest in the elasticity, or incentives, effects of government policies. And incentive effects lay at the heart of supply-side economics" (R. Collins 2000, 189).

To his credit, during his tenure with the Reagan administration, Feldstein was too sophisticated to buy supply-side economics in its entirety. Like the fanatical supply-siders who held sway in the administration, Feldstein vigorously opposed taxes and regulation, but he was also concerned about the ballooning federal deficit.

In particular, Feldstein feared that government deficits would soak up too much of the available national savings, starving private business for credit. His reasoning was similar to the Gale and Orszag study mentioned earlier. Unlike the fervent proponents of the starve-the-beast scenario, Feldstein worried that the financial havoc that high deficits create could cause too much damage before Congress could react. For this reason, Feldstein dissented from the Reagan program to cut taxes rather than the federal budget deficit—a policy that George W. Bush resurrected with a vengeance a couple of decades later.

The Reagan Administration was understandably unhappy with Feldstein's stand. He was told to "shape up or ship out" (Altman 2004, 34; Hoffman 1983). He resigned a few months later, returning to the Bureau and to Harvard, where he has remained ever since. In 2004, Feldstein also became president of the American Economic Association.

Feldstein's influence in Washington still continued long after his departure. A *New York Times* profile even suggested that he "may well be the most influential economist in Washington, even though he has not worked there since 1984, when he returned to the Harvard faculty" (Leonhardt 2002).

A *Fortune* article described how Feldstein cultivated his position of power: "Just as he's rebuilt the NBER, he has systematically and quietly forged connections in the world of business, public policy, and the media. How does Feldstein maintain his vast web of contacts? It's a combination of charm, persistence, and his BlackBerry" (Bernasek 2004). The article paints a vivid picture of how solid Feldstein's influence has become:

> In a certain crowd—make that an elite circle—of power brokers, policy shapers, and politicos in the know, "Marty" is all it takes to identify the country's top conservative economic mind. Since George W. Bush became President, Martin Feldstein has been an economic Merlin of sorts, exerting a veiled influence on policy. "Whenever I go down to a meeting at the White House, Marty is always there sitting next to the President," says one regular participant who refused to be named for fear of not being invited back. The President has plenty of advisors to choose from—Treasury Secretary John Snow and Greg Mankiw, chairman of the Council of Economic Advisors, for instance. Still few people today, with the exception of Federal Reserve chairman Alan Greenspan, have the kind of authority that Feldstein commands. (Bernasek 2004)

In addition to his personal influence, Feldstein's students frequently occupy powerful economic policy positions, leading the *New York Times* to suggest that "the Bush administration's economic team begins to look like a Feldstein alumni club" (Leonard 2002). For example, in the administration of George W. Bush:

> [The president] stocked his economic team with a legion of Professor Feldstein's academic protégés. Mr. Lindsey, once his mentor's deputy on the faculty at Harvard, became the top economic adviser in the White House's inner circle. Professor [Glen] Hubbard, once Professor Feldstein's research assistant, took over his old post: chairman of the Council of Economic Advisers. Among Professor Hubbard's classmates at Professor Feldstein's lectures had been Richard H. Clarida, who became the assistant secretary of the Treasury for economic policy. Professor Clarida's deputy, Mark J. Warshawsky, was also a Feldstein student. (Altman 2004, 41–42)

Feldstein also worked hard to ensure that a new generation of economics students will continue in the conservative tradition through his control of Ec10, the introductory economics course that enrolls 600–900 students each year. Feldstein taught this course for 21 years until 1995, when he passed the baton to N. Gregory Mankiw, who had just resigned as the chief economic advisor to President George W. Bush. The *New York Times* Feldstein profile puts the course in perspective: "thousands of Harvard students who have taken his, and only his, economics class during their Harvard years have gone on to become policy makers and corporate executives" (Leonard 2002).

During the 1960s and early 1970s, before Feldstein's ascendancy, progressives and even radicals were able to participate in the course. Feldstein has done his best to make sure that over the last two decades thousands of Harvard undergraduates were indoctrinated with a decidedly anti-tax, free-market-leaning brand of instruction. An article in the *Harvard Crimson* provides the flavor of the complaints:

> Harvard students have known for nearly two decades that Ec10 is flagrantly biased. Disgruntled students have even gone so far as to organize Students for a Humane and Responsible Economics (SHARE). It is a blotch on the University's academic record that it has allowed Baker Professor of Economics Martin S. Feldstein '61, since he began teaching the class in 1984, to use Harvard's only introductory economics course as a forum to vent his personal views. Given students growing frustration, and the current review of the Core Curriculum, the administration must reform Ec10. . . .
>
> This clearly is an affront to Harvard's rigorous academic standards. By excluding ideas and perspectives which do not match his own, Prof. Feldstein has failed to equip students with the full knowledge they need in order to understand a host of contemporary issues. By presenting a one-sided view of the discipline, he also risks putting off many students who would otherwise have pursued further studies in economics."
>
> But, what is most shameful is Professor Feldstein's intellectual dishonesty. Suppressing the critical examination of alternative ideas is unbecoming of a Harvard professor, and should not be tolerated. Unfortunately, the administration has tolerated this state of affairs for nearly twenty years. (Stafford 2003)

Navigating the Center of Power

The George W. Bush administration policies of tax cuts and privatization of Social Security closely followed a script that Feldstein had written decades ago, except for the ballooning budget deficit. Feldstein, however, has not repeated his earlier mistake of warning that deficits pose a danger.

Instead, Feldstein wrote extensively in support of the Bush administration's policies, often from his position as a regular contributor to the *Wall Street Journal*. His reluctance to stray again from the party line served him well in maintaining his power and prestige. For example, Feldstein was frequently mentioned as a likely successor to Alan Greenspan as head of the Federal Reserve, the same position that Burns had filled earlier (Leonhardt 2002). Those who doubted his chance for the nomination typically mentioned his single lapse in loyalty regarding tax cuts and the deficit.

Feldstein's power as head of the National Bureau of Economic Research cannot be underestimated. About 500 elite economists, mostly conservative, belong to the Bureau. By choosing the subjects of the Bureau's prestigious books and conferences, Feldstein directly shapes the content of economic research and often frames future economic debates.

For example, under Feldstein's leadership the Bureau published a steady stream of books on Social Security—about one book per year since 1998, almost 6 percent of all the books that the Bureau published, not to mention a slew of books on taxation in which programs, such as Social Security, were damned for creating perverse incentives that supposedly undermine the economy. The Bureau's working paper series also signals to other economists what sort of research is considered legitimate and by default what is unacceptable.

The National Bureau of Economic Research even occupies a semi-official position. The Business Cycle Dating Committee of the Bureau determines whether a slowdown should be counted as a recession or a depression or when business cycles begin and end. The government uses the committee's decisions in organizing data. This function does nothing to alter the economy, but it can be important in framing public understanding. For example, if government data could have indicated that the Great Depression had not begun until Roosevelt took office, the politics of the New Deal might have been substantially different.

While the enormity of the Great Depression would have prevented such a blatant distortion, typically the data give a subtler signal, allowing the committee a certain degree of discretion. Although economists may disagree about the details, the committee usually makes its decision according to fairly well-defined parameters.

However, in 2003, the committee made a particularly controversial determination that the recession that had begun in early 2001 ended later that year. This decision had important political implications, because it allowed the Bush administration to take credit in its reelection campaign for having ended a recession early in his administration, even though traditional measures, such as payroll jobs, indicated that the recession was still continuing at the time (see Berry 2003; Strawser 2003).

Feldstein also integrated himself into the corporate sector, acting as an economic adviser to several businesses in the United States and abroad. He serves as a director of three major corporations—the scandal-ridden American International Group, Eli Lilly, and HCA. The latter may be most strategic because its founders were the father and brother of former Senate Majority Leader Bill Frist.

Corporate influence also plays a role at the Bureau. Between 1985 and 2002, Feldstein secured more than $10 million for the National Bureau of Economic Research from the Bradley, Olin, Scaife, and Smith Richardson foundations, which have been among the most active funders of hard right-wing activism (Media Transparency, n.d.).

John Maynard Keynes never met Martin Feldstein. If he had, he would have seen how the influence of economists expands by obediently catering to the madmen in authority. Feldstein is not unique in this respect. He is only perhaps the most successful.

Making Economics Useful

Despite the irrelevance of much of modern economics, many of the practitioners are absolutely brilliant. Over and above their technical proficiency, some economists have an uncanny ability to uncover obscure data sources that offer unexpected information. Yet the discipline of economics has largely painted itself into a corner of irrelevancy.

Rather than casting much needed light on the economy, the economics profession mostly worked to provide cover for the status quo. Turning to the verdict of James Heckman, a Nobel Prize–winning economist from the arch-conservative University of Chicago economics department:

> In economics there's a trend now to come up with cute papers in an effort to be cited as many times as possible. All the incentives point that way, especially for young professors.... In some quarters of our profession, the level of discussion has sunk to the level of a New Yorker article: coffee-table articles about "cute" topics, papers using "clever" instruments. The authors of these papers are usually unclear about the economic questions they address, the data used to support their conclusions and the econometrics used to justify their estimates. This is a sad development that I hope is a passing fad. Most of this work is without substance, but it makes a short-lived splash . . . at the expense of working on hard and important foundational problems. (Douglas 2005)

Heckman, however, does not acknowledge that opening economics up to important foundational problems runs the risk of derailing the dogmatic uniformity that has become the defining characteristic of contemporary economics. Admittedly, vigorous and even contentious debates do occur among economists, but only within a very narrow range of questions. Real foundational questions remain off-limits.

Economists should have a responsibility to be open to all points of view, much like the original mandate of the National Bureau of Economic Research. At all times, society needs a large number of economists to offer critical analysis of current policy. Only with a broad diversity of voices will economists make progress in coming to grips with real problems.

The public has a right to hear about the dangers, or at least the risks that the right-wing takeover poses for the economy—and even for the world at large. In this respect, the current efforts of the right wing to silence critical voices do a grave disservice to society.

Economists would serve society better if they would cease to arrogantly market their ideological goods as absolute truths. Nobody has a monopoly on truth. Principled conservative economists had valuable insights about the shortcomings of the New Deal. The critics of the right wing will certainly be wrong on some points. The best we can hope for in developing good policy is an open dialogue in which all perspectives are aired.

Turning again to Keynes, I am reminded of his hope for economics: "If economists could manage to get themselves thought of as humble, competent people, on a level with dentists, that would be splendid" (Keynes 1930, 331). At this time, both humility and competence are in short supply. Instead, economists, including some of the most brilliant members of the profession, are wasting their sorely needed talents or, worse yet, intentionally or not, actively working against the public good.

Conclusion and Hopefully a New Beginning

This book told the story of the disintegration of the Golden Age, followed by a period of disillusionment and anger, which then helped to usher in the right-wing takeover. The right wing initiated policies that favored the rich and powerful, tearing society apart, while promising a new age of prosperity and growth for everyone.

Instead, the one-sided class war that the right wing has pursued is a recipe for certain disaster. Rather than using its resources to develop productivity gains comparable to the achievements of the Golden Age, business attempted to regain its rate of profit by attacking labor and dismantling regulatory restraints. In addition, after recovering the political confidence shattered by the disaster in Vietnam, the right wing used the power of the state to demand special advantages in international markets.

Here, I can do no better than quote a book, coauthored by Rajan Raghuram G., a University of Chicago Professor who is currently Director of Research Department at the International Monetary Fund, "Capitalism's biggest political enemies are not the firebrand trade unionists spewing vitriol against the system but the executives in pin-striped suits extolling the virtues of competitive markets with every breath while attempting to extinguish them with every action" (Rajan and Zingales 2004, 276).

I suspect that many of the right-wing leaders sincerely believe that their policies promote the welfare of mankind, whether in waging war in the Middle East or eliminating market controls at home. In this environment, education, science, freedom of the press, and even the health and safety of the people must bend to accommodate the greater good of the right-wing revolution. I am reminded of words often attributed to John Adams: "Power always thinks it has a great soul and vast views beyond the comprehension of the weak; and that it is doing God's service when it is violating all his laws" (Morgenthau 1957, xvi).

Rather than fostering prosperity and growth, the right-wing agenda threatens to strangle the forces of economic vitality. Increasing profits by a policy of shooting, looting, and polluting is hardly a recipe for sustained economic progress.

Economists, who should be able to offer guidance in putting the economy back on the right track, have largely sidelined themselves because of a combination of trained incapacity and narrow ideological preconceptions. Hopefully that disaster will unfold slowly enough that we will have time to react.

In a book such as this, the author has an obligation to point to actions that people can take to improve the situation. I can do no better than to suggest a reverse Lewis Powell strategy.

Powell was absolutely correct to insist that a long-term strategy was a prerequisite to success. In addition, he understood that an effective movement requires the construction of fresh, new institutions. Although the right wing has far more money to create conservative foundations and think tanks, progressives have a greater natural constituency. But first, progressives must learn to communicate with that constituency. Surely, telling the truth to the people should be easier than misleading them in the way that the right wing has.

A firm determination to create lasting institutions that can shift the economic and political climate in a more progressive direction will eventually pay great dividends. Two specific victories will be required for success. Both will be challenging. First, real campaign finance reform that prevents wealth from buying elections will be a necessity. Second, we will need a media that acts as a watchdog rather than a lapdog, one that will keep the public informed about government and business activities.

Neither goal is immediately achievable. To move forward we require widespread engagement. The key to the right-wing takeover has been to spread discouragement and disengagement among traditionally progressive forces, while effectively organizing and mobilizing its own base. The future depends upon engaging the public with a solid vision. Sadly, the failure of the Democratic Party to provide such a vision has been as important for the right-wing victory as the organizational successes of the conservatives.

Getting people to work on matters of popular concern will be essential to preventing even more damage. Progressives must always be on the lookout for the possibility of progress—even marginal progress—like stopping a local polluter or becoming involved in some matter of local, national, or even international importance. Each small victory will give the people involved a feeling of empowerment. Others will also take heart from the example of successful activism, creating the possibility of a progressive crescendo. The greatest threat to this strategy is impatience—a sense that all is hopeless unless everything immediately falls your way. Setbacks, certainly many setbacks, will occur before the tide will change.

One further factor works in favor of the progressive outcome. Sooner or later, a good part of the business community will eventually see that its aggressiveness is counterproductive. The election of 2006 may be a sign of things to come. So with time, energy, and patience the country can be put on a better footing, provided we begin before it is too late.

In the longer run, a total rethinking of economics is needed. The managed capitalism of the Keynesians worked well enough during the Golden Age, such policy is not capable of delivering the perpetual prosperity that it had promised. Even the near-full employment that the economy enjoyed during the Golden Age does not come close to what a healthy economy could achieve.

For example, the exceptional productivity that occurred during World War II, when people were inspired to greater efforts out of a sense of patriotism, represents a superior level of performance. Hopefully, we can work together to build something far better—something that can tap people's potential in the manner that William James suggested with his moral equivalent of war—something based on cooperation rather than competition. Economists can make a contribution to this transformation by deemphasizing competition, while learning to understand more humane motives of behavior than profit maximization.

Imagining a new kind of economy becomes easier after considering what individuals can accomplish. The world is full of examples of people who have managed to accomplish extraordinary things despite seemingly impossible odds. Flipping the dial on your television through the sports channels you will see people performing in ways that would seem to defy the laws of physics. Some of the children who are imitating these athletes will no doubt surpass what you see today.

Athletes, scientists, and artists all perform best when they have the opportunity to follow a career that gives them joy. A healthy economy will have to make sure that as many people as humanly possible can find challenging, useful, and pleasurable work. Finally, improved productivity can be turned into more leisure, which can give people the opportunity to improve themselves, eventually making their work more productive and more pleasurable.

References

Abramsky, Sasha. 2006. *Conned: How millions went to prison, lost the vote, and helped send George W. Bush to the White House.* New York: New Press.

Ackerman, Frank, and Lisa Heinzerling. 2004. *Priceless: On knowing the price of everything and the value of nothing.* New York: New Press.

Adam, Stephen. 2001. Transnational education project: Report and recommendations (Confederation of European Union Rectors' Conferences, March). http://www.crue.org/espaeuro/transnational_education_project.pdf.

Alesina, Alberto, and Dani Rodrik. 1994. Distributive politics and economic growth. *Quarterly Journal of Economics* 109, no. 2 (May): 465–90.

Alesina, Alberto, and Roberto Perotti. 1996. Income distribution, political instability and investment. *European Economic Review* 40, no. 6 (June): 1203–29.

Alesina, Alberto, and Edward L. Glaeser. 2004. *Fighting poverty in the U.S. and Europe: A world of difference.* Oxford: Oxford University Press.

Alexander, Lamar. 2005. Interview with Jennifer Ludden. *National Public Radio, All Things Considered,* April 16.

Alliance for Justice. 1993. Justice for sale: Shortchanging the public interest for private gain. http://www.allianceforjustice.org/research_publications/publications/collection/Justice_for_Sale.html?referrer_level_id=7335&ref_color=red&ref_name=research_publications&inform=1.

Alterman, Eric. 2004. Dishonest, moronic or both? *The Nation* (April 26): 26.

Altman, Daniel. 2003. Efficiency and equity (In the same breath). *New York Times,* April 20, p. C4.

———. 2004. *Neoconomy: George Bush's revolutionary gamble with America's future.* New York: PublicAffairs.

Amadae, Sonja Michelle. 2003. *Rationalizing capitalist democracy: The cold war origins of rational choice liberalism.* Chicago: University of Chicago Press.

American Electronics Association. 2005. Losing the competitive advantage? The challenge for science and technology in the United States. http://aeanet.org/Publications/ idjj_CompetitivenessMain0205.asp.

American Tort Reform Association. n.d. http://www.atra.org

Anderson, Jenny. 2006. Atop hedge funds, richest of the rich get even more so. *New York Times,* May 26, p. C1.

Angell, Marcia. 1999. The American health care system revisited—A new series. *The New England Journal of Medicine* 340, no. 1 (January 7): n.p.

Anon. 1929. This time they did not cut wages. *Business Week* (December 31): 23–24.

———. 1980. The new NBER: Has scholarship been hurt? *Business Week* (October 6): 95–98.

———. 2001. Is the university-industrial complex out of control? *Nature* 409, no. 6817 (January 11): 119.

———. 2002. The non-taxpaying class. *Wall Street Journal,* November 20, p. A20.

———. 2006. The million-dollar president, soon to be commonplace? *The Chronicle of Higher Education*, November 24.

Archer, Jules. 1973. *The plot to seize the White House.* New York: Hawthorn Books.

Armstrong, Karen. 2001. *The battle for God: A history of fundamentalism.* New York: Alfred A. Knopf.

Association of American Universities. 2004. Statement and recommendations on visa problems harming America's scientific, economic, and security interests. http://www.aau.edu/homeland/JointVisaStatement.pdf.

Atkinson, Anthony B. 1999. *The economic consequences of rolling back the welfare state.* Cambridge: Massachusetts Institute of Technology Press.

Bailey, Stephen Kemp. 1950. *Congress makes a law: The story behind the Employment Act of 1946.* New York: Columbia University Press.

Baily, Martin Neil. 1978. The effectiveness of anticipated policy. *Brookings Papers on Economic Activity* (1): 11–60.

Bank for International Settlements. 2005. Triennial central bank survey. March. http://www.bis.org/publ/rpfx05t.pdf.

Barber, William J. 1985. *From New Era to New Deal: Herbert Hoover, the economists, and American economic policy, 1921–1933.* Cambridge: Cambridge University Press.

Barrett, Paul M. 1986. A movement called 'Law and Economics' sways legal circles—Judge Richard Posner, others favor basing a decision on its costs and benefits—A threat to personal rights? *Wall Street Journal*, August 4.

Barrow, Clyde W. 1990. *Universities and the capitalist state.* Madison: University of Wisconsin Press.

Bartik, Timothy J. 1999. Will welfare reform cause displacement? *W. E. Upjohn Institute for Employment Research Employment Research*, Spring. http://www.upjohninst.org/publications/newsletter/tjb_s99.pdf.

Bassie, V. L. 1946. Consumers' expenditures in war and transition. *Review of Economic Statistics* 28, no. 3 (August): 121–29.

Bauer, Lynn, and Steven D. Owens. 2004. *Justice expenditure and employment statistics.* Washington, DC: U.S. Department of Justice, Bureau of Justice Statistics. http://www.ojp.usdoj.gov/bjs/pub/pdf/jeeus01.pdf.

Baum, Dan. 1996. *Smoke and mirrors: The war on drugs and the politics of failure.* Boston: Little, Brown.

Baum, Sandy. 2005. The truth about Pell grants. January 18. http://www.inside highered.com/views/the_truth_about_pell_grants.

Baum, Sandy, and Marie O'Malley. 2003. College on credit: How borrowers perceive their education debt: Results of the 2002 National Student Loan Survey. http://www.nelliemae.com/library/research_10.html.

Bebchuk, Lucian A., and Jesse Fried. 2004. *Pay without performance: The unfulfilled promise of executive compensation.* Cambridge, MA: Harvard University Press.

Bebchuk, Lucian, and Yaniv Grinstein. 2005. The growth of executive pay. Discussion Paper 510. John M. Olin Center For Law, Economics, and Business. http://papers.ssrn.com/sol3/papers.cfm?abstract_id=648682#PaperDownload.

Becker, Gary S. 1968. Crime and punishment: An economic approach. *Journal of Political Economy* 76, no. 2 (March–April): 169–217.

Beder, Sharon. 2003. *Power play: The fight to control the world's electricity.* New York: New Press.

Beddoe, John. 1885/1971. *The races of Britain: A contribution to the anthropology of Western Europe.* Bristol and London: J. W. Arrowsmith. Repr. London: Hutchinson. Partially reprinted at http://www.isle-of-man.com/manxnotebook/manxnb/v09p023.htm.

Bégaud, Bernard, and Hélène Verdoux. 2004. Did the U.S. boycott of French products spread to include scientific output? *British Medical Journal* 329(7480): 1430–31.

Benabou, Roland. 1996. Inequality and growth. In *NBER macroeconomics annual,* ed. Ben Bernanke and Julio Rotemberg, 11–74. Cambridge: Massachusetts Institute of Technology Press.

Benoit, Bertrand, Dan Roberts, Gary Silverman, and John Thornhill. 2004. U.S. brand giants suffer a sales slump in "Old Europe." *Financial Times* (London), October 25, p. 19.

Bentham, Jeremy. 1962. Anarchical fallacies. In *The works of Jeremy Bentham,* 11 vols., ed. John Bowring, ii, 489–534. New York: Russell and Russell.

Benton, Sherry A., John M. Robertson, Wen-Chih Tseng, Fred B. Newton, and Stephen L. Benton. 2003. Changes in counseling center cient problems across 13 years. *Professional Psychology: Research & Practice* 34, no. 1 (February): 66–72.

Berdahl, Robert M. 2000. The privatization of public universities. Chancellor's Immediate Office, University of California, Berkeley. http://cio.chance.berkeley.edu/chancellor/sp/privatization.htm.

Berlau, John. 1998. Grover Norquist takes on the tyranny of federal taxation. *Insight,* January 26.

Bernasek, Anna. 2004. The next Greenspan? *Fortune,* June 14.

Bernstein, Irving. 1966. *The lean years: A history of the American worker, 1920–1933.* Boston: Houghton Mifflin.

Berry, John M. 2003.Number crunchers vs. recession; Seeking official end, panel wrestles with one stubborn stat. *Washington Post,* July 11, p. E1.

Binns, Arthur. 1943. Is the Wagner Bill for rebuilding our cities desirable? *National Real Estate Journal* 44 (October): 16–20.

Bivens, L. Josh. 2005. Social security's fixable financing issues: Shortfall in funds is not inevitable. Economic Policy Institute Issue Brief no. 207, April 26. http://www.epinet.org/content.cfm/ib207.

Blank, Rebecca M. 1997. *It takes a nation: A new agenda for fighting poverty.* New York: Russell Sage Foundation.

Blank, Rebecca, and Alan Blinder. 1986. Macroeconomics, income distribution and poverty. In *Fighting poverty: What works, what doesn't,* ed. Sheldon Danziger and Daniel Weinberg, 180–208. Cambridge, MA: Harvard University Press.

Blaug, Mark. 1998. Disturbing currents in modern economics. *Challenge* 41, no. 3 (May/June): 11–34.

Bleifuss, Joel. 1995. Lies, damn lies, and GOP anecdotes. *In These Times* (June 12): 12–13.

Blinder, Alan S. 1988. Richard T. Ely lecture: The challenge of high unemployment. *American Economic Review* 78, no. 2 (May): 1–15.

Blyth, Mark. 2002. *Great transformations: Economic ideas and institutional change in the twentieth century.* Cambridge: Cambridge University Press.

Bok, Derek. 1993. *The cost of talent: How executives and professionals are paid and how it affects America.* New York: Free Press.

Bollier, David. 1991. *Citizen action and other big ideas: A history of Ralph Nader and the modern consumer movement.* Washington, DC: Center for Study of Responsive Law.

Borjas, George J. 2005. The labor market impact of high-dkill immigration. *American Economic Review* 95, no. 2 (May): 56–60.

Bork, Robert H. 1990. *The tempting of America: The political seduction of the law.* New York: Free Press.

Boswell, James. 1934–64. *Life of Johnson.* 6 vols. Oxford: Oxford University Press.

Bowles, Samuel, and Richard Edwards. 1985. *Understanding capitalism: Competition, command, and change in the U.S. economy.* New York: Harper and Row.

Bowles, Samuel, and Herbert Gintis. 1995. Escaping the efficiency equity trade-off: Productivity-enhancing asset redistributions. In *Macroeconomic policy after the conservative era: Studies in investment, saving, and finance,* ed. Gerald A. Epstein and Herbert M. Gintis, 408–40. New York: Cambridge University Press.

Bowles, Samuel, and Arjun Jayadev. 2006. Guard labor. *Journal of Development Economics* 79, no. 2 (April): 328–48.

Boyd, Donald, Hamilton Lankford, Susanna Loeb, and James Wyckoff. 2005. Explaining the short careers of high-achieving teachers in schools with low-performing dtudents. *American Economic Review* 95, no. 2 (May): 166–71.

Boyer, Richard D., and Herbert M. Morais. 1955. *Labor's untold story.* New York: Cameron Associates.

Bracey, Gerald. 1998. The eighth Bracey Report on the condition of public education. *Phi Delta Kappan* 80, no. 2 (October): 112–20.

Bradsher, Keith. 2004. *High and mighty on Arnold Schwarzenegger and the Hummer.* New York: Public Affairs.

Brainard, Jeffrey. 2004. Lobbying to bring home the bacon. *Chronicle of Higher Education* 51, no. 9 (October 22): A26.

Brainard, Jeffrey, and Anne Marie Borrego. 2003. Academic pork barrel tops $2 billion for the first time. *Chronicle of Higher Education* (September 26): n.p.

Bronfenbrenner, Martin, ed. 1969. *Is the business cycle obsolete? Based on a conference of the social science council committee on economic stability.* New York: Wiley-Interscience.

Brookings Institution. 2006. *From poverty, opportunity.* Washington, DC: Brookings Institution.

Bruni, Frank. 2001. Bush promotes education, and in a calculated forum. *New York Times,* August 2, p. A14.

Buffett, Warren. 2004. Annual letter to the shareholders of Berkshire Hathaway, Inc. http://www.berkshirehathaway.com/letters/2003ltr.pdf.

———. 2005. Annual letter to the shareholders of Berkshire Hathaway, Inc. http://www.berkshirehathaway.com/letters/2005ltr.pdf.

Burns, Arthur F. 1979. The anguish of central banking. In *The anguish of central banking,* with commentaries by Milutin Cirovic, Jacques J. Polak. Belgrade: Per Jacobsson Foundation. Reprinted in *Federal Reserve Bulletin* 73, no. 9 (September 1987): 687–98. http://www.perjacobsson.org/lectures/1979.pdf.

Burrough, Bryan, and John Helyar. 1990. *Barbarians at the gate: The fall of RJR Nabisco.* New York: Harper and Row.

Busch, Lawrence, et al. 2004. External review of the collaborative research agreement between Novartis Agricultural Discovery Institute, and the regents of the

University of California. http://www.berkeley.edu/news/media/releases/2004/
07/external_novartis_review.pdf.

Bush, George W. 2004. Remarks at a Bush-Cheney reception in Atlanta, Georgia
(January 15). *19 January Weekly Compilation of Presidential Documents* 40, no. 3.
http://www.presidency.ucsb.edu/ws/index.php?pid=72534.

California Community Colleges Chancellor's Office. 2005. Addendum: Impacts of
student fee increase and budget changes on enrollment in the California community colleges: Analysis of fee increase from $18 to $26 per unit: A report to
the legislature, pursuant to provisions of the 2004-05 Budget Act (December).
http://www.cccco.edu/divisions/tris/rp/rp_doc/impact_study_18_26.pdf.

Callahan, David. 1999. $1 billion for ideas: Conservative think tanks in the 1990s.
National Committee for Responsive Philanthropy (March). http://www
.commonwealinstitute.org/ncrp.callahan.1.htm.

Cannon, Lou. 1982. *Reagan*. New York: Putnam.

Carlson, Bo. 1989. Flexibility and the theory of the firm. *International Journal of
Industrial Organization* 7, no. 2 (June): 179–204.

Carnoy, Martin. 1994. *Faded dreams: The politics and economics of race in America*.
New York: Cambridge University Press.

Center for Media and Democracy. n.d. Mercatus Center. http://www.sourcewatch
.org/index.php?title=Mercatus_Center.

Chellaraj, G., K. E. Maskus, and A. Mattoo. 2004. The contribution of skilled immigration and international graduate students to U.S. innovation. Working Paper
no. 04–10 (September), Department of Economics, University of Colorado Center for Economic Analysis. http://www.colorado.edu/Economics/CEA/WPs-04/
wp04-10/wp04-10.pdf.

Chu, Kathy. 2005. Rising bank fees hit consumers. *USA Today*, October 4.

Clarke, G. R. G. 1995. More evidence on income distribution and growth." *Journal
of Development Economics* 47, no. 2 (August): 403–27.

Clement, Douglas. 2005. Interview with James Heckman. *The Region* [Federal
Reserve Bank of Minneapolis] (June). http://minneapolisfed.org/pubs/region/
05-06/heckman.cfm.

Cochran, Thomas C., and William Miller. 1942. *The age of enterprise: A Social history of industrial America*. New York: Harper.

Coddington, Alan. 1983. *Keynesian economics: The search for first principles*. London: Allen and Unwin.

Colander, David C. 1989. Money and the spread of ideas. In *The spread of economic
ideas*, ed. David C. Colander and A. W. Coats, 229–33. Cambridge: Cambridge
University Press.

Colander, David C., and Arjo Klamer. 1987. The making of an economist. *Journal of
Economic Perspectives* 1, no. 2 (Autumn): 95–111.

Colby, Gerard. 1974. *Du Pont: Behind the nylon curtain*. Englewood Cliffs, NJ: Pren-
tice-Hall.

Collins, Chuck, Mike Lapham, and Scott Klinger. 2004. *I didn't do it alone: Society's
contribution to individual wealth and success*. Boston: United for a Fair Economy.
http://www.responsiblewealth.org/press/2004/notalonereportfinal.pdf.

Collins, Robert M. 1981. *The business response to Keynes, 1929–1964*. New York:
Columbia University Press.

————. 2000. *More: The politics of economic growth in postwar America*. Oxford: Oxford University Press.

Committee on Assuring the Health of the Public in the 21st Century, Board on Health Promotion and Disease Prevention, Institute of Medicine. 2003. *The future of the public's health in the 21st century*. Washington, DC: National Academies Press.

Committee on Recent Economic Changes. 1929. *Recent economic changes in the United States: Report of the committee on recent economic changes of the president's conference on unemployment*. New York: McGraw-Hill.

Court, Jamie. 2003. *Corporateering: How corporate power seals your personal freedom . . . And what you can do about it*. New York: J. P. Tarcher.

Cowie, Jefferson. 2002. Nixon's class struggle: Strategic formulations of the new-right worker. *Labor History* 43, no. 3 (August): 257–83.

Curtis, John W. and Monica F. Jacobe. 2006. Consequences: An increasingly contingent faculty. American Association of University Professors. http://www.aaup .org/AAUP/pubsres/research/conind2006.htm

Curtis, L. Perry. 1997. *Apes and angels: The Irishman in Victorian caricature*. Rev. ed. Washington, DC: Smithsonian Institution Press.

Dalberg-Acton, John Emerich Edward [Lord Acton]. 1877/1907. The history of freedom in antiquity: An address delivered to the members of the Bridgenorth Institute, February 26, 1877. In *The history of freedom and other essays*, 1–29. Repr. London: Macmillan.

Danitz, Tiffany. 2001. States pay $400 million for tests in 2001. Stateline.org. February 27. http://www.stateline.org/live/ViewPage.action?siteNodeId= 136&languageId=1&contentId=14274.

Davis, Bob. 2004. With White House ex-staffers, Mercatus helps zap codes it says restrict business. *Wall Street Journal*, July 16, p. A1.

Deane, Claudia. 2002. Computer-assisted influence? Think tank seeks payoff aiding press with data. *Washington Post*, April 19.

de Figueiredo, John M., and Brian S. Silverman. n.d. Academic earmarks and the returns to lobbying. *The Journal of Law and Economics*, forthcoming.

de Tocqueville, Alexis. 1835. *Democracy in America*. 2 vols. Trans. Henry Reeve. New York: D. Appleton.

Delsohn, Gary. 2005. Governor: Starve state's "Monster." *Sacramento Bee*, January 19.

Derthick, Martha, and Paul J. Quirk. 1985. *The politics of deregulation*. Washington, DC: Brookings Institution.

Dew-Becker, Ian, and Robert J. Gordon. 2005. Where did the productivity growth go? Inflation dynamics and the distribution of income. *Brookings Papers on Economic Activity* (2): 67–127.

Dewald, W., J. Thursby, and R. Anderson. 1986. Replication of empirical economics: The *Journal of Money, Credit and Banking* project. *American Economic Review* 76, no. 4 (September): 587–603.

Diamond, Peter A., and Peter R. Orszag. 2005. Saving social security. *The Journal of Economic Perspectives* 19, no. 22 (Spring): 11–32.

Dillon, Sam. 2004. Ivory tower executive suite gets C.E.O.-level salaries. *New York Times*, November 15.

Dodge, Joseph M., and Jay A. Soled. 2005. Inflated tax basis and the quarter-trillion-dollar revenue question. *Tax Notes* 106, no. 4 (January 24): 453–62.

Doyle, Roger. 1999. Behind bars in the U.S. and Europe. *Scientific American* 281, no. 2 (August): 25.

Draffan, George. 2003. *The elite consensus: When corporations wield the constitution.* New York: Apex Press.

DuBoff, Richard B., and Herman, Edward S. 1972. The new economics: Handmaiden of inspired truth. *Review of Radical Economics* 4, no. 4 (August): 54–84.

Easterbrook, Frank H., and Daniel R. Fischel. 1982. Antitrust suits by targets of tender offers. *Michigan Law Review* 80, no. 6 (May): 1155–78.

Easterly, William. 2002. *The elusive quest for growth.* Cambridge: Massachusetts Institute of Technology Press.

Easton, Nina J. 2002. *Gang of five: Leaders at the center of the conservative ascendancy.* New York: Touchstone Books.

Editors of *Monthly Review.* 1983. Unemployment: The failure of private enterprise. *Monthly Review* 35, no. 2 (June): 1–9.

Edsall, Thomas Byrne. 1984. *The new politics of inequality.* New York: W. W. Norton.
———. 2005. Think tank's ideas shifted as Malaysia ties grew business interests overlapped policy. *Washington Post,* April 17.

Edwards, Lee. 1997. *The power of ideas: The Heritage Foundation at 25 years.* Ottawa, IL: Jameson Books.

Elgar, Frank J., Chris Roberts, Nina Parry-Langdon, and William Boyce. 2005. Income inequality and alcohol use: A multilevel analysis of drinking and drunkenness in adolescents in 34 countries. *The European Journal of Public Health* 15(3): 245–50.

Ely, Richard T. 1883. The past and the present of political economy. *Overland Monthly and Out West Magazine* 2, no. 9 (September): 225–35. http://www.hti .umich.edu/cgi/t/text/text-idx?c=moajrnl;idno=ahj1472.2-02.009;node=ahj1472 .2-02.009:1.
———. 1884. *The past and the present of political economy.* Baltimore: John Hopkins University Studies in the Social Sciences Second Series.
———. 1894. *The strength and weakness of socialism.* New York: Chautauqua Press.
———. 1936. The founding and early history of the American Economic Association. *American Economic Review* 26, no. 1 (March): 141–50.

Engardio, Pete, and Bruce Einhorn. 2005. Outsourcing innovation. *Business Week* (March 21): 86–94.

Epstein, Gerald, and Dorothy Power. 2002. The return of finance and finance's returns: recent trends in renter incomes in OECD countries, 1960–2000. Research Brief 2002–02, University of Massachusetts, Amherst, Political Economy Research Institute. http://www.umass.edu/peri/pdfs/RB2002-2.pdf.

Epstein, Richard A. 1985. *Takings: Private property and the power of eminent domain.* Cambridge, MA: Harvard University Press.

Etzold, Thomas H., and John Lewis Gaddis. 1978. NSC 68: The strategic reassessment of 1950. In *Containment: Documents on American policy and strategy, 1945–1950,* ed. Thomas H. Etzold and John Lewis Gaddis, 383–85. New York: Columbia University Press.

Fabricant, Solomon. 1984. Toward a firmer basis of economic policy: The founding of the National Bureau of Economic Research. National Bureau of Economic Research. http://www.nber.org/nberhistory/sfabricantrev.pdf.

Fabrikant, Geraldine. 2006. Executives take company planes as if their own. *New York Times*, May 10.

Faler, Brian. 2005. Aid to Christian school in Alaska spurs lawsuit. *Washington Post*, May 9, p. A21.

Families USA. 2005. Paying a premium: The added cost of care for the uninsured. *Families USA*. http://www.familiesusa.org/site/PageServer?pagename=Paying _a_Premium_splash.

Feldstein, Martin S. 1974. Social security, induced retirement and aggregate capital accumulation. *Journal of Political Economy* 82, no. 5 (September–October): 905–26.

———. 1993. Clinton's revenue mirage. *Wall Street Journal*, April 6.

———. 1996. The missing piece in policy analysis: Social security reform (Richard T. Ely lecture). *American Economic Review* 86, no. 2 (May): 1–14.

———. 1999. Reducing poverty not inequality. *Public Interest* (Fall): 33–41.

———. 2005a. Rethinking social insurance. *The American Economic Review* 95, no. 1 (March): 1–24.

———. 2005b. Saving social security. *Wall Street Journal*, July 15.

Fernandez, Raquel, and Richard Rogerson. 1996. Income distribution, communities, and the quality of public education. *Quarterly Journal of Economics* 111, no. 1 (February): 135–64.

Feulner, Edwin J. 2002. The Heritage Foundation. In *Think tanks and civil societies: Catalysts for action*, ed. J. G. McGann and R. K. Weaver, 67–85. New Brunswick, NJ: Transaction Press.

Fialka, John J. 1999. How Koch Industries tries to influence judicial system. *Wall Street Journal*, August 9, p. A20.

Field, Alexander J. 2003. The most technologically progressive decade of the century. *American Economic Review* 93, no. 4 (September): 1399–413.

Finn, Michael G. 2003. Stay rates of foreign doctorate recipients from U.S. universities, 2001. Oak Ridge (TN) Institute for Science and Education. http://www.orau .gov/orise/pubs/stayrate03.pdf.

Fite, Gilbert C. 1991. *Richard B. Russell, Jr.: Senator from Georgia*. Chapel Hill: University of North Carolina Press.

Fones-Wolf, Elizabeth A. 1994. *Selling free enterprise: The business assault on labor and liberalism, 1945–60*. Urbana: University of Illinois Press.

Ford, Glen, and Peter Gamble. 2004. "No choice": Wal-Mart prepares to bury the left under a mountain of money. *In These Times* (April 26): 22–23, 29.

Foust, Dean. 2005. "Protection" racket?: As overdraft and other fees become huge profit sources for banks, critics see abuses. *Business Week* (May 2): n.p.

Frank, Robert. 2004. Rising riches stir rivalry for ever-bigger yachts. *Wall Street Journal*, December 14, p. A1.

Franklin, Stephen. 2001. *Three strikes: Labor's heartland losses and what they mean for working Americans*. New York: Guilford Press.

Freeman, Richard B. 1996. Why do so many young American men commit crimes and what might we do about it? *Journal of Economic Perspectives* 10, no. 1 (Winter): 25–42.

Fried, Charles. 1991. *Order and law: Arguing the Reagan revolution—A firsthand account*. New York: Simon and Schuster.

Friedman, Milton. 1968. The role of monetary policy. *American Economic Review* 58, no. 1 (March): 1–17.

———. 1980. The changing character of financial markets. In *The American economy in transition*, ed. Martin Feldstein, 78–86. Chicago: University of Chicago Press.

———. 1988. Why the twin deficits are a blessing. *Wall Street Journal*, December 14, p. A14.

———. 2003. What every American wants. *Wall Street Journal*, January 15, p. A10.

Friedman, Thomas L. 1999. *The lexus and the olive tree*. New York: Farrar Straus and Giroux.

Galanter, Marc. 1992. Pick a number, any number. *American Lawyer* (April): n.p.

Galbraith, John Kenneth. 1961. *The great crash*. Boston: Houghton Mifflin.

Gale, William G., and Peter R. Orszag. 2004. The budget outlook: Projections and implications. *The Economists' Voice* 1, no. 2. http://www.bepress.com/ev/vol1/iss2/art6.

———. Forthcoming. Budget deficits, national saving, and interest rates. *Brookings Papers on Economic Activity*. http://www.brook.edu/views/papers/20040910 orszaggale.htm.

Gapper, John, and Peter Thal Larsen. 2005. Visa rules hurting U.S., warns Gates. *Financial Times*, January 31, p. 1.

Garbarino, Joseph. 1962. *Wage policy and long term contracts*. Washington, DC: The Brookings Institution.

Gelfand, Mark I. 1975. *A nation of cities: The federal government and urban America, 1933–1965*. New York: Oxford University Press.

General Motors, Ford, DaimlerChrysler, and the Canadian Auto Workers. 2002. Joint letter (September 12). http://www.caw.ca/campaigns&issues/ongoing campaigns/jointletter.asp.

Gerth, Jeff, and Tim Weiner. 1997. Arms makers see bonanza in selling NATO expansion. *New York Times*, June 28, p. A1.

Gingrich, Newt. 1990. Language: A key mechanism of control. Partially reprinted as Accentuate the negative. *Harpers Hagazine* 281, no. 1686 (November): 16–17.

———. 2005. *Winning the future: A 21st century contract with America*. Washington, DC: Regnery.

Gladieux, Lawrence, and Laura Perna. 2005. Borrowers who drop out: A neglected aspect of the college student loan trend. National Center for Public Policy and Higher Education. http://www.highereducation.org/reports/borrowing/borrowers.pdf.

Glaeser, Edward L., and Raven Saks. 2004. Corruption in America. Harvard Institute of Economic Research Discussion Paper 2043 (October). http://post.economics.harvard.edu/hier/2004papers/HIER2043.pdf.

Glaeser, Edward L., Jose Scheinkman, and Andrei Shleifer. 2003. The injustice of inequality. *Journal of Monetary Economics* 50, no. 1 (April): 199–222.

Glasser, Ira. 2006. Drug busts = Jim Crow. *The Nation* (July 10): n.p.

Golden, Daniel. 2004. Nonunion teacher groups cost NEA membership and clout. *Wall Street Journal*, July 28, p. A1.

Golden, Soma. 1980. Superstar of the new economists. *New York Times Magazine* (March 23): 30–33, 91–95.

Goldsmith, John A. 1993. *Colleagues: Richard B. Russell and his apprentice, Lyndon B. Johnson.* Washington, DC: Seven Locks Press.

Goodman, Walter. 1981. Irving Kristol: Patron saint of the new right. *New York Times Magazine* (December 6): n.p.

Goodstein, Laurie, and David D. Kirkpatrick. 2004. Conservative group amplifies voice of protestant orthodoxy. *New York Times*, May 22.

Gordon, Colin. 1991. Health care the corporate way. *The Nation* (March 25): 376–80.

Gordon, Robert A. 1969. The stability of the U.S. economy. In *Is the business cycle obsolete? Based on a conference of the social science council committee on economic stability*, ed. Martin Bronfenbrenner, 3–35. New York: Wiley-Interscience.

Gordon, Robert J. 1980. Postwar macroeconomics: The evolution of events and ideas. In *The American economy in transition: A sixtieth anniversary conference*, ed. Martin Feldstein, 101–62. Chicago: University of Chicago Press.

Gould, Eric, Bruce Weinberg, and David Mustard. 1998. Crime rates and local labor market opportunities in the United States: 1979–1995. Working Paper, no. 98–472 (August), University of Georgia.

Greenspan, Alan. 2004. Question-and-answer session after his semiannual testimony on monetary policy before the Senate Banking, Housing and Urban Affairs Committee (July 20).

———. 2005. Question-and-answer session after his semiannual testimony on monetary policy before the Senate Banking, Housing and Urban Affairs Committee (February 16).

Greider, William. 1991. The education of David Stockman. *The Atlantic Monthly* 248, no. 5 (December): 27–54.

Grey, Thomas C. 1986. The Malthusian constitution. *University of Miami Law Review* 41:21–49.

Griliches, Zvi. 1988. Productivity puzzles and R&D: Another nonexplanation. *Journal of Economic Perspectives* 2, no. 4 (Fall): 9–21.

Grogger, Jeff. 1998. Market wages and youth crime. *Journal of Labor Economics* 16, no. 4 (October): 756–91.

Gross, Daniel. 2006. The CEO bought a yacht?: Then it's time to sell. *Slate* (August 15). http://www.slate.com/id/2147788.

Habakkuk, H. J. 1962. *American and British technology in the nineteenth century: The search for labour-saving inventions.* Cambridge: Cambridge University Press.

Hahn, Frank. 1970. Some adjustment problems (Presidential address to the econometric society). *Econometrica* 38, no. 1 (January): 1–17.

Haldeman, H. R. 1994. *The Haldeman Diaries: Inside the Nixon White House.* New York: G. P. Putnam's Sons.

Hammond, Bray. 1957. *Banks and politics.* Princeton, NJ: Princeton University Press.

Harpaz, Beth J. 2000. Billionaire Buffett takes a swipe at trust-fund kids. *Des Moines Register*, September 28, p. 1.

Harrison, Bennett. 1994. *Lean and mean: The changing landscape of corporate power in the age of flexibility.* New York: Basic Books.

Hartung, William D., and Michelle Ciarrocca. 2000. Star wars, continued. *Multinational Monitor* 21, no. 10 (October 1). http://multinationalmonitor.org/mm2000/00october/corp1.html.

Head, Simon. 2003. *The new ruthless economy: Work and power in the digital age.* New York: Oxford University Press.

Healy, Paul M., and Krishna G. Palepu. 2003. The fall of Enron. *Journal of Economic Perspectives* 17, no. 2 (Spring): 3–26.

Heller, Walter W. 1966. *New dimensions of political economy.* New York: W. W. Norton.

Henry, David. 2005. Corporate America's new Achilles' heel. *Business Week* (March 28): 32–33.

Henwood, Doug. 2003. *After the new economy.* New York: New Press.

———. 2005. Social security, revisited. *Left Business Observer,* no. 110 (March). http://www.leftbusinessobserver.com/SocialSecurityRevisited.html.

Herbert, Bob. 2007. Working harder for the man. *New York Times,* January 8.

Heritage Foundation. 2003. *Annual report 2002.* http://www.heritage.org/About/loader.cfm?url=/commonspot/security/getfile.cfm&PageID=39932.

Herman, Edward S. 1993. The politicized "Science." *Z Magazine* (February): 43–48.

Hertzberg, Hendrik. 2004. Reckless driver. *The New Yorker* (March 8): 25–26.

Hey, John. 1997. The economic journal: Report of the managing editor. *Royal Economic Society Newsletter* (January): 3–5.

Himmelstein, David U., Elizabeth Warren, Deborah Thorne, and Steffie Woolhandler. 2005. Illness and injury as contributors to bankruptcy. *Health Affairs,* February. http://content.healthaffairs.org/cgi/reprint/hlthaff.w5.63v1?maxtoshow=&HITS=10&hits=10&RESULTFORMAT=&fulltext=Illness+and+Injury&andorexactfulltext=and&searchid=1&FIRSTINDEX=0&resourcetype=H.

Hoffman, David. 1983. Blames Tax cuts, defense buildup; Feldstein is warned on deficit stance. *Washington Post,* December 1.

Holmes, Oliver Wendell, Jr. 1927. Dissenting opinion, compania general de tabacos de Filipinas v. collector of internal revenue, 275 U.S. 87, 100.

Hoover, Herbert. 1952. *The Great Depression, 1929–1941.* Vol. 3 of *The memoirs of Herbert Hoover.* New York: Macmillan.

Huber, Peter. 1988. *Liability: The legal revolution and its consequences.* New York: Basic Books.

Huntington, Samuel P. 1975. The United States. In *The crisis of democracy: Report on the governability of democracies to the trilateral commission,* ed. Michel Crozier, Samuel Huntington, and Joji Watanuki, 59–117. New York: New York University Press.

Hutchins, Robert. 1944. Threat to American education. *Collier's,* no. 114 (December 30): 20–21.

Jeffries, John Calvin. 1994. *Justice Lewis F. Powell, Jr.* New York: C. Scribner's Sons.

Jenks, Jeremiah. 1890. The economic outlook. *Dial* 10:n.p.

Jensen, Richard J. 1989. The causes and cures of unemployment in the Great Depression. *Journal of Interdisciplinary History* 19, no. 4 (Spring): 553–84.

Johnston, David Cay. 2003. *Perfectly legal: The covert campaign to rig our tax system to benefit the super rich—And cheat everybody else.* New York: Portfolio.

Jones, Del. 2006. Golf bragging rights bittersweet as firms of top CEO golfers often sub-par. *USA Today,* September 6. http://www.usatoday.com/money/companies/management/2006-09-06-golf-ceos_x.htm.

Judis, John B. 2000. *The paradox of American democracy: Elites, special interests, and the betrayal of public trust.* New York: Pantheon Books.

———. 2003. Minister without portfolio. *The American Prospect* 14, no. 5 (May). http://www.prospect.org/print/V14/5/judis-j.html

Juhasz, Antonia. 2006. *The Bush agenda: Invading the world, one economy at a time.* New York: Regan Books.

Kaldor, Nicholas, and Tibor Barna. 1943. The 1943 white paper on national income and expenditure. *The Economic Journal* 53, no. 210/211 (June): 259–74.

Kendall, Douglas T., and Charles P. Lord. 1998. *The takings project: Using federal courts to attack community and environmental protections* (Community Rights Counsel). http://www.communityrights.org/CombatsJudicialActivism/TP/TPcontents.asp.

Keynes, John Maynard. 1924. Alfred Marshall, 1842–1925. In *Essays in biography.* Vol. 10, *The collected writings of John Maynard Keynes,* 161–231. London: Macmillan, 1973.

———. 1930a. Economic possibilities for our grandchildren. *Nation and Athenaeum* (October). Repr. *Essays in persuasion* 9. *Collected works of John Maynard Keynes,* ed. Donald Moggridge, 321–31. London: Macmillan, 1972.

———. 1936. *The general theory of employment, interest and money.* London: Macmillan.

———. 1938. Letter to Roy Harrod (July 4). In *The collected writings of John Maynard Keynes.* Vol. 14, *The general theory and after,* Part II, *Defence and development,* 295-97. London: Macmillan, 1973.

Kiester, Edwin, Jr. 1994. The GI Bill may be the best deal ever made by Uncle Sam. *Smithsonian Magazine* 25, no. 4 (November): 129-32.

Kilgore, Ed. 2003. Starving the beast: If President Bush keeps listening to Grover Norquist, republicans won't have a government to kick around anymore. *Democratic Blueprint* 22:9–11.

King, Tracey, and Ellynne Bannon. 2002. At what cost? The price that working students pay for a college education. The state PIRGs' higher education project. http://www.studentpirgs.org/atwhatcost.pdf.

Kitman, Jamie. 2000. The secret history of lead. *The Nation* (March 20): 11-44.

Knott, Alex. 2005. Industry of influence nets almost $13 billion: Shadowy lobbyists ignore rules and exploit connections. Center for Public Integrity (April 7). http://www.publicintegrity.org/lobby/report.aspx?aid=675&sid=200.

Kogan, Richard, and Robert Greenstein. 2005. President portrays social security shortfall as enormous, but his tax cuts and drug benefit will cost at least five times as much. Center on Budget and Policy Priorities (February 11). http://www.cbpp.org/1-4-05socsec.htm.

Kohl, Herbert. 1967. *36 Children.* New York: New American Library.

Kostinen, Paul. 2004. *Arsenal of World War II: Political economy of American warfare.* Lawrence: University Press of Kansas.

Kozol, Jonathan. 1991. *Savage inequalities: Children in America's schools.* New York: Crown.

———. 2005. *The shame of the nation: The restoration of Apartheid schooling in America.* New York: Random.

Kristof, Nicholas D. 2006. America's laziest man? *New York Times,* November 7.

Kristol, Irving. 1978a. The shareholder constituency. In *Two cheers for capitalism,* 146-50. New York: Basic Books.

———. 1978b. On corporate philanthropy. In *Two cheers for capitalism*,141–45. New York: Basic Books.

———. 1995. *Neoconservatism: The autobiography of an idea*. New York: Free Press.

Krueger, Alan B. 2005. The farm-subsidy model of financing academia. *New York Times*, May 26.

Krueger, Alan B., and Alexandre Mas. 2004. Strikes, scabs and tread separations: Labor strife and the production of defective Bridgestone/Firestone tires.*Journal of Political Economy* 112, no. 2 (April): 253-89.

Krueger, Anne O. 1974. The political economy of the rent-seeking society. *American Economic Review* 64, no. 4 (June): 291-303.

Krugman, Paul. 1996. The spiral of inequality. *Mother Jones* (November/December): n.p.

———. 2002. For richer. *New York Times Magazine* (October 20): n.p.

Kuznets, Simon. 1936. Review of three Brookings Institutions works. *Science and Society* 1, no. 2 (Winter): 241–47.

———. 1955. Economic growth and income inequality. *American Economic Review* 45, no. 1. (March): 1–28.

Laband, David N., and John P. Sophocleus. 1992. An estimate of resource expenditures on transfer activity in the United States. *Quarterly Journal of Economics* 107, no. 3 (Autumn): 959-83.

Landay, Jerry. 2002. Attack on American free enterprise system: How a prominent lawyer's attack memo changed America. mediatransparency.org. http://www .mediatransparency.org/stories/powellmanifesto.htm.

———. 2004. The apparat: George W. Bush's back-door political machine. mediatransparency.org (March 18). http://www.mediatransparency.org/stories/ apparat.html.

Lapham, Lewis H. 2004. Tentacles of rage: The republican propaganda mill: A brief history. *Harpers Magazine* (September): 31–41.

Lebergott, Stanley. 1984. *The Americans: An economic record*. New York: Norton.

Lee, Fred. 2004. History and identity: The case of radical economics, 1945-70. *Review of Radical Political Economics* 36, no. 2 (Spring): 177-95.

Leeson. Robert. 1997. The political economy of the inflation-unemployment trade-off. *History of Political Economy* 29, no. 1 (Spring): 117-56.

Leimer, Dean R., and Selig D. Lesnoy. 1982. Social security and private saving: New Time-series evidence. *Journal of Political Economy* 90, no. 3 (June): 606-29.

Lekachman, Robert. 1966. *The age of Keynes*. New York: Random House.

Lemieux, Thomas, and David Card. 1998. Education, earnings, and the Canadian G.I. Bill. n.p.

Leonhardt, David. 2002. Scholarly mentor to Bush's team. *New York Times*, December 1.

Leontief, Wassily. 1971. Theoretical assumptions and nonobserved facts. *American Economic Review* 61. no. 1 (March): 1–7.

Lesnoy, Selig D., and Dean R. Leimer. 1985. Social security and private saving: Theory and historical evidence. *Social Security Bulletin* 48, no. 1 (January): 14–30.

Levy, David M., and Sandra Peart. 2002. The secret history of the dismal science. http://levine.sscnet.ucla.edu/papers/ip.ch1.pdf.

Lewis, Michael. 1989. *Liar's poker: Rising through the wreckage on Wall Street*. New York: W. W. Norton.

Lindert, Peter H. 2004. *Growing public: Social spending and economic growth since the eighteenth century*. Cambridge: Cambridge University Press.

Lindorff, Dave. 2005. GM's healthcare double standard. *In These Times* (May 9): 8–9.

Livingston, James. 1986. *Origins of the federal reserve system: Money, class, and corporate capitalism, 1890–1913*. Ithaca, NY: Cornell University Press.

Lochner, Lance, and Enrico Moretti. 2004. The effect of education on crime: Evidence from prison inmates, arrests, and self-reports. *American Economic Review* 94. no. 1 (March): 155-89.

Loungani, Prakash. 2004. Getting there first: An economist's lifelong study of the effects of taxes and social insurance. *Finance and Development* (March): 4–7.

Lowe, Janet. 1997. *Warren Buffett speaks: Wit and wisdom from the world's greatest investor*. New York: John Wiley and Sons.

Lucas, Robert E., Jr. 1970. Capacity, overtime, and empirical production functions. *American Economic Review* 60, no. 2 (May): 23–27. Repr. *Studies in business cycle theory*, by Robert E. Lucas, Jr., 146–55. Cambridge: Massachusetts Institute of Technology Press, 1983.

———. 1980a. Methods and problems in business cycle theory. *Journal of Money, Credit, and Banking* 12 (November): 696–715. Repr. *Studies in business cycle theory*, by Robert E. Lucas, Jr., 271–96. Cambridge: Massachusetts Institute of Technology Press.

———. 1980b. The death of Keynesian economics. *Issues and Ideas* (Winter): n.p.

———. 1981. Tobin and monetarism: A review article. *Journal of Economic Literature* 19, no. 2 (June): 558–67.

———. 1987. *Models of business cycles. The Yjiro Jannson lectures*. Oxford: Basil Blackwell.

———. 1988. On the mechanics of economic development. *Journal of Monetary Economics* 22, no. 1 (July): 3–42.

———. 1992. On efficiency and distribution. *Economic Journal* 102, no. 411 (March): 233–47.

———. 2003. The Industrial Revolution past and future. *The Region. Federal Reserve Bank of Minneapolis, Annual Report*. http://www.minneapolisfed.org/pubs/region/04-05/.

Lucas, Robert E., Jr., and Leonard A. Rapping. 1969. Real wages, employment, and inflation. *Journal of Political Economy* 77, no. 5 (September–October): 721–54.

Luthar, Suniya S. 2003. The culture of affluence: Psychological costs of material wealth. *Child Development* 74, no. 6 (November): 1581–93.

McCracken, Jeffrey. 2004. One cost burdens carmakers. *Detroit Free Press* (August 6).

McGann, J. G., and R. K. Weaver, eds. 2002. *Think tanks and civil societies: Catalysts for action*. New Brunswick, NJ: Transaction Press.

McIntyre, Robert S., and T. D. Coo Nguyen. 2004. *Corporate income taxes in the Bush years* (Citizens for Tax Justice: Institute on Taxation and Economic Policy) (September). http://www.ctj.org/corpfed04pr.pdf.

McIntyre, Robert S., and T. D. Coo Nguyen. 2005. *Corporate tax avoidance in the states even worse than federal*. Citizens for Tax Justice: Institute on Taxation and Economic Policy) (September). http://www.ctj.org/pdf/corp0205an.pdf.

MacIver, Robert M. 1955. *Academic freedom in our time*. New York: Columbia University Press.

Magdoff, Harry, and Paul Sweezy. 1983. International finance and national power. *Monthly Review* 35, no. 5 (October): 1–13.

Maier, Charles S. 1987. *In search of stability: Explorations in historical political economy.* New Rochelle, NY: Cambridge University Press.

Makinson, Larry. 2004. *Outsourcing the Pentagon: Who benefits from the politics and economics of national security?* Center for Public Integrity (September 29). http://www.mindfully.org/Reform/2004/Pentagon-Outsourcing-CPI29sep04.htm.

Marcus, Ruth. 1998. Issues groups fund seminars for judges; Classes at resorts cover property rights. *Washington Post*, April 9, p. A1.

Maremont, Mark. 2005. Frequent fliers: Amid crackdown, the jet perk suddenly looks a lot pricier for CEOs. *Wall Street Journal*, May 25, p. A1.

Markusen, Ann R. 2003. The case against privatizing national security. *Governance: An International Journal of Policy, Administration, and Institutions* 16, no. 4 (October): 471–501.

Mas, Alexandre. 2003. Labor unrest and the quality of production: Evidence from the construction equipment resale market. n.p.

Mathewson, Stanley. 1939. *Restriction of output among unorganized workers* Carbondale: Southern Illinois University Press.

Mathiason, Nick. 2005. Super-rich hide trillions offshore. *The Observer* (March 27): n.p.

Mauer, Marc. 2003. *Comparative international rates of incarceration: An examination of causes and trends presented to the U.S. Commission on Civil Rights.* Washington, DC: The Sentencing Project. http://www.sentencingproject.org/pdfs/pub9036.pdf.

Mead, Lawrence. 1986. *Beyond entitlement: The social obligations of citizenship.* New York: Free Press.

Means, Gardiner C. 1975. Simultaneous inflation and unemployment: A challenge to theory and policy. *Challenge* 18, no. 4 (September/October): 6–20. Repr. from *The roots of inflation: The international crisis*, ed. Gardiner Means et al., 1–33. New York: Burt Franklin, 1975.

Meckler, Laura. 2006. Why big airlines are starting a fight with business jets. *Wall Street Journal*, June 1, p. A1.

Media Transparency. (1). n.d. The Powell memo. http://www.mediatransparency.org/story.php?storyID=22

———. (2). n.d. Grants to Pacific Legal Foundation. http://www.mediatransparency.org/search_results/info_on_any_recipient.php?recipientID=760

———. (3). n.d. Grants to the National Bureau of Economic Research. http://www.mediatransparency.org/search_results/info_on_any_recipient.php?recipientID=243.

Merton, Robert K. 1942. Science and technology in a democratic order. *Journal of Legal and Political Sociology* 1, nos. 1–2 (October): 115–26.

———. 1968. The Matthew effect in science. *Science* 159, no. 3810 (January 5): 56–63.

Metcalf, Lee, and Vic Reinemer. 1967. *Overcharge.* New York: D. McKay.

Mill, John Stuart. 1848. *Principles of political economy with some of their applications to social philosophy*, vols. 2–3. *Collected works*, ed. J. M. Robson. Toronto: University of Toronto Press.

Miner, Barbara. 2004. Why the right hates public education. *The Progressive* (January): 22-24.

Minow, Nell. 2001. The use of company aircraft. The Corporate Library. http://www.thecorporatelibrary.com/special/misc/aircraft.html.

Minsky, Hyman P. 1982. Debt deflation processes in today's institutional environment. *Banca Nazionale del Lavoro Quarterly Review* 143 (December): 375–93.

Mirowski, Philip. 2001. *Machine dreams: Economics becomes a cyborg science.* Cambridge: Cambridge University Press.

Mises, Ludwig von. 1955. Inequality of wealth and incomes. Ideas on liberty (May). Repr. *Economic freedom and intervention: An anthology of articles and essays by Ludwig von Mises*, ed. Bettina B. Greaves. Irvington-on-Hudson, New York: Foundation for Economic Education, 1990. http://www.mises.org/efandi/ch9.asp.

Mitchell, Daniel J. 1998. How government policies discourage savings. Backgrounder no. 1185. http://www.heritage.org/Research/PoliticalPhilosophy/BG1185.cfm#pgfId=1005754.

Mitchell, Wesley C. 1936. *Retrospect and prospect: 1920-1935.* New York: National Bureau of Research.

Monbiot, George. 2002. The fake persuaders: Corporations are inventing people to rubbish their opponents on the internet. *The Guardian* (May 14): n.p.

Morgenson, Gretchen. 2005. Only the little people pay for lawn care. *New York Times*, May.

Morgenthau, Hans. 1957. Introduction to *Ethics and United States foreign policy*, ed. Ernest Lefever, xv–xix. New York: Meridian Books.

Mulligan, Casey B. 1998. Pecuniary incentives to work in the United States during World War II. *Journal of Political Economy* 106, no. 5 (October): 1033–77.

Murphy, Kevin M., Andrei Shleifer, and Robert Vishny. 1991. The allocations of talent: Implications for growth. *Quarterly Journal of Economics* 106, no. 2 (May): 503–30.

———. 1993. Why is rent-seeking so costly to growth? *American Economic Review* 83, no. 2 (May): 409–14.

Murray, Alan. 2004. Microsoft foe quits antitrust crusade—With check in hand. *Wall Street Journal*, December 7, p. A4.

———. 2005. Health-care overhaul: GM CEO weighs in. *Wall Street Journal*, February 9, p. A2.

Myers, William Starr, and Walter H. Newton. 1936. *The Hoover administration: A documented narrative.* New York: Charles Scribner.

Naastepad, C. W. M., and Alfred Kleinknecht. 2004. The Dutch productivity slowdown: The culprit at last? *Structural Change and Economic Dynamics* 15:137–63.

Nader, Ralph. 1995. Nader's raid on corporate reports: If tort liability is such a crippler to American industry, why do companies downplay that effect in their SEC reports. *Recorder* (May 10): 8.

Narin, Francis, Kimberly S. Hamilton, and Dominic Olivastro. 1997. The increasing linkage between U.S. technology and public science. *Research Policy* 26(3): 317-30.

National Intelligence Council. 2005. Mapping the global future: Report of the National Intelligence Council's 2020 Project. http://www.foia.cia.gov/2020/2020.pdf.

National Resources Committee. 1939. *The structure of the American economy*. Washington, DC: National Resources Committee.

Neal, Alfred C. 1981. *Business power and public policy*. New York: Praeger.

Nelson, Emily, and Laurie P. Cohen. 2002. Why Grubman was so keen to get his twins into the Y: Rich and famous New Yorkers see preschool as a passport to success. *Wall Street Journal*, November 15.

Netburn, Deborah. 2002. Panic rooms of New York. *New York Observer*, April 1.

Noble, David. 1979. *America by design*. Oxford: Oxford University Press.

Norquist, Grover. 2001. Interview with Mara Liasson, *National Public Radio, Morning Edition*, May 25.

O'Brien, Anthony Patrick. 1989. Behavioral explanation for nominal wage rigidity during the Great Depression. *Quarterly Journal of Economics* 104, no. 4 (November): 719–36.

O'Connor, Michael J. L. 1944. *Origins of academic economics in the United States*. New York: Garland, 1974.

O'Leary, James J. 1945. Consumption as a factor in postwar employment. *American Economic Review* 35, no. 2 (May): 37–55.

O'Reilly, Kenneth. 1995. *Nixon's piano: Presidents and racial politics from Washington to Clinton*. New York: Free Press.

Oglesby, Carl. 1976. *The Yankee and cowboy war: Conspiracies from Dallas to Watergate*. Mission, KS: Sheed Andrews and McMeel.

Okun, Arthur M. 1970. *The political economy of prosperity*. New York: W. W. Norton.

———. 1980. Postwar macroeconomic performance. In *The American economy in transition: A sixtieth anniversary conference*, ed. Martin Feldstein, 162–69. Chicago: University of Chicago Press.

Olmstead, Frederick Law. 1856. *A journey in the seaboard slave states in the years 1853–1854*. New York: Dix and Edwards. http://docsouth.unc.edu/nc/olmsted/olmsted.html.

Olson, Keith. 1974. *The G.I. Bill, the veterans, and the colleges*. Lexington: University Press of Kentucky.

Oreskes, Michael. 1990. For G.O.P. arsenal, 133 words to fire. *New York Times*, September 9, p. A30.

Organisation for Economic Co-operation and Development. 2004. *OECD economic outlook* no. 75, chap. 5. *Recent growth trends in OECD countries*. http://www.oecd.org/dataoecd/42/49/2087393.pdf.

———. 2004b. *2004 employment outlook*. http://www1.oecd.org/media/econsurv/EMO_e_04.pdf.

———. 2004c. *Clocking in and clocking out: OECD policy brief* (October). http://www.oecd.org/dataoecd/42/49/33821328.pdf.

Palmeri, Christopher. 2006. Snarl in the sky. *Business Week* (June 5): 26–29.

Paral, Rob, and Benjamin Johnson. 2004. Maintaining a competitive edge: The role of the foreign-born and U.S. immigration policies in science and engineering. *Immigration Policy in Focus* (American Immigration Law Foundation) 3, no. 3 (August). http://www.ailf.org/ipc/ipf081804.asp.

Parenti, Christian. 2003. *The soft cage: Surveillance in America from slavery to the war on terror*. New York: Basic Books.

———. 2004. Fables of the reconstruction. *The Nation* (August 30–September 6): 16–20.

Payne, A. Abigail. 2002. Do congressional earmarks increase research productivity at universities? *Science and Public Policy* 29, no. 5 (October): 314–30.

Peltzman, Sam, 1980. The growth of government. *Journal of Law and Economics* 23, no. 2 (October): 209–87.

Perelman, Michael. 1989. *Keynes, investment theory and the economic slowdown: The role of replacement investment and q-ratios.* London: Macmillan.

———. 1999. *The natural instability of markets: Expectations, increasing returns, and the collapse of markets.* New York: St. Martin's Press.

———. 2001. *The pathology of the U.S. economy revisited: The intractable contradictions of economic policy.* New York: Palgrave.

———. 2002. *Steal this idea: The corporate confiscation of creativity.* New York: Palgrave.

———. 2006. *Railroading economics: The creation of the free market mythology.* New York: Monthly Review Press.

Perlstein, Rick. 2001. *Before the storm: Barry Goldwater and the unmaking of the American consensus.* New York: Hill and Wang.

Persson, Torsten, and Guido Tabellini. 1994. Is inequality harmful for growth? *American Economic Review* 84, no. 3 (June): 600–21.

Pertschuk, Michael. 1982. *Revolt against regulation: The rise and pause of the consumer movement.* Berkeley: University of California Press.

Piketty, Thomas, and Emmanuel Saez. Forthcoming. Income inequality in the United States, 1913–1998. In Top incomes over the twentieth century: A contrast between the European and English speaking countries, ed. Anthony B. Atkinson and T. Piketty. Oxford: Oxford University Press. http://emlab.berkeley.edu/users/saez/piketty-saezOUP04US.pdf.

———. 2006. The evolution of top incomes: A historical and international perspective. *American Economic Review* 96, no. 2 (May): 200–205. http://elsa.berkeley.edu/~saez/TabAEA3.xls.

Pimpare, Stephen. 2004. What business wanted from welfare reform. *Counterpunch* 11, no. 16 (September 16–30): n.p.

Pizzigati, Sam. 2004. *Greed and good: Understanding and overcoming the inequality that limits our lives.* New York: Apex Press.

Pollin, Robert. 2003. *Contours of descent: U.S. economic fractures and the landscape of global austerity.* New York: Verso.

Posner, Richard A. 1977. *Economic analysis of law.* Boston: Little, Brown.

Powell, Lewis F., Jr. 1967. Civil disobedience: Prelude to revolution? *U.S. News and World Report* (October 30): 66–69.

President of the United States. 2006. *Economic report of the president.* Washington, D.C.: U.S. Government Printing Office.

Press, Eyal, and Jennifer Washburn. 2000. The kept university. *Atlantic Monthly* 285, no. 3 (March): 39–54.

Prins, Nomi. 2004. *Other people's money: The corporate mugging of America.* New York: New Press.

Quist, David, and Ignacio Chapela. 2001. Transgenic DNA introgressed into traditional maize landraces in Oaxaca, Mexico. *Nature* 414 (November 29): 541–43.

Rajan, Raghuram, and Julie Wulf. 2004. Are perks purely managerial excess? NBER Working Paper no. w10494 (May).

Rajan, Raghuram G., and Luigi Zingales. 2004. *Saving capitalism from the capitalists: Unleashing the power of financial markets to create wealth and spread opportunity*. Princeton, NJ: Princeton University Press.

Rajghatta, Chidanand. 2005. Watch out for the Indian era: Intel CEO. *Economic Times* (India) (March 7): n.p.

Rampton, Sheldon, and John Stauber. 2004. *Banana republicans*. New York: Tarcher.

Rattner, Steven. 1979. Volcker asserts U.S. must trim living standard. *New York Times*, October 18, p. A1.

Roberts, Sam. 2006. Panel recommends change in census prisoner count. *New York Times*, September 15.

Robinson, Joan. 1962. The Keynesian revolution. In *Economic Philosophy*, 75–100. Garden City, NY: Doubleday Anchor.

Rogers, Jesse. 2004. Inventor emphasizes power of engineering. *The Daily Pennsylvanian* (December 9). http://www.dailypennsylvanian.com/vnews/display.v/ART/2004/12/08/41b6b66ed7c52

Romer, Christina D., and David H. Romer. 1989. Does monetary policy matter? A new test in the spirit of Friedman and Schwartz. In *NBER macroeconomics annual*, ed. Olivier Jean Blanchard and Stanley Fischer, 121–70. Cambridge: Massachusetts Institute of Technology Press.

Rosenberg, Nathan. 2000. *Schumpeter and the endogeneity of technology: Some American perspectives*. New York: Routledge.

Rosenberg, Samuel. 2003. *American economic development since 1945: Growth, decline, and rejuvenation*. New York: Palgrave.

Rosenthal, Robert. 2002. Interpersonal expectancy affects: A 30-year perspective. *Current Directions in Psychological Science* 3:176–79.

———. 2003. Covert communication in laboratories, classrooms, and the truly real world. *Current Directions in Psychological Science* 12, no. 5 (October): 151–96.

Rothstein, Richard. 2001. Lessons: Reducing poverty could increase school achievement. *New York Times*, March 7.

Saez, Emmanuel. 2004. Interview with Michael Perelman, July 15.

St. Clair, Jeffrey. 2005. *Grand theft Pentagon*. Monroe, ME: Common Courage Press.

Samuelson, Paul A. 1977. Liberalism at bay (Second Gerhard Colm memorial lecture). March 5. *Social Research*, 16–31. Repr. *The collected scientific papers of Paul A. Samuelson*, vol. 4, ed. Hiroaki Nagatani and Kate Crowley, 865–80. Cambridge: Massachusetts Institute of Technology Press, 1977.

———. 1997. Credo of a lucky textbook author. *Journal of Economic Perspectives* 11, no. 2 (Spring): 153–60.

Sanger, David E. 2001. President asserts shrunken surplus may curb congress. *New York Times*, August 25, p. A1.

Santa-Clara, Pedro, and Rossen Valkanov. 2003. The presidential puzzle: Political cycles and the stock market. *Journal of Finance* 58, no. 5 (October): 1841–72.

Santini, Laura. 2004. Drug companies look to China for cheap R&D. *Wall Street Journal*, November 22, p. B1.

Santoni, G. J. 1986. The Employment Act of 1946: Some history notes. *Economic Review of the Federal Bank of St. Louis* 68, no. 9 (November): 5–16.

Savage, John. 1999. *Funding science in America: Congress, universities, and the academic pork barrel*. Cambridge: Cambridge University Press.

Sawicky, Max B. 2006. Do-it-yourself tax cuts: The crisis in U.S. tax enforcement. In *Bridging the tax gap: Addressing the crisis in federal tax administration*, ed. Max B. Sawicky, 1–20. Washington, DC: Economic Policy Institute.

Schoenhof, Jacob. 1893. *The economy of high wages: An inquiry into the cause of high wages and their effects on methods and cost of production.* New York: G. P. Putnam's Sons.

Schumpeter, Joseph Alois. 1954. *History of economic analysis.* New York: Oxford University Press.

Scott, Janny. 2006. Cities shed middle class, and are richer and poorer for it. *New York Times*, July 23.

Segal, Adam. 2004. Is America losing its edge? *Foreign Affairs* (November/December): n.p.

Select Committee to Study Governmental Operations with Respect to Intelligence Activities. U. S. Senate. 1976. *Supplementary detailed staff reports on intelligence activities and the rights of americans.* Book III. Final Report. Washington, DC: U.S. Government Printing Office.

Sennett, Richard, and Jonathan Cobb. 1972. *The hidden injuries of class.* New York: Knopf.

Shapin, Steven. 2002. Dear prudence: Review of return to reason by Stephen Toulmin. *London Review of Books* 24, no. 2 (January 14): n.p.

Simons, Algie Martin. 1925. *Social forces in American history.* New York: Macmillan.

Skocpol, Theda. 1998. The G.I. Bill and U.S. social policy, past and future. In *The welfare state*, ed. Ellen Frankel Paul, Fred D. Miller, Jr., and Jeffrey Paul, 95-115. Cambridge: Cambridge University Press.

Smith, Adam. 1776. *An inquiry into the nature and causes of the wealth of nations.* 2 vols. Ed. R. H. Campbell and A. S. Skinner. New York: Oxford University Press. Repr. 1976.

Smith, James Allen. 1989. Think tanks and the politics of ideas. In *The spread of economic ideas*, ed. David C. Colander and A. W. Coats, 175-94. Cambridge: Cambridge University Press.

———. 1991. *The idea brokers: Think tanks and the rise of the new policy elite.* New York: Free Press.

Solow, Robert M. 1997. How did economics get that way and what way did it get? *Daedalus* 126, no. 1 (Winter): 39–58.

Staehle, Hans. 1955. Technology, utilization and production. *Bulletin de l'Institue Internationale de Statistique* 34, Part 4: 112–36.

Stafford, Eoghan W. 2003. Spotlight on Marty. *Harvard Crimson*, February 10.

Stefancic, Jean, and Richard Delgado. 1996. *No mercy: How conservative think tanks and foundations changed America's social agenda.* Philadelphia: Temple University Press.

Stein, Ben. 2006. In class warfare, guess which class is winning. *New York Times*, November 26.

Stein, Herbert. 1969. *The fiscal revolution in America.* Chicago: University of Chicago Press.

———. 1984. *Presidential economics: The making of economic policy from Roosevelt to Reagan and beyond.* New York: Simon and Schuster.

Stigler, George J. 1969. Does economics have a useful past? *History of Political Economy* 1, no. 2 (Fall): 217–30. Repr. *The economist as preacher and other essays*, ed. George J. Stigler, 107–18. Chicago: University of Chicago Press, 1982.

———. 1982. Do economists matter? In *The economist as preacher and other essays*, ed. George J. Stigler, 54–67. Chicago: University of Chicago Press, 1982.

Stiglitz, Joseph E. 2004. *The roaring nineties: A new history of the world's most prosperous decade*. New York: W. W. Norton.

Stille, Alexander. 2001. Grounded by an income gap. *New York Times*, December 15, p. A15.

Strassman, W. P. 1959. *Risk and technological investment*. Ithaca, NY: Cornell University Press.

Strauss, Gary. 2003. Pricey perk lets executives fly high. *USA Today*, August 5, p. A1.

Strawser, Cornelia. 2003. This is economic recovery? Letter to the editor. *Washington Post*, July 22, p. A16.

Strunk, Bradley C., and James D. Reschovsky. 2004. *Trends in U.S. health insurance coverage, 2001–2003*. Center for Studying Health System Change Tracking Report no. 9 (August). http://www.hschange.org/CONTENT/694/.

Swanson, Diane L., and Marc Orlitzky. 2005. Executive preference for compensation structure and normative myopia: A business and society research project. In *The Ethics of Executive Compensation*, ed. R. W. Kolb. Malden, MA: Blackwell.

Taylor, John. 1814. *An inquiry into the principles and policy of the government of the United States*. New Haven, CT: Yale University Press. Repr., 1950.

Thomas, Dana. 1976. On the right side. *Barron's* (February 2): 3, 8, 14.

Thurgood, Lori. 2004. Graduate enrollment in science and engineering fields reaches new peak; First-time enrollment of foreign students declines. Science Resource Statistics, National Science Federation, InfoBrief 326 (June). http://www.nsf.gov/sbe/srs/infbrief/nsf04326/start.htm.

Titmuss, Richard M. 1962. *Income distribution and social change: A study of criticism*. London: Allen and Unwin.

Tolstoy, Leo. 1970. *Anna Karenina*. New York: W. W. Norton.

Union of Concerned Scientists. 2004. *Scientific integrity in policymaking: An investigation into the Bush administration's misuse of science*. (February). http://www.ucsusa.org/global_environment/rsi/report.html.

U.S. Bureau of Labor Statistics. 2007. International comparisons of manufacturing productivity and unit labor cost trends, supplementary tables. http://www.bls.gov/fls/prodsupptabletoc.htm.

U.S. Chamber of Commerce. 2007. NCLC celebrates 30 years of service to the business community. http://www.uschamber.com/nclc/about/anniversary.htm.

U.S. Department of Commerce. Bureau of economic analysis. 2006. National Income and Product Accounts (October). http://www.bea.gov/bea/dn/nipaweb/TableView.asp?SelectedTable=85&FirstYear=2004&LastYear=2006&Freq=Qtr.

U.S. Department of Education. Digest of education statistics, 2002, Washington, DC, 2002. http://nces.ed.gov/programs/digest/d02.

U.S. Department of Justice. 2004. *Profile of jail inmates 2002*. Washington, DC: U.S. Department of Justice, Office of Justice Programs, NCJ-2011932 (July). http://www.ojp.usdoj.gov/bjs/pub/pdf/pji02.pdf.

U.S. Department of Justice, Bureau of Justice Statistics. 1996. *Sourcebook of criminal justice statistics*. Washington, DC: U.S. Department of Justice.

U.S. Department of Justice, Bureau of Justice Statistics. 2003. *Sourcebook of criminal justice statistics, 2002*. Washington, DC: U.S. Department of Justice.

U.S. Department of Justice. Office of Justice Programs. 2004. *Bureau of justice statistics*. http://www.ojp.usdoj.gov/bjs.

U.S. General Accounting Office. 1996. *School facilities: America's schools report differing conditions*. GAO/HEHS-96-103. Washington: DC: U.S. Government Printing Office.

U.S. National Security Council. 1950. NSC 68: United States objectives and programs for national security. Repr. *Containment: Documents on American policy and strategy, 1945-1950*, ed. Thomas H. Etzold and John Lewis Gaddis, 385–442. New York: Columbia University Press, 1978.

U.S. Senate, Committee on the Judiciary, Subcommittee of Separation of Powers. 1970. *The Philadelphia plan*, 91st Cong., 1st Sess. October.

Veblen, Thorstein. 1914. *The instinct of workmanship and the state of the industrial arts*. New York: Macmillan. Repr. New York: Augustus M. Kelley, 1964.

———. 1915. *Imperial Germany and the Industrial Revolution*. New York: Macmillan.

Vedder, Richard K., and Lowell Gallaway. 1991. The Great Depression of 1946. *Review of Austrian Economics* 5(2): 3–32.

———. 1993. *Out of work: Unemployment and government in twentieth-century America*. New York: Holmes and Meier.

Vidal, Gore. 1992. Time for a people's convention. *The Nation* 254, no. 3 (January 27): 73, 88–94.

Viner, Jacob. 1933. *Balanced deflation, inflation or more depression*. Day and Hour Series, no. 3. Minneapolis: University of Minneapolis Press.

Vinzant, Carol. 2002. The democratic dividend: The stock market prefers democratic presidents to republicans. Why? *Slate* (October 4). http://slate.msn.com/id/2071929.

Viscusi, W. Kip. 2004. The blockbuster punitive damages award. John M. Olin Center for Law, Economics, and Business, Discussion Paper no. 473.

Vogel, David. 1989. *Fluctuating fortunes: The political power of business in America*. New York: Basic Books.

Vogel, David, and Leonard Silk. 1976. *Ethics and profits: The crisis of confidence in American business*. New York: Simon and Schuster.

Volcker, Paul A. 1981. Testimony before the committee on banking, finance and urban affairs of the U.S. House of Representatives, July 21, 1981. *Federal Reserve Bulletin* 67, no. 8 (August): 613–18.

———. 1982. Testimony before the Joint Economic Committee, January 26, 1982. *Federal Reserve Bulletin* 68, no. 2 (February): 88–90.

Waldrop, M. Mitchell. 1992. *Complexity: The emerging science at the edge of order and chaos*. New York: Simon and Schuster.

Walker, Francis A. 1889. Recent progress of political economy in the United States. *Publications of the American Economic Association* 4:17–40.

Wallis, John, and Barry R. Weingast. 2004. Equilibrium impotence: Why the states and not the American national government financed infrastructure investment in the antebellum era. http://www-hoover.stanford.edu/research/conferences/collective/01132004.pdf.

Walsh, Lawrence E. (Independent Counsel). 1993. Final report of the independent counsel for Iran/Contra matters. Volume I: Investigations and prosecutions (U.S. Court of Appeals for the District of Columbia Circuit. Division for the

Purpose of Appointing Independent Counsel Division, no. 86–86 (August 4). http://www.fas.org/irp/offdocs/walsh/.

Walsh, Sharon. 2004. Berkeley denies tenure to ecologist who criticized university's ties to the biotechnology industry. *The Chronicle of Higher Education* (January 9): n.p.

Wanniski, Jude. 1976. Taxes and a two-Santa theory. *National Observer* (March 6): n.p.

———. 1979. *The way the world works.* New York: Simon and Schuster.

———. 1999. Memo to: Ed Crane, president of CATO (April 19). http://www .wanniski.com/showarticle.asp?articleid=329

———. 2003. The Laffer curve. http://www.wanniski.com/showarticle.asp? articleid=2965

Warren, Peter N. 1994. Delta force: Conservatism's best young economists. *Policy Review* (Heritage Foundation), no. 70 (Fall): 72–79.

Washburn, Jennifer. 2005. *University, Inc.: The corporate corruption of American higher education.* New York: Basic Books.

Weiner, Tim. 2004. Lockheed and the future of warfare. *New York Times,* November 28.

Weinstein, Henry. 1975. Defending what? The corporations' public interest. *Juris Doctor* 3, no. 1 (June): 39–43.

Weiss, Gaudio, Andrea Del, and John W. Fantuzzo. 2001. Multivariate impact of health and caretaking risk factors on the school adjustment of first graders. *Journal of Community Psychology* 29, no. 2 (March): 141–61.

Welch, Finis. 1999. In defense of inequality. *American Economic Review* 89, no. 2 (May): 1–17.

Wells, David A. 1889. *Recent economic changes, and their effect on the production and well-being of society.* New York: Da Capo Press. Repr., 1970.

Wells, Tom. 1994. *The war within: America's battle over Vietnam.* Berkeley: University of California Press.

Whaples, Robert. 2006. Do economists agree on Aanything? Yes! *The Economists' Voice* 3(9): article 1. http://www.bepress.com/ev/vol3/iss9/art1.

White, Theodore H. 1965. *The making of the president 1964.* New York: Athenaeum.

Wilkinson, Richard G. 1997. *Unhealthy societies: The afflictions of inequality.* London: Routledge.

Williamson, Jeffrey, and Peter H. Lindert. 1980. *American inequality: A macroeconomic history.* New York: Academic.

Wills, Garry. 1971. *Nixon Agonistes.* New York: New American Library.

Winerip, Michael. 2006. Standardized tests face a crisis over standards. *New York Times,* March 22, p. A21.

Winter, Greg. 2004. Students to bear more of the cost of college. *New York Times,* December 23, p. A18.

Wise, Tim. 1989. Radical surgery: The consensus builds for national health coverage. *Dollars and Sense,* no. 150 (October): 6–9.

Wolfe, Alan. 1981. *America's impasse: The rise and fall of the politics of growth.* New York: Pantheon.

Wolff, Edward N. 2004. Changes in household wealth in the 1980s and 1990s in the U.S. Levy Economics Institute working paper, no. 407 (May): n.p.

Woodward, Bob. 1994. *The agenda: Inside the Clinton White House.* New York: Simon and Schuster.

Woolhandler Seffie, T. Campbell, and D. U. Himmelstein. 2003. Costs of health care administration in the United States and Canada. *The New England Journal of Medicine* 349: no. 8 (August 21): 768–75.

Woolhandler, Steffie, and David U. Himmelstein. 1997. Costs of care and Administration at for-profit and other hospitals in the United States. *The New England Journal of Medicine* 3336, no. 11 (March 13): 769–74.

———. 2001. Paying for national health insurance and not getting it. *Health Affairs* 21, no. 4 (July/August): 88–98.

Wright, Gavin. 1990. The origins of American industrial success, 1870–1940. *American Economic Review* 80, no. 4 (September): 651–68.

Wright, Philip G. 1915. The contest in congress between organized labor and organized business. *Quarterly Journal of Economics* 29, no. 2 (February): 235–61.

Wright, Richard W. 2003. Hand, Posner, and the myth of the "Hand formula." *Theoretical Inquiries in Law* 4. http://ssrn.com/abstract=362800.

Yergin, Daniel, and Joseph Stanislaw. 1997. *The commanding heights: The battle between government and the marketplace that is remaking the modern world.* New York: Simon and Schuster.

Yermack, David. 2004. Flights of fancy: Corporate jets, CEO perquisites, and inferior shareholder returns. New York University Stern School of Business. http://public.kenan-flagler.unc.edu/faculty/shivdasani/unc-duke%20corporate%20finance/David_Yermack_Aircraft0904.pdf.

Ziobrowski, Alan J., Ping Cheng, James W. Boyd, and Brigitte J. Ziobrowski. 2004. Abnormal returns from the common stock investments of the United States Senate. *Journal of Financial and Quantitative Analysis* 39, no. 4 (December): 661–76.

Index